UNJUST Transition

The Future for
Fossil Fuel
Workers

EDITED BY:
Emily Eaton, Andrew Stevens & Sean Tucker

FERNWOOD PUBLISHING
HALIFAX & WINNIPEG

Copyright © 2024 Emily Eaton, Andrew Stevens, and Sean Tucker

All rights reserved. No part of this book may be reproduced or transmitted in any form by any means without permission in writing from the publisher, except by a reviewer, who may quote brief passages in a review.

Copyediting: Jenn Harris
Cover design: Jess Koroscil
Text design: Lauren Jeanneau
Printed and bound in the UK

Published by Fernwood Publishing
Halifax and Winnipeg
2970 Oxford Street, Halifax, Nova Scotia, B3L 2W4
www.fernwoodpublishing.ca

Fernwood Publishing Company Limited gratefully acknowledges the financial support of the Government of Canada through the Canada Book Fund and the Canada Council for the Arts. We acknowledge the Province of Manitoba for support through the Manitoba Publishers Marketing Assistance Program and the Book Publishing Tax Credit. We acknowledge the Nova Scotia Department of Communities, Culture and Heritage for support through the Publishers Assistance Fund.

Library and Archives Canada Cataloguing in Publication
Title: Unjust transition : the future for fossil fuel workers / edited by: Emily Eaton, Andrew Stevens & Sean Tucker.
Names: Eaton, Emily, 1980- editor. | Stevens, Andrew (Lecturer in the sociology of work and employment), editor. | Tucker, Sean (Lecturer in leadership and occupational health and safety), editor.
Description: Includes bibliographical references and index.
Identifiers: Canadiana (print) 20240281071 | Canadiana (ebook) 20240281179 | ISBN 9781773636726 (softcover) | ISBN 9781773636740 (EPUB) | ISBN 9781773636733 (PDF)
Subjects: LCSH: Strikes and lockouts—Petroleum industry—Saskatchewan—Regina. | LCSH: Collective bargaining—Saskatchewan—Regina. | LCSH: Labor unions—Saskatchewan—Regina. | LCSH: Petroleum industry and trade—Saskatchewan—Regina. | LCSH: Petroleum refineries—Saskatchewan—Regina.
Classification: LCC HD5329.P42 2019 U55 2024 | DDC 331.892/822338209712445—dc23

CONTENTS

ACKNOWLEDGEMENTS v

ABOUT THE AUTHORS vi

1 | REFINERY TOWN IN THE PETRO-STATE
Co-opting the Just Transition
Emily Eaton, Andrew Stevens, and Sean Tucker 1

2 | HORIZONS OF SOLIDARITY
The Regina Refinery Pension Lockout
Kevin Skerrett 22

3 | "THEY HAD NO INTENTION OF EVER COMING TO AN AGREEMENT"
Voices of Unifor 594 Workers
Interviews by Emily Eaton, Andrew Stevens, and Sean Tucker 46

4 | CLASS POWER AND LEGAL COERCION
Refinery Workers Confront the Limits of the "Right to Strike"
Charles Smith and Lisa Wanlin 68

5 | UNGOVERNABLE
How a Refinery Became "Too Big to Fail" —
and What it Means to the People of Saskatchewan
Patricia W. Elliott 88

6 | "YOU'RE NOT BOILING MILK"
Health and Safety at the Co-op Refinery
Sean Tucker 117

7 | WHERE IS THE "LABOUR BEAT REPORTER"?
The Regina Refinery Lockout and the Many Crises of Journalism
Doug Nesbitt and Emily Leedham 142

8 | TOWARDS A JUST TRANSITION FOR REFINERY WORKERS?
Taking Control of the Change
Emily Eaton 165

9 | TRANSITION PATHWAYS
Workers Before Profits
Emily Eaton, Andrew Stevens, and Sean Tucker 189

INDEX 213

We dedicate this book to the members of Unifor Local 594.

ACKNOWLEDGEMENTS

We thank current and former members of Unifor 594 who spoke with us about their experience of the lockout and working conditions at the refinery, as well as others who shared first-hand information about the Co-op Refinery Complex. Now three years on, it is still difficult for many workers to talk about the dispute and the deep-seated feeling of betrayal. We hope this book can help these and other workers mobilize strategically around growing employer engagement with the politics of energy transition. We hope Local 594 members see their voices reflected in this book.

We appreciate the support and guidance of editor Wayne Antony at Fernwood Publishing. Thanks also to the rest of the Fernwood staff for design and promotion. Finally, thanks to Jenn Harris for carefully copyediting this book.

ABOUT THE AUTHORS

Emily Eaton is a professor of geography and environmental studies at the University of Regina, where she studies the power and influence of the fossil fuel industries and the possibilities for just transition. Her books include *The End of This World: Climate Justice in So-Called Canada* (2023), *Fault Lines: Life and Landscape in Saskatchewan's Oil Economy* (2016), and *Growing Resistance: Farmers and the Politics of Genetically Modified Wheat* (2013).

Patricia W. Elliott is an investigative journalist and the Distinguished Professor of Investigative and Community Journalism at First Nations University of Canada. Since 2017 she has been a lead collaborator in the award-winning Price of Oil investigative journalism project, uncovering the environmental and health impacts of oil.

Emily Leedham is the Prairie reporter for *PressProgress* and editor of *Shift Work*, *PressProgress*' weekly national labour newsletter. Emily has years of labour reporting experience as a former editor of *RankandFile.ca* and host of the labour news podcast *Rank and File Radio*. Her work can also be found in *Vice*, *Briarpatch*, and *Canadian Dimension*.

Doug Nesbitt is a labour activist and historian in Kingston, Ontario. He is a co-founder and editor of *Rankandfile.ca* and a founding member of the Kingston Workers' History Project.

Kevin Skerrett is a research officer at CUPE and adjunct research professor at Carleton University's Institute of Political Economy. He is co-editor of *The Contradictions of Pension Fund Capitalism* (2018).

Charles Smith is an associate professor in the Department of Political Science at St. Thomas More College, University of Saskatchewan. His research interests include Canadian and International political economy, public law, labour unions, and federal and provincial public policy. He is the author of *Transforming Provincial Politics* (2015) and *Unions in Court: Organized Labour and the Charter of Rights and Freedoms* (2017). He has also authored numerous articles on Saskatchewan politics, labour in court, and labour history. Charles is also co-editor of Canada's foremost labour studies journal, *Labour/Le Travail*.

Andrew Stevens is an associate professor at the University of Regina's Faculty of Business Administration. His research focuses on labour relations, migrant worker policies, and collective action.

Sean Tucker is a professor of occupational health and safety in the Faculty of Business Administration at the University of Regina.

Lisa Wanlin is a law student at the University of Saskatchewan. She grew up on a farm near Eastend, Saskatchewan. Lisa obtained a master of arts in political studies at the University of Saskatchewan and will be articling with Legal Aid Saskatchewan in 2024.

1

REFINERY TOWN IN THE PETRO-STATE
Co-opting the Just Transition

Emily Eaton, Andrew Stevens, and Sean Tucker

ON A BITTERLY COLD DAY in January 2020, dozens of Regina Police Service officers attempted, unsuccessfully, to clear a barricade set up at the Co-op Refinery Complex (CRC) in Regina by locked-out oil refinery workers. The confrontation led to Jerry Dias, then national president of Unifor, Canada's largest private sector union, being arrested, loaded into a police wagon, and taken into custody. Dias and hundreds of Unifor representatives from across Canada were in town as part of an effort to reinforce the picket lines blockading entrances to the refinery, thereby forcing the company to get serious about negotiating an end to the dispute. That night, news outlets across Canada rolled the footage of the national union leader being detained, evoking expressions of solidarity from allies as well as vitriol from those who wanted "eastern" labour leaders to stay out of local oil and gas affairs.

The lockout would drag on for another five months. For many workers, the long dispute, which divided the community, was about maintaining their pension plan and ensuring the survival of their local union, Unifor 594. We believe this lockout was also a bellwether event for fossil fuel workers in an industry being forced to respond to the deepening climate emergency.

In the years leading up to and during the lockout, the employer justified its demands in terms of cost savings that were necessary for investments to shift to a low-carbon economy. Two weeks prior to the lockout, in an open letter, the company reasoned that pension concessions were needed "because we understand that a shift in our traditional fossil fuel market is already taking place and we must be prepared to address the challenges with significant investment in our refinery."[1] And yet local media and analysts who covered the historic dispute left the company's stated reasons for locking out their workers largely unexamined.

This dispute provides a window into the ways that other fossil fuel companies may manage their labour relations as they respond to new climate change–driven government regulations and position themselves as part of the coming net-zero future. Ultimately, this is a story about a powerful fossil fuel company — ironically, of an enterprise that began its story as a consumer co-operative — trying to break its workers' union under the guise of climate action, a story that may become more familiar in the decades ahead if oil and gas workers, their unions, and civil society are unsuccessful in winning a transition to a low-carbon economy centred on principles of justice.

As we see it, energy transition is happening now — industries are having to respond to changing regulations and consumer demands — but exactly *how* companies respond remains an open question. The CRC is responding by engaging in greenwashing and delaying action through far-off promises it may not be serious about achieving, while using the spectre of the coming low-carbon future to attempt to break the collective power of the union. The six-and-a-half–month lockout at the Co-op Refinery serves as a cautionary tale and, hopefully, motivation for workers and broader civil society to push for a transition that is more just, humane, and supports a livable planet well into the future. This experience also illustrates the complexity of change and the hopes and fears of refinery as well as other oil and gas workers.

The CRC is a wholly owned subsidiary of Saskatoon-based Federated Co-operatives Limited (FCL), which in turn is owned by over 164 retail co-ops from British Columbia to northern Ontario. The CRC was founded in 1935 as the Consumers' Co-operative Refineries Limited, with 632 shareholding members. Nine years later, in 1944, it joined the FCL. Today FCL had the second highest total sales revenue of all Saskatchewan companies.

The dispute with its workers occurred within the broader climate politics and regulations that emissions-intensive energy industries are attempting to shape and navigate. Regional politics in fossil fuels have evolved from a time when energy unions worked to chart independent policy positions on the oil economy to the current "petro-populism" of western Canada in which labour has often aligned itself with corporate interests. In this political economy, are unions representing workers employed in the oil and gas sector, like Local 594, equipped to lead a transition to different but equally well-paid jobs? Especially in what political scientist Angela Carter describes as a "petro-province"?[2]

FEDERAL CLIMATE CHANGE REGULATION SPURS A RESPONSE

Since the CRC opened in 1935, the concentration of CO_2 in the Earth's atmosphere has increased from 308 to 417 parts per million (a 35 percent increase).[3] Over this same period, the average temperature on the planet has increased by 0.8 Celsius.[4] The consensus among scientists is that this warming is due to human activities, primarily burning fossil fuels.[5] In response to worsening climate change, and as part of global efforts to reduce greenhouse gas (GHG) emissions, Canada has committed to reducing its emissions 40–45 percent below 2005 levels by 2030 and reaching net zero by 2050. The federal government's emissions reduction plan, released in March of 2022,[6] includes several new regulations with which the oil and gas industry will have to comply and on which fossil fuel companies have been consulted for some time. A new clean fuel standard, methane reduction measures, and a cap on oil and gas emissions are among the new and coming regulations targeting the sector. Whether these regulations will deliver the GHG reductions to match Canada's commitment, it is clear that fossil fuel–intensive industries are in a period of adjustment. If they can't produce operating plans that show a path to net-zero emissions and performance models to match these plans, refineries risk being phased out.

Like other oil and gas operations, the CRC, which emits about 2.1 million tonnes of carbon dioxide per year, is attempting to maintain its social licence by promising it will use carbon capture technology and biofuels to reduce its emissions 40 percent by 2030.[7] It says it is "aspiring for net neutral by 2050."[8] However, it appears that the CRC's commitment to sustainability is mostly an exercise in "greenwashing." There has been no meaningful investment into winding down their fossil fuel business in line with the global goal of transitioning to a near-zero future.[9] This response is hardly unique.

Fossil fuel companies must also adapt to a consumer demand for electrification of vehicles and heating, along with changing patterns of global investment in environment, social, and corporate governance. Both the refinery and its parent company, FCL, know this.[10] Currently, about 5 percent of all new vehicle sales in Canada are fully battery electric.[11] This is forecast to increase to 60 percent by 2030,[12] and 100 percent of all new light-duty vehicle sales will be "zero emissions" by 2035 under the new federal mandate.[13] Whether economies are actually able to transition off of oil and gas and meet their GHG targets, the industry is already in the throes of a profound transition. This is a transition that oil and gas companies in the US and Canada have been planning for — while also actively resisting and delaying — for decades. The CRC is no exception.[14] Refineries are valued at several billion dollars each and they risk becoming stranded assets with huge environmental cleanup liabilities in the coming decades.

THE POLITICAL ECONOMY OF OIL AND GAS IN SASKATCHEWAN

The Government of Saskatchewan, led by Premier Scott Moe, has vocally opposed Ottawa's regulations for the oil and gas sector, with particular venom directed toward the federal price on carbon emissions and environmental protection regulations. One of the pillars of the province's "30 Goals for 2030" growth plan, released in the fall of 2020, is increasing "oil production by 25 percent to 600,000 barrels per day."[15] This flies in the face of reports, such as the International Energy Agency's *Net Zero by 2050*, that call for no new investments in fossil fuel supply, instead focusing on winding down production.[16]

Many commentators have pointed out that the province is in a perpetual state of conflict with Ottawa over how to reach Canada's international GHG emissions reduction goals. This barb from the Saskatchewan minister of energy, in 2021, is illustrative:

> [T]he constitutional treatment of Saskatchewan can no longer be based on economic punishment. When it comes to the energy conversation, the whole world is tearing up the script

and we're adjusting to what the Bank of America is calling the new energy world order.... Our stability has been in spite of, and not because of, the federal government, as provinces like Saskatchewan have fought the energy fight.[17]

Oil and gas have become celebrated industries in Saskatchewan since global commodity prices began to rise in the early 2000s.[18] This has helped to create what scholars describe as the "petro-state," whereby the political geography of a region or country is defined by its economic relationship with oil.[19] Indeed, governments of all political stripes in the province have worked to empower the oil industry as a matter of public policy.[20] As Carter writes, "successive governments in Saskatchewan — socialist and conservative — have championed the oil and gas industry, starting with the CCF in 1944."[21] Western Canada's position as a centre of "carbon capital" has certainly aided this trend, particularly due to its surging bitumen exports and branding of Canadian oil as the world's "most ethical."[22] Business-friendly royalty and taxation regimes are thus configured to entice capital investment in an effort to compete with other oil-producing provinces and regions.[23] In this context, the political consensus is that expanding oil and gas pipelines destined for export markets will benefit all communities, businesses, and workers in the region — part of what Stuart Trew labels "pipeline populism."[24] Broader questions of labour rights and wealth distribution are subordinated to the interests of employers in the petro-state's new common sense, wherein workers' interests and corporate interests are framed as one and the same, exemplified by the slogan "I love Canadian oil and gas."[25]

Regina can be described, as Steve Early puts it, as a "refinery town," with the CRC dominating the political, economic, and social spheres of the prairie municipality.[26] The facility is listed as the second largest property taxpayer at the municipal level,[27] and it has become a significant patron of cultural and social programs, even financing a municipal public emergency notification system.[28]

In Saskatchewan, questioning the hegemony of this industry is met with severe consequences. A short-lived decision by Regina's city council in early 2021 to ban fossil fuel companies from sponsoring civic infrastructure and events demonstrated the province's ideological commitment to oil and gas. While the policy would have had no material effect on the industry other than disrupting one avenue for the CRC to influence public opinion through corporate social responsibility initiatives, it was enough to mobilize the refinery, industry organizations like Canadian Association of Petroleum Producers, and Conservative government–backed advocacy groups like Alberta's Canadian Energy Centre against the municipal council. Saskatchewan premier Scott Moe went so far as to threaten the province's second largest city with a suspension of yearly grants in lieu of property taxes from SaskPower and SaskEnergy in an effort to turn the public against their elected local representatives.[29]

In Saskatchewan, and arguably in much of western Canada, conservative forces have successfully positioned fossil fuel workers (and at times the unions that represent them) as inherently aligned with the interests of industry leaders — or what some political economists have described as the "carbon-capital elite."[30] However, oil-producing states like Norway, which is heavily reliant on fossil fuels as a staple of employment and national revenue, reveal a different trajectory. There, a close alliance exists between the social democratic establishment, oil workers, and their respective unions and labour federations. Politicians who recognize the need to accelerate the green transition actively invite these workers to become "heroes of tomorrow" in their narratives about the role of fossil fuel labour.[31] Tensions certainly exist when it comes to phasing out the oil industry and what this means for Norwegian jobs, but conservative groups have not successfully achieved hegemony among this important constituency as they have in Canada. It is within this political and economic context that FCL and Unifor 594 began negotiating a new collective agreement in 2018.

NEGOTIATING TRANSITION

Until about 2010, the CRC largely reflected the co-operative principles that have governed most of its existence.[32] While marking the eightieth anniversary of the refinery in 2015, FCL boasted, "The Refinery units continue to stand as towers of hope, embodying not only what has been done, but also what can be done … when people work together."[33] Article 4 of the Local 594 collective agreement speaks to the value of cooperation in the context of labour relations, binding both parties to a commitment to "foster and promote the highest level of employee morale and employee-employer relationships." Signage celebrating this relationship even appears at an entrance to the facility.

Despite FCL's espousal of co-operative values and principles in its public relations strategy, power and decision making have become increasingly centralized and undemocratic. Along with this centralization, a cultural shift has led to growing antagonism between management and workers. Throughout the lockout, FCL and CRC aligned their messaging with the political discourse of the Government of Saskatchewan: Unifor was an eastern union interested in stirring up trouble in the province. This strategy proved highly successful in winning public support.

In the years leading up to the dispute, CRC leadership insisted that the refinery needed to transition the facility to meet new fuel standards, cope with a federal carbon tax, and respond to an anticipated decline in fossil fuel consumption.[34] Former FCL CEO Scott Banda situated pension concessions in the context of preparing for a downturn in refinery profits due to carbon pricing and slowing demand for fossil fuels. "It's real; it's happening; it's going to impact us. It will be at the refinery," he remarked in a 2017 interview.[35] FCL's VP of energy, Cal Fichter, expressed similar concerns: "We recognize that the world is changing and there is a political momentum to transition away from fossil fuels."[36] Ironically, in 2021, FCL acquired 171 Husky Energy retail fuelling stations.[37]

The company's supposed financial constraints also framed the previous round of negotiations with Local 594, but at that time the company pointed to the downturn in oil prices, rather than federal regulations, as the main cause of concern. As bargaining commenced in 2016, the company announced that FCL's revenues were being hit by the recent slide in oil prices and the general weakening of the energy sector.[38] Amid this turmoil, Banda wrote in a letter sent directly to refinery employees, "While we cannot isolate ourselves from challenges in today's western Canadian economy, co-ops are uniquely positioned to answer those challenges." Much of this correspondence was aimed at pressuring workers to accept a defined contribution pension plan for new hires.[39] "New pipelines," the letter continued, "are putting pressure on the cost of our crude supply," suggesting that increased capacity could result in increased prices of refinery inputs, thereby jeopardizing the bottom line.[40] Labour costs, the company insisted, were spiralling out of control compared to competitors. Workers recognized this move as a historic turning point in labour-management relations.

But the company was attempting to mask the facility's financial success. Regina's Co-op Refinery Complex benefits from its proximity to the cheaper Western Canadian Select (WCS) crude oil stream — a fact that is largely kept quiet by both the provincial government and FCL — by way of reduced product costs and, therefore, higher profits.[41] As a process operator remarked during an interview, "It's the cheapest of the cheap. It's the difference of what it costs us now — because everyone is complaining that raw crude is so cheap. Yeah if you're a driller, it's shitty. It's awful, because your raw crude is cheap. But for us we buy it cheap from you but we can still make the same item at the end of the day."[42] The CRC is also at the financial heart of the co-operative system. In 2022, FCL's Energy Segment,[43] of which the CRC is a part, accounted for 64 percent of the co-operative's overall sales or $7.96 billion, and 75 percent of FCL's net income.[44] As Canada's fifth largest refinery, processing oil was a significant contributor to FCL's $1.1 billion profit in 2018 — the most profitable year in its ninety-one-year history.

Despite its record profitability in the lead-up to the historic lockout, FCL attempted to create a sense of looming financial hardship, citing increased competition, new pipelines, and the potential for new federal emissions standards. It mobilized these future threats as reasons for its assault on Local 594,[45] and particularly for its position that pension concessions were crucial for the co-op's continued existence. Management was ready for this fight, having spent years setting up the issues and playing into prevailing attitudes in Saskatchewan that see environmental regulation as a threat to livelihoods and prosperity. But it wasn't always like this in Saskatchewan. Through the history of the CRC we can trace a story that mirrors the broader trajectory of western Canadian politics. Starting with principles of cooperation and workers developing independent energy policy, it ends up today in an era of petro-populism where workers have made difficult concessions and been appropriated in the narratives and interests of their employers.

TRANSITIONING AWAY FROM ENERGY POLICY INDEPENDENCE AND CO-OPERATIVE VALUES

Until the early 1980s, unionized oil workers in Canada forged their own political trajectory centred on public ownership and control, with strong roots in the anti-corporate and co-operative movements of Saskatchewan. In 1942, workers at the farmer-established co-op refinery unionized with no contest from the employer and began agitating for their interests in national energy policy. Notably, they became Local 1 of the newly formed Oil Workers' Industrial Union (OWIU). The union was formed on the cusp of the socialist Co-operative Commonwealth Federation (CCF) being elected to office in 1944, with Tommy Douglas as premier.

Neil Reimer, who was involved in the initial union drive at the CRC, was the leader of the refinery workers' union from the early 1950s to 1980. According to Reimer, "the movement was so politicized and because the role of co-ops was so important, we had to decide what role the union movement would play. The role of co-ops, socialism, and democracy were all part of it."[46] Reimer's experience led him to conclude that the CCF and the co-operatives could not be trusted to uphold the interests of refinery workers, or workers more generally — unions would be required to protect labour's interests despite the social democratic mantra of the government. Throughout the 1940s and 1950s, Canada's first refinery union — which became Local 594 of the OWIU in 1948 — proceeded to define labour organizing and political mobilization throughout the sector, with the CRC functioning as its operational base.[47]

By the 1960s, Canadian oil worker unions had flagged the problems of foreign ownership and the necessity of a Canadian energy strategy, part of the wider left-nationalist tendency that defined the era.[48] Two major strikes against the energy companies in 1965 and 1969, involving "hot oil" boycotts, illegal walkouts, and sympathy strikes, implemented national-pattern bargaining.[49] By the 1970s, OWIU (now the Oil, Chemical, and Atomic Workers International Union, or OCAW) had crafted its own national energy policy, which advocated for the expansion of PetroCanada, investment in solar, wind, and biomass research and development, along with conservation programs as an alternative to pricing mechanisms such as a general pollution tax because the union viewed "market-based" solutions as hurting ordinary working people.[50] These developments represented the maturation of several ideas that can be traced back to the union's original base at the co-operative refinery in Regina.

However, national-pattern bargaining became severely fragmented and weakened throughout the 1980s and 1990s, and the OWIU's energy policies of the late 1970s have now been all but abandoned. After breaking away from OCAW in 1979, the independent Energy and Chemical Workers Union (ECWU) developed their 1980 energy strategy. While the strategy remained on the union's agenda through the decade, there was no accompanying rank-and-file education campaign to rally the membership around these ideas. In 1992 the ECWU merged with other unions to form the Communications, Energy and Paperworkers (CEP) union. The CEP's subsequent energy strategy, published in 2002, reiterated many of the points made in the ECWU's 1980 policy position. The climate crisis was in the foreground, but the document contained no demand for nationalization. Caught between recessions, unemployment, and concerted anti-unionism by governments and employers alike, refinery workers were hardly alone in retreating from the militancy of the previous decades. Ultimately, the ECWU and subsequent CEP would effectively abandon its own proposals for transforming the oil industry in Canada and follow the prerogatives of industry.

In Regina, workers told us that shifting attitudes within the leadership of FCL and CRC have unsettled decades of stable labour relations. For one Local 594 member, "Everything is negative. I called it the 'house of hatred'.... They hate the workers. Anything that you come up with, they don't want to hear. Any safety issue you bring up, they don't wanna hear.... There's no incentive there to do your job better." Prior to beginning the lockout in early December 2019, one 594 member remarked to one of the editors of this book that the "plant is in the toilet."

COLLECTIVE BARGAINING — 2016–2020

A dispute in the 2019–2020 round of bargaining was predictable, but few Local 594 members anticipated the scope of the struggle that would ensue. The CRC had established the groundwork for a protracted dispute during the last round of bargaining in 2016. At that time, the company demanded pension concessions and the elimination of the most skilled and experienced job in the bargaining unit, the master operator (MO). Tasked with authorizing work and maintenance, as well as overseeing safety-sensitive operations, the elimination of the MO position from the bargaining unit could severely weaken the union at the bargaining table. The union gave ground on their pension but not the MO.

Rank-and-file members of Local 594 recognized that neither the workers nor the union leadership were prepared to challenge the employer in 2016: "I think why we settled last time is we weren't as prepared as we should have been," said a 594 member during an interview. "We didn't really think that they were willing to spend hundreds of millions of dollars to save $30 million worth of wages." Ultimately the members agreed to the employer's offer, which included the creation of a two-tier pension scheme, and avoided a dispute. But the employer's push for concessions would not abate. Due to the delay in negotiating the 2017 deal, discussion of the next contract began only one and half years later.

Weeks before the 2019 lockout, Gil Le Dressay, VP of refinery operations, stated: "Bringing trailers on-site [to house replacement workers] is not something we want to do, but is something we have to do for the safety of our people and our community.... We must be prepared to safely run our refinery in the event of a labour disruption."[51] After failed attempts at bargaining and mediation, the union served the company with the required forty-eight-hour notice of job action on December 4, 2019. The company responded by declaring a lockout before the strike could commence.[52]

Prior to the union's strike notice, the co-op said it had no plans to lock out employees before Christmas, but the threat of uncertain disruptions, like work-to-rule, forced its hand. The CRC was racing to secure occupancy permits for its "scab camp," situated on land leased from the City of Regina for the stated purpose of a temporary work camp, as it wrestled with fire codes and other building standards even after the lockout had commenced. Senior managers noted that the camp had been filling up before the local authorities had granted all the permits, pointing to the significance of the camp for the refinery.[53] Picket lines were immediately established at all entrances and exits to the plant, with fuel trucks delayed thirty minutes or more in some cases.

The delay of fuel trucks in and out of the refinery complex prompted the CRC to seek an injunction against the union on December 17, claiming that picketers had been involved in improper and illegal conduct on the picket lines and had threatened violence and assault.[54] While Unifor's legal counsel requested time to prepare a response, the court immediately instituted a five-minute limit on the blockade of vehicles used to shuttle replacement workers, fuel, and supplies into and out of the facility.[55] Helicopters were already being deployed to outflank the picket line, even at the early stage of the lockout.

Both the summary of injunction affidavits and statements from workers on the line suggest that the company was needlessly dispatching fuel trucks to the site to exaggerate the hardship faced by the employer, drivers, and contracted trucking companies and to build a case for legal action.[56] As one worker alleged in court documents, "fuel trucks [were] leaving the Complex empty or underloaded." In-scope dispatchers also said that it is not uncommon for truckers to wait extended periods of time in the fuel marshalling area of the refinery, further indicating that the employer may have deliberately created a sense of urgency that could be used against Local 594.[57]

Through the injunction, a long-standing legal tool, the employer sought to debilitate labour's capacity to disrupt business operations while nominally supporting the right to picket — provided it had no meaningful effect. "In a labour dispute," Banda made clear, "everyone understands that there's two rights: there's the right for the union to picket in a peaceful way and there's the right for the business to operate, and what we have been denied is the ability to operate."[58] Documents submitted by the employer's legal team reveal the company's interest in criminalizing the activities of the union, its members, and even community allies. Evidence drawn from access to information documents reveals that the company wanted the provincial government to go even further by involving the Ministry of Corrections, Policing, and Public Safety directly if the municipal police force and courts failed to uphold the company's business interests.[59]

In mid-December, Unifor's national leadership called for a boycott of all FCL-affiliated co-op businesses.[60] By the New Year, the public face of the dispute quickly shifted from Local 594 members and its executive team to Unifor's national leadership, marking a turning point in the lockout. Bargaining was now taking place in full public view, as both sides launched comprehensive advertising campaigns defending their respective positions. Unifor's national executive largely took over decision making, putting a community unionism strategy developed by Local 594 in jeopardy as securing public sympathy gave way to militant confrontation with the employer. The stated reason for the lockout — the need for savings to transition the refinery to compete in a "low-carbon" economy — was no longer being discussed.

In January 2020, companies affected by the picket lines began coming to the aid of the refinery. Owners of trucking companies made a public appeal to municipal and provincial leaders to crack down on locked-out workers, specifically demanding the Regina Police Service (RPS) investigate alleged acts of sabotage against trucks.[61] This resulted in trucking companies staging their own act of civil disobedience by blocking traffic in the city's downtown corridor for a day as a protest against the government's unwillingness to dismantle the picket lines. Similar allegations surfaced as local residents accused union members of using caltrops to spike the roadways adjacent to the refinery.[62] Trucking companies continued their appeal by writing to the premier, provincial ministers, mayor and city council, and the Regina police chief to escalate pressure on the union. Little was said in the media of the employer's role in the lockout.[63]

In an effort to pressure both the company and provincial government to take action, Unifor barricaded all entrances to the refinery on January 20, 2020. Hours later the labour relations terrain shifted considerably when Unifor's national president, Jerry Dias, was arrested by the municipal police, along with several picketing workers, for violating the injunction.[64] Dias's arrest signalled the significance of the dispute to labour leaders across Canada. Prior to the arrests, unions in the province had been officially silent, as Unifor was unaffiliated with the Saskatchewan Federation of Labour and the Canadian Labour Congress. The lack of solidarity undermined attempts to build a broader campaign not only in support of Local 594, but also for workplace pensions and benefits in a profitable oil and gas industry. Dias's detainment catalyzed a protracted assault by the employer on Unifor's "eastern Canadian" roots at a time when the latest western separatist movement, known as #Wexit, was gaining traction in the region and premiers Moe and Kenney, in Alberta, were constantly attacking Ottawa. The CRC continued to cast Unifor as an outsider, not aligned with the interests of western Canadians; it silenced efforts to build rapport with members of the public and further alienated Local 594 from mainstream Saskatchewan.[65] Tension increased in the community and many 594 members felt unsupported walking the line during the cold prairie winter.

By February 2020, pressure for increased police presence on the picket lines escalated as union blockades began to inflict gas shortages at Co-op and other service stations in Manitoba, Saskatchewan, and Alberta. Regina's police chief had long struggled to resist attempts by political leaders to involve themselves in the RPS's affairs, despite being cast by the union as working in the interests of the refinery. Calls from the premier demanding the RPS enforce an injunction order issued a month earlier made the chief of police's hands-off approach less tenable.[66] At the time, self-identified farmers even threatened to detonate a bomb in order to break up the blockade, according to a letter uncovered through a freedom of information search.⁶⁷ Furthermore, FCL's CEO seemed to accept support from United We Roll — a conservative movement with far-right supporters — in response to confrontations at Alberta Co-op Cardlock stations.⁶⁸ Opponents of Local 594 also used social media to shift the narrative about the dispute, casting workers as entitled union "thugs" working against the interests of rural Saskatchewan. Additional picket line arrests and a permanent police presence at the blockade soon emerged. Throughout all of this, there was no discussion of the energy transition that is upon us.

Leading up to a court decision in February, the CRC asked for an unprecedented $1 million fine and the imprisonment of two 594 union leaders who they claimed had instigated the blockades.⁶⁹ Ultimately the union was found guilty of contempt of court and served with a $250,000 fine, along with community service for one of the local's vice-presidents. The minister of labour refused to order the parties back to work despite calls from the municipal council and Local 594 members, instead appointing special mediators to help resolve the conflict.⁷⁰ Veteran mediators Vince Ready and Amanda Rogers provided written recommendations, which Local 594 members subsequently approved with 98 percent support. However, Ready and Rogers noted in their report: "The Employer makes clear in its submission that it has no appetite to resolve the present dispute without achieving its bargaining objectives,"⁷¹ chief among them elimination of the MO position.

Amid these significant challenges, the COVID-19 pandemic hit Saskatchewan in March of 2020. Worries of the virus infecting replacement workers housed in the CRC's camp mounted, and calls for health authority inspections resulted in some government action.⁷² Escalating financial hardship associated with the initial COVID lockdown, sharp decline in fuel demand, and the length of the dispute resulted in waning public interest. Media attention was punctuated by periodic reporting. The discovery that 60,000 litres of oil sludge from the refinery had been seeping into the municipal sewer system (and partially into a local waterway called Wascana Creek) attracted considerable media attention.⁷³

On April 29, Local 594 members voted against the company's "best and final offer." The refinery insisted on continuing the lockout and self-servingly used the pandemic to gain even more concessions. By this point all legal avenues had been exhausted by the union and a meaningful legal disruption of the employer's supply and distribution line was effectively silenced. This left locked-out workers in the unusual position of lobbying the government for back-to-work legislation with an arbitrated resolution.

However, the minister of labour, Don Morgan, resisted pressure to intervene, arguing that "we'd like to see at the end that this becomes a negotiated settlement that was arrived at between the two parties, not negotiated on the floor of the [Legislative] Assembly."[74] By June, Local 594 and the CRC returned to the table, and with further intervention from the mediators, workers eventually accepted a contract containing concessions that 594 had fought for over four years. A contentious return-to-work agreement outlining the use of discipline and grievances to handle recalcitrant and militant workers was maintained after the seven-year contract was signed.

The deal was a bitter pill to swallow for refinery workers. However, and most importantly, the union had managed to uphold solidarity: no workers are known to have crossed the picket line during the dispute. They also maintained the MO position in the Local, something that the CRC had, since 2016, sought to eliminate in the name of "operational efficiency." But workers did experience injustices when they returned to the plant in July 2020: the company swiftly terminated several workers (later, these dismissals were reversed by an arbitrator) and the CRC also laid off the MOs (later, in 2021, it eliminated the position entirely). The union accused the refinery of bad-faith bargaining and the Saskatchewan Labour Relations Board concurred. In October 2022, the board found that CRC had misled the union when it failed to disclose a decision to eliminate the MO position while bargaining was taking place in March 2020. In their unanimous decision, the board stated: "All of the evidence that leads to this conclusion is too voluminous to spell out in detail."[75]

RAMIFICATIONS OF THE LOCKOUT

The 2019–2020 CRC lockout holds multiple implications for the transition that will take place in the coming two decades. It is noteworthy that through all the twists and turns of the dispute there was virtually no discussion — in the media or by elected officials, the union, rank-and-file members, or the company — of the CRC's initially stated reason for its bargaining position: the need for cutting labour costs to fund the refinery's transition. Imagining the future of fossil fuel refining comes first and foremost from the voices of Local 594 workers themselves. They are best situated to narrate what was lost and gained through the lockout and how the transition can be just. But the CRC's plans for a low-carbon future are suspect.

The refinery's aim to achieve net-zero emissions is far-fetched and serves as cover for endless concessions, including workforce reductions. Workers cannot rely on the CRC, or any other employer, to advance a transition agenda that balances the interests of workers with environmental stewardship. A close look at the refinery's environmental and health and safety track records compared with facilities elsewhere in Canada shows that it lags far behind and potentially poses a significant threat to surrounding communities. Despite significant occupational disease and other health hazards for refinery workers, the CRC has been successful at deflecting political and public scrutiny of safety issues at the plant — all at the expense of workers.

It is clear that unions and workers must mobilize if they are to achieve a transition that is truly just. The pension plan dispute illustrates this point. While the employer claimed existential financial hardship should workers not concede to changes at the bargaining table, it continued to be highly profitable leading up to and after the labour conflict. While often seemingly less central than wages and working conditions, the struggles over pensions, not just in this conflict but in the wider history of labour negotiations, are important. For the most part, the media propped up the CRC's narrative around pensions and allowed many of the company's talking points to go unchecked for much of the dispute.

Finally, we must not forget the role that the state played in this situation. The police, the courts, and the government all worked to protect the interests of capital over that of labour — this, despite the pretext of the Saskatchewan government's stance of neutrality throughout the lockout and successive Supreme Court of Canada decisions that have upheld the constitutional right to strike and picket. The courts rendered the picket line ineffective and elevated the company's right to protect its business interests over the labour rights of the workers.

On the whole, this begs the question: Will the trajectory of the fossil fuel sector be one of a "just transition" toward a less carbon-intensive economy with the needs of oil and gas workers front and centre, or will the winding down of extractive industries lead to acrimonious labour relations and social injustice? Coverage of the lockout generally failed to dig deeper into issues such as labour's role in transition and the costs workers bear when they are forced into things like pension concessions. This paints a dire picture of an unjust transition towards what the oil industry has defined for itself as a sustainable future. Both workers' interests and the environment are sacrificed to assist in industry's attempt to delay its evitable demise.

But another way is possible. To build a just future for workers and the environment, energy sector unions will need to become both environmental actors and stewards of good jobs as part of a genuinely "just transition." Labour will need to build its power and advocate for itself and its communities loudly, and it must take its place at the policy tables when governments and employers are making decisions about the future of fossil fuels.

ENDNOTES

1. Federated Co-operatives Limited (FCL), "Open Letter: Preparing for the Future." November 18, 2019, <fcl.crs/news-reports/news/article/open-letter-preparing-for-the-future>.
2. Angela Carter, *Fossilized: Environmental Policy in Canada's Petro-Provinces* (Vancouver: UBC Press, 2020).
3. CO2.Earth, "CO_2 Proxy Data," <co2levels.org/>.
4. NASA, "Global Temperature," <climate.nasa.gov/vital-signs/global-temperature/>.
5. NASA, "How Do We Know Climate Change is Real?," <climate.nasa.gov/evidence/>.
6. Government of Canada, *Canada's 2030 Emissions Reduction Plan* (Ottawa: Government of Canada, 2022), <canada.ca/en/services/environment/weather/climatechange/climate-plan/climate-plan-overview/emissions-reduction-2030/plan.html>.
7. FCL, *Annual Report 2022*. Saskatoon: FCL, 2022, <fcl.crs/wcm/connect/www.fcl.crs-14309/e626b7d3-a1c6-41ed-8f5c-aa84684d72f4/2022-Annual-Report.pdf?MOD=AJPERES&CVID=opwcP2e>.
8. FCL, *Annual Report 2022*.
9. Reuters, "Canada's Federated Co-operatives Plans C$510 Million Carbon Capture Facilities," October 21, 2021, <reuters.com/business/energy/canadas-federated-co-operatives-plans-c510-million-carbon-capture-facilities-2021-10-21/>.
10. FCL, "FCL Purchases True North's Assets," April 9, 2021, <fcl.crs/news-reports/news/article/fcl-purchases-true-norths-assets>.
11. Electric Autonomy Canada, "CharIN Stages North American Launch of its Universal Charging Standard for Commercial Heavy-Duty Electric Vehicles," October 13, 2022, <electricautonomy.ca/2022/10/13/charin-megawatt-charging-system-standard-north-america/>.
12. Prime Minister of Canada, "Helping More Canadians Drive Electric Vehicles," April 11, 2022, <pm.gc.ca/en/news/news-releases/2022/04/11/helping-more-canadians-drive-electric-vehicles>

13 Government of Canada, "Zero Emission Vehicles Infrastructure Program," October 26, 2023, <nrcan.gc.ca/energy-efficiency/transportation-alternative-fuels/zero-emission-vehicle-infrastructure-program/21876>.
14 Frontline, *The Power of Big Oil*, PBS, 2022, <pbs.org/wgbh/frontline/documentary/the-power-of-big-oil/>.
15 Government of Saskatchewan, *Saskatchewan's Growth Plan* (Regina: Government of Saskatchewan, 2022), <pubsaskdev.blob.core.windows.net/pubsask-prod/114548/Saskatchewan%2527s%252BGrowth%252BPlan%252BExecutive%252BSummary.pdf>.
16 nternational Energy Agency, *Net Zero by 2050: A Roadmap for the Global Energy Sector*, 2021, <iea.blob.core.windows.net/assets/deebef5d-0c34-4539-9d0c-10b13d840027/NetZeroby2050-ARoadmapfortheGlobalEnergySector_CORR.pdf>.
17 Greg Nikkel, "Minister Eyre Decries Federal 'Contempt' for Saskatchewan," *SaskToday*, June 3, 2022, <sasktoday.ca/south/local-business/minister-eyre-decries-federal-contempt-for-saskatchewan-5440829>.
18 Emily Eaton and Val Zink, *Fault Lines: Life and Landscape in Saskatchewan's Oil Economy* (Regina: University of Regina Press, 2016).
19 Angela V. Carter and A. Zalik, "Fossil Capitalism and the Rentier State: Towards a Political Ecology of Alberta's Oil Economy," in *First World Petro-Politics: The Political Ecology and Governance of Alberta*, ed. Laurie E. Adkin (Toronto: University of Toronto Press, 2016).
20 Erin Weir, *Saskatchewan at a Crossroads: Fiscal Policy and Social Democratic Politics* (Regina: Canadian Centre for Policy Alternatives — Saskatchewan, 2004), <policyalternatives.ca/sites/default/files/uploads/publications/Saskatchewan_Pubs/sk_taxcuts.pdf>.
21 Carter, *Fossilized*, 65.
22 William K.Carroll, "Canada's Carbon-Capital Elite: A Tangled Web of Corporate Power," *Canadian Journal of Sociology* 42, no. 3 (2017); Paul Kellogg, *Escape from the Staple Trap: Canadian Political Economy after Left Nationalism* (Toronto: University of Toronto Press, 2016).
23 Laurie E. Adkin, "Ecology and Governance in a First World Petro-State," in *First World Petro-Politics: The Political Ecology and Governance of Alberta*, ed. Laurie E. Adkin (Toronto: University of Toronto Press, 2016).
24 Stuart Trew, "Pipeline Populism," *The Monitor* (Ottawa: Canadian Centre for Policy Alternatives, July–August, 2019), 2. <policyalternatives.ca/sites/default/files/uploads/publications/National%20Office/2019/07/CCPA%20Monitor%20Jul%20Aug%202019%20WEB.pdf>.
25 Shane Gunster, "Extractive Populism and the Future of Canada," Canadian Centre for Policy Alternatives, July 2, 2019, <policyalternatives.ca/publications/monitor/extractive-populism-and-future-canada>.
26 Steve Early, *Refinery Town: Big Oil, Big Money and the Remaking of an American City* (Boston: Beacon Press 2017).
27 City of Regina, *Annual Reports* (Regina: City of Regina, 2018), <open.regina.ca/dataset/5e011351-3612-4a51-919d-914dcef52ffb/resource/bbdcf839-f9f5-4675-a618-383280365376/download/final-2018-annual-report-may-28-v18-compressed.pdf>.
28 Federated Co-operatives Limited, "Co-op Refinery Complex Supports 'notifynow,'" May 3, 2016, <fcl.crs/news-reports/news/article/Co-op-Refinery-Complex-supports-notifynow>.

29 PressProgress, "Scott Moe, Oil Industry Stoke 'Fear and Anger' Over Climate Motion, Regina Councillors Say," December 17, 2021, <pressprogress.ca/scott-moe-oil-industry-stoked-fear-and-anger-over-climate-motion-regina-councillors-say/>.
30 Nicolas Graham, "Fossil Knowledge Networks: Science, Ecology, and the 'Greening' of Carbon Extractive Development," *Studies in Political Economy: A Socialist Review* 101, no. 2 (2020): 93–113.
31 Andreas Ytterstad, Camilla Houeland, and David Jordhus-Lier, "Heroes of the Day After Tomorrow: 'The Oil Worker' in Norwegian Climate Coverage 2017–2021," *Journalism Practice* 16, no. 2–3 (2021).
32 As a signatory to the International Cooperative Alliance, CRC's parent organization, FCL, has committed to the following set of values: "Co-operatives are based on the values of self-help, self-responsibility, democracy, equality, equity and solidarity. In the tradition of their founders, co-operative members believe in the ethical values of honesty, openness, social responsibility and caring for others."
33 FCL, "The Story of the Co-op Refinery Complex," June 9, 2015, <fcl.crs/news-reports/news/article/The%20story%20of%20the%20Co-op%20Refinery%20Complex>.
34 FCL, "The CRC Unable to Accept Special Mediators' Recommendations in Full," March 22, 2020, <fcl.crs/news-reports/news/article/crc-unable-to-accept-recommendations-in-full>.
35 Brett Fairbairn, *Risk and Relevance: The Transformation of Canada's Co-operative Retailing System* (Regina: Canadian Centre for the Study of Co-operatives, 2018), 394.
36 Fairbairn, *Risk and Relevance*, 394.
37 FCL, "FCL Purchase of Husky Retail Fuel Sites Approved," August 25, 2022 <fcl.crs/news-reports/news/article/FCL-purchase-of-Husky-retail-fuel-sites-approved>.
38 Brian Cross, Brian, "Oil Slide Cuts Revenue at Federated Co-op," *The Western Producer*, December 21, 2015, <producer.com/daily/oil-slide-cuts-revenue-at-federated-co-op/>.
39 Co-op Refinery Complex, "Staying Competitive in a Changing Market," company correspondence (Regina: Co-op Refinery Complex, 2016).
40 Co-op Refinery Complex, "Staying Competitive."
41 National Energy Board, *Canadian Refinery Overview: Energy Market Assessment* (Ottawa: National Energy Board, 2018).
42 This interview with a Local 594 member is drawn from a study conducted on the union by one of the authors in 2018.
43 The "Energy segment" includes refining, manufacturing, distribution and marketing of petroleum products, as well as exploration for and production of crude oil and natural gas.
44 FCL, *Consolidated Financial Statements* (Saskatoon: FCL, 2022) <fcl.crs/wcm/connect/www.fcl.crs-14309/2c196290-a31b-48db-8e57-0556d2078556/2022+Annual+Report+Consolidated+Financial+Statements.pdf?MOD=AJPERES&CVID=oq3QTHy>.
45 Vince Ready and Amanda Rogers, *Report of the Special Mediator: Consumer's Co-operative Refineries Limited and Unifor Canada Local 594*, March 19, 2020.
46 Wayne Roberts, *Cracking the Canadian Formula: The Making of the Energy and Chemical Workers Union* (Toronto: Between the Lines, 1990), 252–53.
47 Ray Davidson, Ray, *Challenging the Giants: A History of the Oil, Chemical and Atomic Workers International Union* (Denver: OCAW, 1988).

48 Daphne Taras, "Impact of Industrial Relations Strategies on Selected Human Resource Practices in a Partially Unionized Industry: The Canadian Petroleum Sector" (unpublished doctoral dissertation, University of Calgary, 1994); J.M. Freeman, *Biggest Sellout in History* (Edmonton: Alberta New Democratic Party, 1966).
49 Roberts, *Cracking the Canadian Formula*, 252–53.
50 Laurie Adkin, *The Politics of Sustainable Development: Citizens, Unions and the Corporations* (Montreal: Black Rose Books, 1998), 134–36.
51 FCL, "The CRC to Bring Trailers On-site to Construct a Work Camp," October 15, 2019, <fcl.crs/news-reports/news/article/CRC-brings-trailers-to-construct-work-camp>.
52 Katherine Hill, "Co-op Refinery Union Workers Vote in Favour of Strike," CTV News, December 3, 2019, <regina.ctvnews.ca/co-op-refinery-union-workers-vote-in-favour-of-strike-1.4713006>.
53 Correspondence between the City of Regina and FCL secured through a freedom of information request, "Regina Co-Op Temporary Camp Permit Application," January 22, 2019–August 14, 2019.
54 Heather Polischuk, "Refinery Labour Dispute Moves to Courtroom as Injunction Sought," *Regina Leader-Post*, December 18, 2019, <leaderpost.com/news/local-news/refinery-labour-dispute-moves-to-courtroom-as-injunction-sought/>.
55 The five-minute restriction was later extended to ten minutes.
56 Andrew Stevens, "Regina Refinery Lockout is No 'Tea Party,'" *Rankandfile*.ca, December 30, 2019, <rankandfile.ca/regina-refinery-lockout-is-no-tea-party/>.
57 *Consumer's Co-operative Refineries Limited v. Unifor Canada, Local 594*, QBG 3302, December, 24, 2019.
58 Jason Herring, "Co-op Seeks Injunction to Break Up Union Barricade at Carseland Fuel Terminal," *Calgary Herald*, February 6, 2020, <calgaryherald.com/news/local-news/co-op-executive-seek-injunction-to-bust-union-barricade-at-carseland-fuel-terminal/>.
59 PressProgress, "An Oil Company Was Angry Police Would Not Stop Picketing Workers. The CEO Claims Scott Moe's People Offered to Help," October 20, 2020, <pressprogress.ca/an-oil-company-was-angry-police-would-not-stop-picketing-workers-the-ceo-claims-scott-moes-people-offered-to-help/>.
60 Jennifer Ackerman, "Locked out Refinery Workers Union Calls for Nation-Wide Boycott of All Things Co-op," *Regina Leader-Post*, December 16, 2019, <leaderpost.com/news/local-news/locked-out-refinery-workers-call-for-nation-wide-boycott-of-all-things-co-op/>.
61 Mark Melnychuk, "Truckers Servicing Refinery Reporting Sabotage, Regina Police Investigating," *Regina Leader-Post*, January 2, 2020, <leaderpost.com/news/local-news/truckers-servicing-refinery-reporting-sabotage-regina-police-investigating/>.
62 No evidence was provided and to date no criminal charges have been laid related to these incidents.
63 Arthur White-Crummey, "Trucking Companies Pushed for Police Action on Day of Refinery Crackdown," *Regina Leader-Post*, January 22, 2020, <leaderpost.com/news/saskatchewan/trucking-companies-pushed-for-police-action-on-day-of-refinery-crackdown/>.
64 Alec Salloum, "Unifor National President Jerry Dias Taken Into Custody at Refinery Picket Line," *Regina Leader-Post*, January 21, 2020, <leaderpost.com/news/

local-news/no-one-will-be-going-in-unifor-president-vows-escalation-in-picket-actions/>.
65 Omar Mosleh, "Is Regina's Co-op Lockout a Watershed Moment for Canada's Labour Movement?" *Toronto Star*, February 9, 2020, <thestar.com/edmonton/2020/02/09/this-fight-between-a-union-and-a-co-op-is-threatening-to-divide-the-province-that-birthed-the-canadas-labour-movement.html>.
66 Heidi Atter, "Regina Police Say They are Investigating Unifor Blockades, Independent of Politics." CBC News, February 4, 2020, <cbc.ca/news/canada/saskatchewan/regina-police-independent-unifor-co-op-refinery-1.5451012>.
67 Arthur White-Crummey, "Bomb Threat Was Made Against Unifor Blockades in February," *Regina Leader-Post*, May 19, 2022, <leaderpost.com/news/local-news/bomb-threat-was-made-against-unifor-blockades-in-february>.
68 Emily Leedham, "Strange New Allies for FCL CEO Scott Banda." *Rankandfile.ca*, February 6, 2020, <rankandfile.ca/strange-new-allies-for-banda/>.
69 Arthur White-Crummey, "CRC Asks for 'Historic' Fine Against Unifor 594, Threat of Jail for 2 Leaders," *Regina Leader-Post*, February 7, 2020, <leaderpost.com/news/saskatchewan/crc-asks-for-historic-fine-against-unifor-threat-of-jail-for-local-leaders/>.
70 Roberta Bell, "Regina Councillor Wants to Call on Province for Binding Arbitration to End Refinery Labour Dispute," Global News, February 24, 2020, <globalnews.ca/news/6588420/regina-councillor-wants-to-call-on-province-for-binding-arbitration-to-end-refinery-labour-dispute/>.
71 Ready and Rogers, *Report of the Special Mediator*.
72 Bryan Eneas, "Co-op Refinery Complex has Adequate Measures to Prevent Spread of COVID-19, Health Authority Says," CBC News, April 12, 2020, <cbc.ca/news/canada/saskatchewan/co-op-refinery-complex-covid-19-pandemic-measures-sha-report-1.5530487>
73 Bryan Eneas, "Co-op Refinery Complex Leaks Sludge Into City of Regina Wastewater System," CBC News, May 30, 2020, <cbc.ca/news/canada/saskatchewan/co-op-refinery-complex-oil-wastewater-system-1.5591956>.
74 Don Morgan, Hansard, Legislative Assembly of Saskatchewan, June 15, 2020.
75 *Unifor Canada Local 594, Applicant v. Consumers' Co-operative Refineries Limited, Respondent*, LRB File No. 173-20; October 17, 2022, para. 138.

2

HORIZONS OF SOLIDARITY
The Regina Refinery Pension Lockout

Kevin Skerrett

WHEN THE SIX-MONTH LOCKOUT OF some 730 unionized workers at Regina's Co-operative Refinery Complex finally ended on June 22, 2020, local media described it as "one of the most bruising and contentious labour disputes in Regina's history."[1] Indeed, this bitter lockout turned primarily on the employer's demand for major concessions on the defined benefit (DB) pensions provided to the members of Unifor Local 594. It was probably the most significant labour fight over pensions anywhere in Canada in more than a decade.

The lockout played out with intense surface drama — from helicopters carrying managers and temporary workers into an on-site employer-built scab camp to union-built picket line blockades, arrests of picketing workers, multiple court injunctions against the union, failed mediation, and long stretches of sub–30-degree Celsius winter temperatures. To top it off, the lockout ran headlong into the March 2020 arrival of the COVID-19 pandemic, which made the work of running picket lines and convening membership meetings far more difficult. The capacity of the rank-and-file members to hold together as long as they did, sustaining round-the-clock picket lines for extended periods, showed a remarkable depth of commitment.

A deeper look at the lead up to the 2019 lockout shows an even more important sequence of bargaining exchanges that merit closer scrutiny.

The outcome of this battle has to be acknowledged as a major defeat for the union. The terms of the June 2020 agreement that ended the lockout showed that the CRC refinery operation, and its parent company, Federated Co-operatives Limited (FCL), had achieved their stated goals of moving from 100 percent employer funding to a fifty-fifty sharing of pension costs with members, eliminating inflation protection on future pension earned, and significant spending reductions on its employee savings plan.

But the outcome of the lockout for Unifor 594 included another, less recognized, defeat. The reduced DB pension plan that survived the lockout will only cover those union members that were in service prior to the plan's earlier closure to new hires in 2017. A controversial concession by the union in the previous round of bargaining provided that all post-agreement hires would be enrolled in an individualized defined contribution (DC) plan with substantially lower employer contributions and no benefit security. That deal, agreed to in the face of aggressive employer lockout threats, conceded a two-tier pension structure and the gradual phasing-out of DB pension provision once the pre-2017 generation retires. This outcome raises difficult questions, not just for Unifor 594 but for the labour movement as a whole. How did this highly profitable employer — a success of the Depression-era co-operative movement — achieve such a dramatic rollback of its unionized workers' pensions? What were the challenges faced by the union, and were other strategic directions available? Finally, given the context of this volume, what lessons does this fossil fuel industry labour story have to offer for the ongoing struggle to tackle the climate crisis with a meaningful "just transition"?

In the broader context of pension bargaining, the details of this experience are instructive for launching a successful defence of pension plans. Such a defence will require unions to resist divisive proposals of two-tier pension schemes, reject employer definitions of "sustainability," and develop a class-wide perspective on pensions. Further, such a class-wide perspective will be vital for the project of developing a serious strategy for establishing economic security for all workers in the context of the climate crisis and the urgency of a "just transition." Clearly, if the left is unable to protect workers from the known risks and material uncertainty of retirement, it will have no credibility in its promises to workers negatively impacted by just transition measures so badly needed.

PENSIONS AND COLLECTIVE BARGAINING IN CANADA

Twentieth-century struggles to win adequate social provisioning in Canada involved, as elsewhere, intense debates about the role of the state. For many years prior to the Depression, the socialist left and sections of the labour movement had fought for a universal and public pension system, such as that proposed in the Co-operative Commonwealth Federation's (CCF's) 1933 Regina Manifesto. This followed important examples from western Europe at the time. Not unlike in other regions, conservatives in Canada resisted this pressure and insisted that retirement income was fundamentally a responsibility of individuals — a function of thrift.[2]

Once unions and collective bargaining had achieved legality and some legitimacy in the 1940s, a major strategic and political debate emerged over the traditional demand for adequate public pensions versus what might be achieved — more quickly — through a collectively bargained "private welfare state."[3] The achievement of major pension breakthroughs at General Motors and US Steel in 1950 were followed quickly across large private companies in the United States and Canada.[4] Canadian unions reproduced what the United Auto Workers (UAW) and United Steelworkers (USW) had negotiated with major employers. In the public sector, parallel pressures led many employers themselves to establish employee pension plans, most of which would eventually be subject to collective bargaining.

The rapid growth of workplace pension coverage in the 1950s and 1960s took some of the labour movement's energy away from the campaign for universal public pensions. This allowed organized opposition from the insurance and banking industries to limit the scope of both Old Age Security and the Canada and Québec Pension Plans (CPP and QPP), established in 1952 and 1966 respectively.[5] For a time, improving union density even pushed some non-union employers to establish pensions to prevent organizing. By 1977, about 46 percent of paid workers had some form of non-CPP pension coverage.[6] However, global economic crises — persistent low growth plus inflation — put an end to these positive trends and reopened basic issues of public policy.

NEOLIBERALISM HITS WORKPLACE PENSIONS

The policy shifts of the 1980s, along with the concession bargaining by large corporate employers, demonstrated a new resolve on the part of private capital to downsize and weaken both the established "welfare state" and the "private welfare state" achieved through collective bargaining at many workplaces. A range of liberalizing and deregulatory policy initiatives — and particularly the US-Canada FTA (1988) and NAFTA (1994) — facilitated capital mobility, intensified international competition, and put a squeeze on both wages and the tax base. This period has been aptly labelled an "employers' offensive."[7]

For employers unable to easily relocate, this offensive focused on wage concessions and, where possible, subcontracting work to non-union labour. In the 1990s, a significant number began to focus their cost-cutting on pensions. The mainstream press began to highlight the significant difference in retirement prospects between those workers with decent (DB) workplace pensions and the large number of workers forced to rely on public pensions paying benefits at or barely above recognized poverty lines. By the late 1990s, large Canadian employers with no unions began following the example of many US and UK employers by closing their DB pension plans. The difference between the two is stark. Where DB plans generally establish a guaranteed benefit that is calculated as a percentage of a worker's earnings, DC plans provide no guarantee of benefit levels at all. Employers had decided that the risks involved in backstopping DB plans — the risk that their pension contribution level may be increased by legal mandate to secure the benefit promise — was no longer worth bearing. The DC alternative involved simple individual investment accounts that eliminate all employer funding risk by fixing their cost at a percentage of payroll that is usually lower than the cost of a good DB plan. Converting an existing DB plan to a DC plan effectively transfers these funding and investment risks to individual plan members because DC plans have no mechanism to mandate additional funding after periods of negative investment or similar economic experience. This employer strategy was greatly facilitated by the stock market boom of the 1990s and the mass marketing of mutual funds and retirement savings schemes (RRSPs) that were promoted as an easy path to retirement riches.

By the market mini-crash of the early 2000s, and particularly after the massive stock market crash of 2007–2008, a number of new pension cost factors combined to accelerate employer interest in either cutting back or dumping their DB pensions. These factors can be considered in two different categories: those reflecting the "financialization" of pensions and those rooted in changes to actuarial valuations of pension plans. First, there are factors that flowed directly from pension plan "financialization." After decades of a mandated low-risk investment framework, pension law was liberalized. In the 1980s and 1990s, pension fund investing shifted significantly from relatively low risk bond portfolios into the higher risk stock markets and even into more exotic areas such as real estate and infrastructure. Once foreign investment restrictions were eased in the late 1990s, and eliminated by the mid-2000s, significant portions of fund portfolios moved offshore. While this shift initially paid off — the market boom of the 1990s led to huge fund surpluses — the downturns of the 2000s and the major 2007–2008 crisis left most plans with large deficiencies. Many employers, after years of taking so-called "contribution holidays" by drawing on surplus to pay their contributions, suddenly had to pay not only their regular contributions but also amortization payments on fund deficiencies.

A second set of pension cost factors is also worth highlighting. Starting in the early 2000s, pension actuaries began to revise several assumptions in valuations that increased plan costs. In some cases, such as recognizing improving life expectancies, these changes were good news for plan members. But they increased plan costs by up to 15 percent and more. Actuaries also had to recognize the effects of the decline in the long-term interest rates on which certain pension valuations depend. That decline was a result of both the market pricing of government debt and aggressive new monetary policies that aimed to revive growth and profitability through ever cheaper credit. An unintended consequence of these policies was to increase the cost of plan benefits on the "solvency" valuations used to secure plan benefits in the event of bankruptcy. Finally, the discount rates used by actuaries — their assumptions about future investment returns — were also reduced to reflect more cautious views.[8]

These pension cost factors combined to raise DB pension costs substantially. For workers, some of these costs must be recognized as legitimate and worth paying. If we retire at the same age but live and receive pensions longer, it will cost more. For many, a longer retirement is worth paying for through higher contribution rates. However, some employers have shown a propensity to guide the actuarial recognition of these costs in ways that generate sudden spikes. Employers then use those spikes as a rationale for deep benefit cuts or even closure of a DB plan. In the same vein, several "activist actuaries" with a conservative bent have been publicly arguing that DB pension plans should shift to a "risk-free" investment structure that essentially eliminates the risk of even short-term investment losses. Such a move would rest on a highly secure but very low-yielding bond portfolio that would in turn inflate pension costs so massively that most plans would become impossibly expensive.[9] These shifts in actuarial practice, and the abusive control of plan administration by many employers, have made recent collective bargaining over pensions a far more fraught and technical challenge for unions than it had previously been.

It was in this context that even more pension-sponsoring employers began to scale back or eliminate their DB plans. For large employers without unions — in the banking and retail sectors, for example — this was as easy as announcing that they were converting their pensions to fixed-cost DC plans or closing their plans to new hires.[10] While plan closure may have been less drastic than forcibly converting all workers to DC, it was still controversial. Closure creates a "two-tier" pension that provides inferior pension benefits to the next generation of workers who are still doing work of equal value. By the early 2000s, even unionized corporate employers with strong unions began to bring proposals for two-tier closures of DB pensions into collective bargaining.[11] From there, it was inevitable that public sector employers, constrained by austerity and budget cuts, would begin to take up the same strategies. The pressure on public sector employers to scale back their DB pensions was actively fostered by conservative think tanks such as the Fraser Institute and the C.D. Howe Institute, along with the Canadian Federation of Independent Business.[12]

Two notable episodes of union pension negotiations illustrate the difficult new landscape in which Local 594 found itself. At Inco, renamed Vale-Inco in 2006 following a takeover by Brazilian mining giant Vale, the employer brought a DB plan closure proposal to the bargaining table in 2009, prompting its venerable union — USW Local 6500 — to launch what would become the "largest private sector strike in Canada in over 30 years." After a year of bitter and protracted picket-line struggle and a restart of nickel production with scab labour, the strike was defeated. In a detailed analysis of the strike, John Peters argues that the union's strategy was inadequate for a struggle with a much larger corporate owner and a shifting balance of class power in collective bargaining.[13]

A second example of employer aggression is also instructive. In 2016, Unifor entered bargaining with the Canadian affiliates of the "Detroit Three" auto companies with a challenging agenda. Despite GM's post-crisis return to profitability in 2016, the company proposed eliminating the remaining DB pension element from the hybrid plan then in place for new hires. The company proposal would, in time, end DB pension coverage — leaving the pre-agreement hires with a closed DB plan and post-agreement hires with an inferior DC plan.

Unifor ended up settling a pattern-setting deal with GM in September 2016 without job action. The company achieved its two-tier DB plan closure and dealt a complete defeat to the union, which had, until that point, always insisted on the superiority of the DB pension model. Then-president Jerry Dias argued that the deal was a victory because it included commitments from the company to make new investments in Canadian operations, "securing jobs" for Unifor's membership. The substantive value of these investment commitments was quickly exposed as empty. Within just two years, GM announced the closure of their flagship production facility in Oshawa.[14]

Unifor's climbdown on two-tier and DC pensions had an impact on the entire labour movement. Employers across the country took note, and right-wing media pundits celebrated the deal as an employer triumph. One jubilant conservative trumpeted it as a breakthrough:

> [The agreement] represents something of a watershed, as representatives for thousands of autoworkers finally abandoned their tenacious battle to remain among the dwindling number of private-sector industries offering rich pension benefits to new employees. Under the agreement, new hires will be offered a defined contribution plan, which does not guarantee a set return when they eventually retire. It's the first time new employees at the three big US automakers will be limited to such a plan, in place of more secure defined-benefit pensions…. That in itself may mark *a new milestone in union acceptance of economic reality.*[15]

Within seven weeks, the framework of the Unifor-GM agreement, including the two-tier pension structure, was reproduced and ratified at both Chrysler and Ford. The provision of secure DB pensions to newly hired auto workers was gone, conceded by Unifor without a strike. As retired Unifor representative Herman Rosenfeld put it, the deal was "a message to other employers in Canada that decent pensions are fair game."[16]

These episodes demonstrate that even where historically strong unions exist and where corporate employers are reporting substantial profits, the balance of power between unions and employers has swung heavily against unions. Aggressive employers had become determined to achieve pension cost (and risk) reductions and saw that two-tier pensions had the additional advantage of dividing and weakening the union's membership.

PENSION PROVISION AT CRC-FCL

The Regina oil refinery that came to be known as the CRC was first established as a farmer-based consumer co-operative in 1935. Its workers unionized not long after, in the context of World War II and rising political support for both the co-operative movement and the social democratic CCF led by Tommy Douglas. Established in a period of intense political struggle and organizational creativity, the union representing these refinery workers has a colourful and militant history.[17]

According to the legal plan text document filed with regulatory authorities, a DB pension plan was established at the CRC in 1971.[18] This was undoubtedly a result of the ongoing spread of similar pensions across all large-scale energy operations and, indeed, more and more private sector employers were becoming unionized and establishing DB pensions. While the pension plan provided coverage only to CRC employees, was administered by the parent co-operative federation known as Federated Co-operatives Limited (FCL). For all practical intents and purposes, those involved in pension decision making and collective bargaining have been from FCL management.[19]

The benefits provided through the CRC-FCL plan were very typical of the private sector DB-type pensions established in the high-growth postwar period. Put simply, these plans set out an employer promise to pay retiring employees a specified pension directly linked to pre-retirement earnings.[20] In this case, after a thirty-five-year career, an employee on typical earnings would be eligible for a benefit worth about 63 percent of their pre-retirement earnings (later improved to 70 percent), though reduced by a relatively small Canada Pension Plan (CPP) offset of about 7 percent on average. For most full career members, this design would produce a decent pension benefit in the range of 55 percent to 63 percent of pre-retirement earnings. These benefits were also guaranteed to be indexed annually at 50 percent of the rate of inflation for retirees age sixty or older (increased to 75 percent on all service for post-2007 retirees, with a 5 percent cap).

This is a strong benefit but reflective of the pensions established in the private sector in Canada and the US from the 1950s to the early 1970s. The CRC plan's relative generosity should also be viewed in the context of the higher incidence of disease and higher mortality rates that are recognized among workers in petrochemical operations and related industries.[21] While there is no published record on the origins of the CRC plan, it is very likely a direct product of collective bargaining achievements secured over several decades. It is known that the plan was established and service began to be earned as of 1971. A record of plan amendments from the 1980s to the 2000s suggests it was a regular subject of negotiated improvements.[22]

In its early years, the cost of this plan was relatively low (11.43 percent of covered payroll in 1995). However, this cost was — like many private sector plans — entirely employer funded.[23] In fact, as a result of high investment returns in the 1990s, even this basic premium cost was eliminated for at least four and possibly six full years between 1996 and 2001 as a result of "contribution holidays" — a draw on pension surplus of at least $7 million, possibly as much as $12 million.[24] Employers generally defend this practice on the theory that they bear the risk of future deficiencies.

In the years following the 2007–2008 financial crisis, that theory would be tested. For the first time, significant deficiencies triggered temporary employer "special payment" obligations to amortize them. CRC-FCL also took their first step in the direction of a two-tier pension structure in 2007 when it closed the DB pension plan for new hires into management positions. Despite its continuing profitability, CRC-FCL responded to post-crisis cost increases with a proposal to eliminate their DB pension plan during the 2016 round of bargaining.[25]

PENSION BARGAINING WITH CRC-FCL

The foregoing historical context of pension provision at CRC-FCL underscores the historic character of the next crucial steps for the union. Given its colourful ninety-year history, it is surprising that Local 594 itself had never experienced a work stoppage of any kind until the 2019 lockout.

Whether due to its reputation, the growth and general financial success of the refinery, or other factors, collective bargaining appears to have been successfully used to establish strong wages, a DB pension plan, and important achievements on workplace health and safety without major disputes. As a participant in the merger between Communications, Energy and Paperworkers Union and the Canadian Auto Workers in 2013, the Local came to be affiliated to Unifor, the largest private sector union in the country. It is important to note that the stage for the 2019 lockout was set not in that year but in the previous (2016–2017) round of bargaining over pensions.[26]

Round One

Having raised concern about rising pension costs over several years and demanding a zero percent wage increase in the prior round,[27] FCL came to the 2016 round of bargaining with Local 594 with a package of serious pension concessions that boiled down to two proposals: closure of the DB plan to new hires and the introduction of member cost-sharing in its previously "non-contributory" structure. According to union negotiators, the company argued that a new actuarial valuation report showed a solvency funding deficiency that required substantial extra-company payments. FCL claimed that these new obligations meant that the plan was no longer "sustainable." In their four-page document of monetary proposals the word "sustainable" was used ten times.[28]

This employer claim was, however, without merit. The company's actuarial filings show that the employer filed a new valuation a full year sooner than required (just in time for bargaining). However, that valuation also contained a sudden adjustment to a key actuarial assumption: the discount rate used for ongoing plan liability measurement. This was a change that significantly increased both the special payment obligations and the ongoing current service cost payments.[29] Notably, the following valuation report filed in 2017 returned the discount rate to nearly the previous level, lowering both costs to more manageable levels.[30]

The union leadership had anticipated both employer proposals and began preparing its membership for a fight. In an August 2016 issue of Local 594's newsletter, *The Conciliator*, the union reports, the company had "broached the idea of placing new hires in a DC plan in the past," but the union had always "steadfastly rejected that proposal."[31] The argument sent out to members by union bargaining team chair Dan Josephson was especially eloquent:

> What's so bad about new hires going into a different pension plan? The short answer is, *that is the first step down the road to losing your DB pension plan.* It will not take very many years before the number of members in the lower cost, lower benefit DC plan outnumber the members in the higher cost, higher benefit DB plan. When the Company comes and says it wants to end the DB plan, who will stand up for you? Why would the majority fight to keep a pension for a minority that they will never receive?[32]

In January 2017, the union took a strike vote and obtained a strong mandate.[33] In the weeks following this vote, FCL obtained a municipal permit for a temporary housing "scab camp" that would be built on the grounds of the refinery — a clear indication of the company's preparations for a stoppage. The stakes were high, and bargaining reached impasse in advance of the strike-lockout deadline of March 30, 2017. In a show of strength, the membership overwhelmingly voted down the employer's final offer on March 20.[34]

On March 29, the day before the deadline, the union announced that it had changed course and reached a tentative agreement with the company. It had backed down on the two-tier pension issue. Under this agreement, new hires would be placed in a DC pension plan that was significantly less costly to the employer: between 6 and 10 percent of payroll, compared to over 22 percent for the DB plan. The level of benefits and the contribution structure for existing tier-one members had been protected. In a statement to members, the bargaining team admitted that it was "not the deal we wanted," but recommended acceptance.[35] It was ratified in a membership vote two days later.

Several union leaders have explained this decision on the basis that the union was not ready to face a lengthy lockout and feared the prospect of standing on picket lines to defend the pension rights of workers who were "not yet members of the union."[36] The bargaining team had also received assurances from the company that accepting the DB plan's closure would satisfy the company's needs for changes to the pension and resolve the issue for good. FCL vice-president Vic Huard had publicly declared on a popular radio talk show that if the union would accept the change for new hires, "every single employee who currently is in the defined benefits plan will remain in that plan from now until when they retire.... None of the existing 777 employees would be removed from their current defined benefits plan."[37]

The union's acceptance of this concession was clearly a defeat given their declared intention to resist a two-tier outcome. Beyond positional principle, there was a strong economic argument to be made that such changes were unnecessary. The union pointed out that their ultimate employer, FCL, was deriving the bulk of its substantial profits from its refinery subsidiary despite its pension bill. The financial data shows not only substantial reported profits for FCL from 2010 to 2021 but also a very large accumulation of retained earnings over the past several decades (see Table 3-1). At the time of pension bargaining in 2016, the company had stockpiled over $3 billion in retained earnings. The refinery's relatively modest $60 million solvency liability (as of the end of 2018) could have easily been injected into the plan, using just 2 percent of FCL's retained earnings, to return the plan to surplus.[38] Regardless, FCL management saw this round of bargaining as their opportunity to move against the pension plan, and they seized it.

Table 3-1 — FCL Profits and Retained Earnings

YEAR	TOTAL SALES	PROFITS	RETAINED EARNINGS
2010	$7,109,559,000	$497,977,000	$1,760,338,000
2011	$8,266,661,000	$839,355,000	$2,062,265,000
2012	$8,832,000,000	$827,000,000	$2,287,000,000
2013	$9,400,000,000	$879,000,000	$2,625,000,000
2014	$10,834,000,000	$655,400,000	$2,758,000,000
2015	$9,104,000,000	$539,000,000	$2,948,000,000
2016	$8,400,000,000	$515,000,000	$3,023,000,000
2017	$9,800,000,000	$575,000,000	$3,203,000,000
2018	$9,600,000,000	$1,100,000,000	$3,522,000,000
2019	$9,177,000,000	$959,000,000	$3,782,000,000
2020	$7,900,000,000	$177,000,000	$3,824,000,000
2021	$9,100,000,000	$495,000,000	$4,019,000,000

Note: Data drawn from annual company financial statements

Round Two

Just two years after the introduction of the new two-tier DC plan, FCL and Unifor Local 594 began another round of bargaining. The company made it clear that it would betray its prior promises and once again target the DB pension in place for pre-2017 hires. The second part of its original agenda from 2017 — imposing full cost-sharing and cutting indexation for tier-one DB plan members — became the CRC's primary focus. At very early points in the process, key spokespeople for the employer even began to claim that their need for pension cost savings was driven, in part, by the company's need to "transition" to an operation with lower greenhouse gas emissions and more aligned with environmental commitments.[39]

The employer's proposal sought to cut its ongoing costs of just under 23 percent of payroll by more than half. They would achieve this by eliminating the plan's indexation provision and by reducing employer costs through a new fifty-fifty cost-share with members.[40] They also proposed eliminating a (non-pension) savings plan that matched member contributions of up to 6.5 percent of payroll. Taken together, these proposals represented very large concessions for the tier-one members.

Local 594's leadership spent its time in 2018 and early 2019 preparing for what it knew could be another negotiation with a looming work stoppage. The on-site "scab camp" from 2017 was already being rebuilt by FCL in October of 2019.[41] After Local 594 secured a 97 percent strike vote from its membership, the company issued a pre-emptive notice and locked out the workers on December 5, 2019.

The lockout generated plenty of headlines and picket-line drama — solidarity rallies, a national boycott, union blockades, police blockades, court injunctions against union blockades, and at least eighteen arrests, including that of Unifor National president Jerry Dias.[42] But there appears to have been very little substantive negotiation during the first two months of the dispute. Instead, the company used aggressive legal tactics to apply pressure on the union and picketing workers. It was only after a full-scale plant blockade by the union that the parties finally sat down to a single day of formal bargaining on January 31, 2020. The union made a new monetary proposal, with movement, and the company responded by adding back concession items to their proposals that they had withdrawn in previous exchanges.[43] The negotiations collapsed after just one day.

It was not until February 12 that Saskatchewan's Minister of Labour Relations and Workplace Safety, Don Morgan, appointed Vince Ready and Amanda Rogers as "special mediators" to facilitate a settlement.[44] After hearing detailed proposals from both sides, the mediators issued a report on March 21 with eight recommendations for a "compromise middle ground" on key issues.[45] This included a new, fixed-member contribution rate to the DB plan of 8 percent for tier-one members, elimination of future indexation, a reduced cap (from 5 percent to 2 percent) on indexing for the accrued pension service, but maintaining the 6.5 percent employee savings plan. While the company's proposals would have reduced employer costs by roughly 17.5 percent of payroll,[46] the mediators' recommendations would have reduced employer retirement and savings plan costs by roughly 11 percent.

The union accepted the mediators' recommendations on March 23 following a 98 percent positive membership vote, despite the significant new pension contributions involved and the loss of indexation.[47] FCL immediately rejected the recommendations, arguing that it did not provide "certainty" in an "uncertain industry." It responded with its own new proposal on March 25 containing higher member contributions and a full fifty-fifty cost- and risk-share for the ongoing "current service cost," estimated to be 9.75 percent of payroll. The union eventually rejected the company's "final offer" in a membership vote of 89 percent.[48] When the union's appeals to the provincial government to impose a legislated resolution were ignored, FCL must have known they had the upper hand.[49]

In the end, a tentative agreement was reached on June 18 and ratified on June 22. Concerning the pension, the agreement was a near-complete employer victory, which resulted in gains for the company beyond the special mediators' recommendations. The employer achieved a full fifty-fifty cost-share on its future "current service cost" along with the elimination of indexing from future earned benefits. They even added a reduction of the cap on indexing for service already accrued from 5 percent to 2 percent — though this was later rejected by the province's superintendent of pensions as a breach of provincial pension law.[50] The 6.5 percent savings plan — left in place in the special mediators' recommendations — was reduced to a 4 percent employer match. Finally, an "opt-out" system was implemented allowing current tier-one DB plan members to opt out of the DB plan, to which they would otherwise be required to contribute, in favour of the DC plan with no required member contributions.

Unifor 594 pension arrangements over these two rounds of bargaining are summarized in Table 3-2.

Table 3-2 — CRC-FCL Pension and Savings Plan Provisions, 2017–2022

	ORIGINAL SINGLE-TIER STRUCTURE		
Up to April 3, 2017	Benefit	= 2 percent / year service (60 percent replacement after 30 years)	
	Employer contribution	= 100 percent current service (~20 percent payroll) = 100 percent deficits payments	
	Member contribution	= 0 percent	
	Indexation	= 75 percent of CPI (max 5 percent)	
	Savings Plan	= 6.5 percent match	
		TIER ONE (HIRED BEFORE 2017)	**TIER TWO (HIRED AFTER 2017)**
After April 3, 2017	Benefit	= 2 percent / year service (60 percent replacement after 30 years' service)	**No guarantee**
	Employer contribution	= 100 percent current service (~23 percent payroll) = 100 percent deficit payments	**6 percent – 10 percent (matching)**
	Member contribution	= 0 percent	**0 percent – 4 percent (optional)**
	Indexation	= 75 percent of CPI (max 5 percent)	**0 percent**
	Savings Plan	= 6.5 percent match	6.5 percent matched
After June 22, 2020*	Benefit	= 2 percent / year service (60 percent replacement after 30 years' service)	No guarantee
	Employer contribution	**= 50 percent current service (~9.6 percent)** = 100 percent deficit payments	6 percent – 10 percent (linked to optional member rates)
	Member contribution	**= 50 percent current service (~9.6 percent)**	0 percent – 4 percent
	Future indexation**	**= 0 percent**	0 percent
	Savings Plan	**= 4 percent**	**4 percent matched**

Notes: Elements shown in boldface were subject to bargained changes in 2017 and 2020.
* Elements in the "after June 22, 2020" category reflect projected plan terms once the June 22, 2020, ratified agreement was fully implemented as of February 1, 2022.
** The settlement ratified on June 22, 2020, provided for both the elimination of indexation on future DB pension service and an extraordinary reduction of indexation on accrued DB pensions from a 5 percent cap to a 2 percent cap. The legality of that element of the agreement has been challenged by a retired plan member through the superintendent of pensions for Saskatchewan (who rejected it as illegal). As of this writing, the dispute continues in the courts.

The employer achievements from this round were subsequently extended even further when they reported to plan members in May 2023 that a massive surplus had accumulated in the plan and that they intended to use that surplus to fund a full, 100 percent employer "contribution holiday" (worth $6.2 million) until the end of December 2025. While member rates were also to be slightly reduced (by just 2.38 percent of payroll), member contributions of 7.29 percent will be the only funding for the plan until the end of 2025 — and possibly beyond.[51] For FCL, their truncated, two-tier DB pension plan is now free and could remain so for the foreseeable future.

Given the intensity of Unifor 594 members' commitment and the unique challenges of trying to continue their lockout picket lines amid an unprecedented global pandemic, this outcome is surely devastating. It aligns this episode with the outcomes of USW 6500 (Vale-Inco) and the Unifor–Detroit Three pension disputes as yet another major defeat resulting in a "two-tier" closed DB pension. Most importantly, it offers the labour movement a vital opportunity to draw strategic lessons.

LOCKOUT LESSONS

The tenacity of the Unifor 594 membership in defending their pension plan makes understanding its ultimate defeat that much more important. In reflecting on the lockout nearly one year following its settlement, Local 594 president Nathan Kraemer points out that FCL's aggression showed that its "end goal was to break the union." It was "about union busting, but they didn't succeed."[52]

Kraemer is certainly right that the survival of a union in the wake of a battle like this matters. Some unions do collapse. Equally important to ensuring unions' survival, along with the broader labour movement, is drawing lessons from confrontations that enable a regeneration of membership confidence and bargaining strength. There are three pension-specific strategic lessons that can be taken from this dispute.

Lesson one is the importance of resisting two-tier pensions in the interest of not only the "tier-two" new hires but also, crucially, the supposedly protected "tier-one" members. When employers propose two-tier pensions they are inviting unions to limit the horizon of their solidarity to their current members only and to allocate the cost of the concession to other workers who will have no vote in the ratification. It is essentially an invitation by employers for unions to betray their future members and risk weakening internal cohesion in the short and long term. This dynamic is no secret. It was explicitly recognized in Unifor 594's newsletter in the midst of the crucial 2017 negotiations ("round one"). In a sharp commentary about the employer's pension proposals — including the two-tier aspect — shop steward Jason Kelly observed:

> It is more important than ever to continue to improve the working conditions of the plant for the future generations who don't even work here yet. Imagine if the previous union leaders gave in to pressure about pension, or the savings plan, or seniority rights?[53]

This point underlines the intergenerational compact that gives past union struggles and strength a legacy that endures. Being hired into a unionized position is so valuable precisely because new members are immediately (or very quickly) granted the wages and working conditions that had been won by previous generations through hard struggle and sacrifice. In a world where two-tier pensions become accepted by unions, the consequences for "union consciousness," let alone class consciousness, are obvious. From that point, even a union that *declares* that its fight is for "pension security for every worker" — as Unifor 594 said in the weeks before the 2019 lockout — will be compromised.[54]

This erosion of union consciousness poses a very serious risk to the integrity of the union. A universal union struggle is for the principle of equal pay for work of "equal value" — a job wage rate (despite classification and wage hierarchies) and common provisions for pensions, benefits, and working conditions. As with two-tier wage systems, two-tier pensions involve unequal compensation for the same work.[55] As the second tier of new hires arrives and grows, they will learn of their substandard pension and will want to know whether *their union* accepted this division or resisted it. In turn, as the second tier cohort grows, the employer gains a stronger position to move against the first tier, knowing that the union may struggle to muster a strike vote or other membership action in defence of the older, tier-one members and their now-shrinking and less risk-pooled plan.[56]

For unions that do end up inheriting or accepting two-tier pension provisions, it should be an explicit goal to find a path back to one tier, even if this means asking those in tier one to compromise. This is in part a matter of principle but also a recognition that membership resentment of the differential will weaken the union's bargaining strength — even for non-pension issues.[57] Unions that end up with or inherit two-tier compensation of any sort must resist employer attempts to introduce any more, and publicly oppose them, not only to protect their future members but to protect themselves. To take just one example, the principled opposition to two-tier pensions within USW 6500 (Vale-Inco) reported above survived the 2010 defeat of their strike. When Vale proposed a two-tier provision for retiree health benefits in June 2021, the union struck again, this time successfully.[58] Making this a union priority will involve serious mass membership education work to ensure that members understand the past experiences and consequences of two-tier systems.

Second, a meaningful union pension defence requires a class-wide perspective. The fact that an enormously profitable operation like FCL would prioritize the closure and phase-out of its DB pension plan reopens fundamental questions about how pension provisioning is most efficiently organized and how workers should fight for it. The move in the 1950s to bargain for workplace pensions led many unions to turn at least partly away from previous commitments to fight for an adequate social security or pension system for all workers. Ultimately, this resulted in a fragmented system in which fewer than 25 percent of workers now have a DB pension at work, and fewer than 10 percent of private sector workers have one. As a result, very significant pension inequality is often viewed as normal. That acceptance clearly undercuts union efforts to generate broader public support for their defence of existing plans. In this context, a continued reliance on simple union militancy in support of an essentially sectional strategy to protect existing pensions, while most workers face grim retirement prospects, will not attract public support.[59] Unless other workers feel some sense that a pension win for unionized workers could have a positive spillover effect for non-union workers (as was the case from the 1950s to the 1970s), broader solidarity is difficult to win.

These points highlight the fact that the political support for a universal health care system came originally from the class-wide perspective of the socialist left. The argument for universal health care was made popular by showing the simple logic and cost efficiency of risk pooling. Unlike the situation in the US, Canadian unions and the organized left succeeded in socializing the risks and costs of medicare. Medicare is an example of a system whose universality is the source of both financial efficiency and popular legitimacy. Today, it is clearer than ever that the most efficient and comprehensive "risk pool" for pension provision is society as a whole, and it is all workers — indeed, all members of society — who share a need for basic income security in retirement. Unions need to integrate a class-wide perspective into their efforts. This means recognizing that the deteriorating pension situation of the broader working class and of the population in general is not just unfortunate but a major problem for all unionized workers with pensions. Responding to this problem needs to become a visible, genuine priority for all unions and particularly those that have managed to hang on to DB pensions. Rather than limiting union "solidarity work" and outreach to United Way and charitable fundraising, unions could take up advocacy for workers in precarious jobs without pensions — disproportionately racialized workers, migrant workers, and women. They could also focus on the need to rebuild the income support programs that have been such targets of neoliberal policies — social assistance, unemployment insurance, and workers' compensation. Such a shift would also ask all unions to view every major pension fight — such as those taken up by Unifor Local 594 and the 2009 USW strike at Inco — as deserving of much greater support than was provided.

To be sure, such a shift towards universal pension benefits will not be easy, and it will require unions to take politics more seriously. It will also mean a reorientation in how unions function and a meaningful effort to engage in political organizing and membership mobilization. Having achieved an important but quite limited expansion of the CPP (and QPP) in 2016, the labour movement could reaffirm its prior ambitions and go further — back to the Regina Manifesto's call for a public pension system that pays enough for everyone to live with dignity in retirement. The class basis for such a plan is as clear as it is for public health care — but the political commitment behind it still needs to be built. For those who fear that such an agenda is too ambitious, or too political, the final outcome of the FCL pension lockout offers more than enough evidence that "business as usual" pension bargaining is not working.

Finally, a third lesson emerging from this dispute involves the need to fully extend our "horizon of solidarity" so as to include even the planetary ecosystem on which we all depend. This means rejecting attempts by fossil fuel industry employers such as FCL to cloak their moves in a greenwashed language of "sustainability." As is the case with virtually all employers and pension administrators who propose major pension cuts, FCL made frequent reference to the need for "sustainable" pensions. They argued that the rising cost of their DB pension plan and the fact that other employers in the oil and gas sector had already reduced or eliminated their DB pension commitments made the long-standing plan for Unifor 594 members "unsustainable." But what does this mean inside a business whose operation is itself fundamentally unsustainable?

Of course, as shown here, this employer's financially driven notion of "sustainable" was itself a fabrication. The CRC and FCL had been hugely profitable for several decades leading up to the purported pension crisis. By 2016 they had banked over $3 billion ($4 billion, as of October 2022) in retained earnings.[60] Instead parent company FCL was giving its labour competitiveness strategy a seemingly technical veneer that aimed to convince observers that its pension plan had somehow become unaffordable — when it had not. Genuine pension cost increases, when shown to be fairly determined, can generally be absorbed over time and integrated into the usual tradeoffs of wage bargaining.

In this context, it is no coincidence that the language of "sustainability" was adopted by the management of a refinery operation embedded in the production of the fossil fuels now recognized as central to the climate crisis. In fact, leading up to and during the lockout, FCL even attempted to argue that it needed its pension costs savings because the future of the refinery is being jeopardized by the "transition to a low-carbon economy."[61] This attempt by FCL to blend their bogus financial argument about pension "sustainability" with a vague reference to environmental concerns is revealing. It underlines the danger of allowing corporate employers — particularly those operating in these industries — to control the narrative through a greenwashing campaign.

The reality is that maintaining secure DB pension plans for workers who may be transitioning to other functions or jobs will be more important than ever if we are to generate the support from vulnerable workers for a truly "just" transition for refineries and other oil and gas operations. These are issues that unions, along with social and environmental movements, must wrest away from the hands of employers. Otherwise, the real economic insecurity of workers — and particularly those working in the most climate-threatening industries — will continue to worsen and leave them viewing disruptive but supposedly "just" transition measures as another threat to their livelihoods. In that sense, this episode underlines the importance of building both an adequate pension system for secure retirement and an effective transition income mechanism that operates outside of the control of profit-driven employers and independent of the uncertain bargaining power of unions. Such a mechanism has been abstractly contemplated but not, as of yet, put into place. The work of doing so is urgent and should be guided by the many lessons offered by the struggle reviewed here.

Endnotes

1. CBC News, "Coop Refinery Complex, Union Sign Deal to End Labour Dispute." June 22, 2020, <cbc.ca/news/canada/saskatchewan/labour-co-op-refinery-unifor-local-594-regina-deal-signed-1.5622636>.
2. Elizabeth Shilton's legal work underlines the continuity of this logic through the system's early evolution. See Elizabeth Shilton, *Empty Promises: Why Workplace Pension Law Doesn't Deliver Pensions* (Montreal: McGill-Queen's University Press, 2016).
3. See Sam Gindin, "Rethinking Unions, Registering Socialism," in *Socialist Register 2013: The Question of Strategy* (Halifax: Fernwood Books, 2012).
4. See Kevin Skerrett and Sam Gindin, "The Failure of Canada's Financialized Pension System: An Alternative Proposal for Retirement with Dignity," in *The Contradictions of Pension Fund Capitalism*, eds. Kevin Skerrett, Johanna Weststar, Simon Archer, and Chris Roberts (Ithaca: Cornell University Press, 2018).
5. Skerrett and Gindin, "The Failure," 260.
6. Marie Drolet and René Morrissette, "New Facts on Pension Coverage in Canada," *Insights on Canadian Society* (Statistics Canada fact sheet), December 18, 2014, 2.
7. Greg Albo and Dan Crow, "Neoliberalism, NAFTA, and the State of the North American Labour Movements," *Just Labour* 6/7, no. 13 (2005).
8. For a recent industry snapshot of these trends, see Watson Towers Wyatt, "Pension Finance Watch: Fourth Quarter 2021," January 25, 2022, <wtwco.com/en-CA/Insights/2022/01/pension-finance-watch-fourth-quarter-2021>.
9. See Fred Vettese, "The Biggest Myth About Defined Benefit Pensions is How Much They Cost," *Financial Post*, September 6, 2014. Vettese references similar work prepared for the C.D. Howe Institute by retired actuary Malcolm Hamilton.
10. For data and commentary on the re-emergence of two-tier compensation systems, see Michael MacNeil, "Two-Tier Workplace Compensation: Issues and Remedies." *Canadian Labour and Employment Law Journal* 17, no. 1 (2013).
11. Between 1991 and 2006, the number of workers participating in DC pension plans almost doubled (from 466,000 to 899,000), while the number in DB plans fell by 192,000 despite an overall employment increase of 29 percent. See Philippe Gougeon, "Shifting Pensions." *Perspectives on Labour and Income*, Statistics Canada, May 2009.
12. For example, see Jim Leech and Jacquie McNish, *The Third Rail: Saving Canada's Pension System* (Toronto: Signal, 2013).
13. John Peters, "Down in the Vale: Globalization, Unions on the Defensive, and the

USW Local 6500 Strike in Sudbury, 2009–2010," *Labour / Le Travail* 66 (Fall 2010).

14 The two-tier wage and pension aspects of the 2016 GM agreement were examined by Sam Gindin's piece, "Big Three Bargaining: Different Ways of Making History." *The Bullet*, October 17, 2016. Gindin's article generated a provocative exchange about the merits of the agreements and the definition of "two-tier" wages. See Bill Murnighan, "Unifor and Big Three Bargaining: A Response to Gindin's 'Different Ways of Making History,'" *The Bullet*, October 31, 2016, and Gindin's response, "Misreading the Historical Moment." *The Bullet*, November 1, 2016. GM began a partial restart of production at the Oshawa assembly plant in November 2021.

15 John Robson, "The Unifor-GM deal is a watershed moment," *National Post*, September 20, 2016 (emphasis added).

16 See Herman Rosenfeld, "Ford Unifor Agreement Ratified — Voted Down at Oakville Unit, Local 707," *The Bullet*, November 11, 2016.

17 For a history of this local, see Doug Nesbitt and Andrew Stevens, "Local 594 and the Lost History of Oil Worker Unionism," *Rank and File*, December 12, 2019, <rankandfile.ca/local-594-history/> as well as the history published on the Local's website at: <unifor594.com/history/>.

18 According to one retiree activist, the pension plan established in 1971 was a reorganization of a prior "superannuation plan." Personal communication, November 11, 2022.

19 Reference to the employer as a pension plan negotiator and decision-maker here will be to CRC-FCL unless distinguishing the two levels is relevant.

20 Available plan documents show that the 2 percent accrual rate has been applicable to all service since 2002, with the a CPP "offset" proportionate to service, but not to exceed 50 percent of the maximum CPP retirement benefit ($7,521 in 2022).

21 See A. Schnatter et al., "Mortality Update of a Cohort of Canadian Petroleum Workers," *Journal of Occupational and Environmental Medicine* 61, no. 3 (March 2019).

22 Historical detail of plan amendments taken from "CCRL Petroleum Employees' Pension Plan," Unofficial Consolidation October 16, 2020 as well as a summary compiled by Local 594 as "CCRL Pension Plan History," March 16, 2022. Both documents provided by Local 594.

23 Actuarial figures taken from filed actuarial reports for 1995 and 1998. The full extent of the contribution holidays would only be possible with a copy of the 2001 report, unavailable at time of writing. Valuation reports provided by Local 594.

24 If the employer decided to "opt for a contribution holiday" for the period from 1998–2001, the value would have been at the high end of this range.

25 "CCRL Pension Plan History," 2.

26 Technically, contract negotiations are carried on with Consumers' Co-operative Refineries Limited (CCRL), and the pension plan is limited to employees of CCRL. Institutionally, the ownership of its CCRL subsidiary by Federated Co-operatives Limited (FCL) positions FCL as the managerial decision maker for practical purposes. The plan's actuaries formally report to regulatory authorities that their work is carried out "at the request of" both FCL and CCRL. For these reasons, all references to the employer will be to FCL.

27 See Daryl Schwartz, "Actual Actuary Analysis," *The Conciliator*, March 2017, 3.

28 See "Company's Opening Monetary Proposals," August 31, 2016, provided by Local 594.

29 The discount rate employed in actuarial practice establishes what is effectively an assumed long term-rate of return on invested assets of the pension plan.

30 For details, see Mercer (Canada), "CCRL Petroleum Employees' Pension Plan: Report on the Actuarial Valuation for Funding Purposes as at December 31, 2015," October 31, 2016. Notably, the discount rate used for that valuation was 5.2 percent, following use of a 5.6 percent rate two years previously. This change alone increased the plan's going concern liabilities by over $28 million. In the next valuation (2017), the discount rate was adjusted back up to nearly the 2014 level, at 5.5 percent, reducing liabilities again by $24 million.
31 Dan Josephson, "Special Pension Edition," *The Conciliator*, August 2016, 1.
32 Josephson, "Special Pension Edition," 4, emphasis added.
33 Without specifying the specific vote result, Dan Josephson reports getting "clear direction" from the membership on January 9, 2017. See *The Conciliator*, February 2017, 3.
34 "Co-op Refinery Workers Reject Latest Offer," *Canada NewsWire*, March 21, 2017.
35 See comments in Brian Fitzpatrick, "Refinery Workers to Vote on New Labour Agreement," *Regina Leader-Post*, April 3, 2017.
36 Anonymous interviews were conducted with current and former leaders of Local 594 on January 8 and 10 and on March 16, 2022.
37 According to former officials of Local 594 interviewed anonymously for this chapter, this comment from Vic Huard was made on the Gormley show on CKOM radio the week of March 20, 2017. FCL reinforced this message in a March 27 open letter, which stated that their offer to the union included "retention of their industry-leading defined benefit pension plan for all current employees." See "Open Letter from FCL," webpost, March 27, 2017, <fcl.crs/news-reports/news/article/open-letter-from-FCL>.
38 Notably, 87 percent of FCL's net income came from its energy unit, primarily the CRC. See Sean Tucker, "More to Refinery Conflict than Defined Pension," *Saskatoon StarPhoenix*, January 28, 2020.
39 For an example, see CRC media release posted to the FCL website: "The CRC Disappointed Unifor 594 Membership Votes to Reject Best and Final Offer," April 29, 2020. See <fcl.crs/news-reports/news/article/the-crc-disappointed-unifor-594-votes-to-reject-offer>.
40 The level of employer pension contributions at this point was described as roughly 23 percent in the "Report of the Special Mediators," published by Vince Ready and Amanda Rogers on March 19, 2020. This figure is consistent with the 23.38 percent current service cost figure reported in valuation report from Mercer (Canada), "CCRL Petroleum Employees' Pension Plan: Report on the Actuarial Valuation for Funding Purposes as at December 31, 2019," February 2020.
41 See comments by Terry Glavin, "Scabbery Pours Gas on Refinery Dispute," *National Post*, January 30, A8.
42 Details on arrests and injunctions found in Omar Mosleh, "Is Regina's Co-op Lockout a Watershed Moment for Canada's Labour Movement?," *Toronto Star*, February 9, 2020.
43 According to Unifor spokesperson Scott Doherty, FCL had "brought back concessions that they'd withdrawn from the table months ago." See Lynn Giesbrecht, "Unifor Reimposes Refinery Blockade, Calls on Premier for Action," *Regina Leader-Post*, February 2, 2020.
44 See "Province Appoints Special Mediator to Assist in Co-op/Unifor Dispute," *Regina Leader-Post*, February 12, 2020, <leaderpost.com/news/local-news/province-appoints-special-mediator-to-assist-in-co-op-unifor-dispute>.

45 Figures and details drawn from Vince Ready and Amanda Rogers, "Report of the Special Mediators," March 19, 2020, 15–18.
46 This 17.5 percent figure includes the value of the new member contributions, the reduction of cost associated with reduced indexation guarantees, as well as the elimination of the employee savings plan.
47 See Alec Salloum, "Unifor, Union Remain at Odds After Mediator's Proposals," *Saskatoon StarPhoenix*, March 25, 2020.
48 Reported in Alec Salloum, "89 Per cent of Unifor Local 594 Members Reject Co-op Refinery Offer," *Regina Leader-Post*, April 29, 2020.
49 Unifor's appeals to the provincial government to intervene with legislation reported in Brian Rodgers, "Unifor Rejects 'Final' Contract Offer from Regina Co-op Refinery," CBC News, April 29, 2020, <cbc.ca/news/canada/saskatchewan/unifor-rejects-final-contract-offer-co-op-refinery-1.5549669>.
50 See decision of the Saskatchewan superintendent of pensions, Roger Sobotkiewicz, posted to the website of the Saskatchewan pension regulatory authority, March 11, 2022: <fcaa.gov.sk.ca/consumers-investors-pension-plan-members/pension-plan-members/regulatory-actions>.
51 Peter Gruening, "Notice of Intention to Use Surplus Assets to Fund Employer Contributions to the Plan," letter to plan members, May 18, 2023. While this notice indicates that the full employer contribution is a legal requirement of the *Income Tax Act*, they omit mention of the alternative option the employer had to allocate that proscribed ("excess") surplus to benefit improvements.
52 See Nathan Kraemer, "Voices from the Picket Line — Case Study 1: Co-op Refinery and Unifor Local 594," website posted interview, May 10, 2021, <unifor.org/news/all-news/voices-picket-line-case-study-1-co-op-refinery-unifor-local-594-0>.
53 Jason Kelly, "Solidarity Forever," *The Conciliator*, February 2017, 2.
54 See "Refinery Workers Frustrated No Fair Deal Reached after Mediation Breakdown," Unifor media release, November 13, 2019, <unifor.org/news/all-news/refinery-workers-frustrated-no-fair-deal-reached-after-mediation-breakdown>.
55 For a brief summary of the introduction of two-tier wage and pension systems at the Detroit Three auto companies, see Sam Gindin, "Big Three Bargaining."
56 The inefficiencies and the increase in costs from DB plan closures are widely acknowledged by actuaries. For example, see Robert Brown and Craig McInnes, *Shifting Public Sector* DB *Plans to* DC: *The Experience So Far and Implications for Canada*, Canadian Pension Policy Leadership Council, October 2014.
57 For an example of the corrosive divide between different tiers within the same union, see Greg Keenan, "Middle Class Squeeze: In the Factories of Michigan, a Two-tiered Version of America's Future is Playing Out on the Assembly Line," *Globe and Mail*, November 3, 2012.
58 Colleen Romaniuk, "Steelworkers, Vale Looking Forward with New Contract in Hand," *Sault Star*, August 5, 2021.
59 For the Statistics Canada report of this data, see Statistics Canada, "Pension Plans in Canada, as of January 1, 2020," *The Daily*, June 29, 2021, <www150.statcan.gc.ca/n1/daily-quotidien/210629/dq210629c-eng.htm>.
60 See FCL Consolidated Financial Statement for 2021, available at <fcl.crs/news-reports/reports>.
61 See CRC media release posted to the FCL website: "The CRC Disappointed Unifor 594 Membership Votes to Reject Best and Final Offer."

3

"THEY HAD NO INTENTION OF EVER COMING TO AN AGREEMENT"

Voices of Unifor 594 Workers

Interviews by Emily Eaton, Andrew Stevens, and Sean Tucker

WORKER REFLECTIONS ABOUT THE LOCKOUT are critical for understanding the state of labour rights and the dispute itself. This chapter draws from interviews conducted by Emily Eaton, Andrew Stevens, and Sean Tucker with eleven Local 594 members. Some of these workers are still employed at the refinery, while others have since retired after decades of employment; still others moved on to find work elsewhere after the lockout. To maintain their confidentiality and well-being we have removed their names and any identifiers, as we believe that workers and university researchers face the threat of retribution by the Co-op Refinery Complex.[1] The University of Regina's ethics review board process that was required before commencing interviews with the workers deemed the interviews "high risk." Our application received a full board review and the university's lawyer was consulted about our application. In the end, the board granted us clearance to proceed under strict measures to ensure confidentiality. Labour journalist Steve Early's commentary about the influence wielded by refineries on local politics and institutions is not just noteworthy but prescient.[2] Regina is indeed a refinery town in a province where oil and gas interests dominate.

The refinery workers we spoke with made clear that the lockout functioned as a political-economic awakening of sorts. They were forced to think about a demise of their sector and confront a political terrain that very much aligns with corporate, not worker, interests. Indeed, oil and gas–dependent workers expressed their rejection of the hegemonic view that this industry is inherently positive and beneficial to the region and the labour force as a whole. Rick Fantasia called this *class consciousness*, wherein "solidarity is created and expressed by the process of mutual association."[3]

Interviews involved fifteen semi-structured questions related to the lockout, media coverage, the role of government, views about their fossil fuel–sector employer, and co-operatives. Workers offered ideas about what they would need in a "just transition" and shared their skepticism that a phasing out of fossil fuels was on the immediate horizon. They also reflected on their understanding of the dispute, as well as the roles that unions, the employer, and government should play in energy transition in Saskatchewan.

MAKING SENSE OF THE DISPUTE

Workers readily concluded that the employer's offensive could be characterized in two ways: first, as an attempt to break their union; second, as an attempt to undermine their defined benefit pension plan. They also highlighted the refinery's efforts to remove the important master operator (MO), the most skilled position in the local, from the bargaining unit, replacing the function of this safety-sensitive role with duties assigned to out-of-scope supervisors. As a class of worker empowered to authorize safe-work permits and maintenance work, the loss of this unionized position could compromise the power of the bargaining unit during negotiations and in the event of a work stoppage. The proposed removal also demonstrated the employer's aim to weaken the union and cut costs. In 2022, the Saskatchewan Labour Relations Board ruled that the CRC had committed an unfair labour practice by attempting to unilaterally disband the MO position outside of bargaining.[4]

What Was the Dispute About?

> Initially the union, back in 2007, negotiated some improvements in the pension plan, and the company, although they agreed to them, didn't like them.... But ultimately they agreed and every bargaining since that time they've tried to push back on those improvements. (Worker 3)

> [T]he push was really to get our costs down … as they were benchmarking against other producers … and getting our operating costs down, and doing that [while] trying to set themselves up for things that were coming down the line, cleaner cars, cleaner energy standards. (Worker 1)

> At one point they put it back in that they wanted to get rid of the process MO … it sounded more like they just wanted to kind of get rid of the union, 'cause it does seem like they almost wanna sell the refinery at some point. (Worker 2)

> So, ultimately they were prepared, I mean, they had been building their lockout camp in 2016. So when 2019 came around and the bargaining started, they actually, in my opinion, they had no intention of ever coming to an agreement, they started building their lockout camp right from day one of bargaining. (Worker 3)

What Was at Stake?

> At stake was the loss of the union, was them just breaking us and just like, breaking us financially so that we couldn't fight anymore. You know, I'll admit there was a lot of, what's the word, negativity and doubt on the picket lines. (Worker 9)

> Like, our salary is good but it's kind of industry standard, but the pension and the benefits kind of is what keeps people there for the thirty-plus years and they wanted to attack those. (Worker 8)

> I think our long history of working with the Co-op — that was something that FCL [Federated Co-operatives Limited] decided was not how they were going to operate anymore as

"They Had No Intention of Ever Coming to An Agreement" 49

a co-operative and they were going to take the co-operative in a new direction and operate it more like a corporation. (Worker 10)

POLICE ON THE PICKET LINES

Many workers saw law enforcement as advancing the employer's interest. This speaks to the role of the state and government agencies in protecting the objectives of capital over those of labour in the deceptively civil and mature stages of industrial pluralism (see Chapter 4). Put another way: while workers have the right to bargain collectively and engage in strike activity, the interests of employers and capital are decidedly privileged in the current judicial and labour relations regime. In the end, the Regina Police Service (RPS) — and, by extension, the municipal government — was seen by many workers as an arm of the CRC and its private security force, AFIMAC.[5] That relationship has yet to be reconciled, according to some workers.

> Well, there was a marked change over time in the police response. At the start of the dispute, the police were basically taking a hands-off approach [to] try and ensure that there just simply wasn't any escalation or any violence in any way... there was a marked shift in January 2020, when the police went from a hands-off type approach to an aggressive one ... the way they tried to break up the picket lines, the incessant ticketing of cars that were parked legally ... from what I understand, most [tickets] have been completely thrown out now because they were illegal to begin with.... Now if it's a labour dispute, I have zero faith in the police at all. (Worker 3)

> A lot of people don't realize this, those security companies that the Co-op used, a lot of them are companies that are formed by retired police officers, we were dealing with retired [law enforcement] guys doing security. So, they're sitting there retired on a defined benefit pension busting us for ours. So, I don't have a lot of sympathy for the police at all. (Worker 6)

> It was an eye opener, that's for sure.... 'Cause I was on a couple times, picketing and all of a sudden, they hauled, like, three people away. And it's like, "what did they do?" and it's like,

"Oh they didn't do anything, they were just there walking." It's almost like an intimidation factor. (Worker 8)

I think RPS took a role that maybe they thought they had to take, but given what we know with the freedom of information requests and some of the conversations that have been happening before, I think that there was definitely talks that we weren't part of between the Co-op and police in preparing for this dispute. (Worker 10)

It might be a little extreme but I have used the term "class traitors." I know you have a job to do, but that "just following orders" thing doesn't sit well with me. You chose your career path and I don't have a lot of love for the RPS after that experience. (Worker 12)

So, you tell me that's right, handing out three hundred tickets knowing that you're going to drop them later, that's a misuse of justice, right, and authority? But they did it, and it worked for them, but to me it's one of those things that, "why are you picking sides?," you know, let it play out. (Worker 4)

MEDIA COVERAGE

As Doug Nesbitt and Emily Leedham point out in Chapter 7, the absence of a labour journalism beat leaves the media ill-equipped to offer meaningful, in-depth coverage of labour disputes and collective bargaining. Press releases, rather than informed investigative journalism, steer the narrative.

The workers speak about the shallow knowledge of labour issues demonstrated in many stories and how some corporate media stations refused to air messages from the union, for fear of losing advertising revenue from FCL and the CRC. Right-wing radio personality and former member of Parliament John Gormley provided a constant stream of mostly anti-labour messaging that resonated in urban and rural Saskatchewan.

I'll tell you, it was sure as heck demoralizing. Every night I had to go, so every night I was on the picket line … the twelve-hour nights. For some of those nights it was hella cold. It definitely didn't make it any better, driving down Ring Road, and seeing all the [CRC] billboards that were, well, a little bit misleading. Or the information in the newspaper — "Oh, they make this much, and they make this much" — when really there's no context to a lot of what they're putting in. And even people's lack of forethought and being like, "I'm just going to accept what I am reading and not really think about it in any other context" 'cause that's just my confirmation bias. (Worker 1)

Uh, well, Gormley was obviously very against us, which unfortunately is the majority of the old farmer base. That's the only radio station to listen to, so, seemed very biased, if you've heard any of his radio casts. Otherwise, the other stuff I saw seemed okay. But like I said, I think that's another reason why they kinda did eventually sign that agreement, was because they were getting too much negative press. (Worker 2)

A bunch of radio stations wouldn't play the union's ads because they didn't wanna lose the Co-op as ad revenue ... I heard there were several stations that wouldn't allow that to happen.... They said they'd stand up for truckers [loading up at the refinery] or whoever they think was fossil fuels. But they were more sticking up not for fossil fuel workers, but for fossil fuel companies. (Worker 2)

[The media] simply took everything that this [CRC] spokesperson said as gospel and the absolute truth, and occasionally they would go to the union for an opposing opinion, but it seemed to me, watching the media reports, that anything the company said was gospel and anything the union said was suspect.... They should be unbiased; they should be critical and analytical about what is being said. (Worker 3)

I had a lot of arguments with my friends that keep spouting shit about the liberal media bias 'cause I don't know where the hell it is.... If companies are paying for commercials like the Co-op does, that media outlet is going to bend over for the paying customer and that's what happened. They're not going to run a bad story. They're not going to dig, if I send them pictures of ambulances going in and out of there [the

> Refinery Complex], which I did, they're not going to show them. (Worker 6)

> Right, so they [the CRC] totally tipped the media off to publish a story about the numbers because they knew that if you told people in the general public that my pension might be worth a million dollars that nobody will have sympathy for me. Well, of course they're not going to have sympathy for me, right, so it was totally garbage and we fed the media all sorts of things that were going on that were wrong, they never published a thing. (Worker 4)

THE ROLE OF GOVERNMENT

Governments and the state play an often-oppositional role in Canada's labour relations system (explained in some detail in Chapter 4). Workers provided front-line accounts of how it felt to see the interests of capital and the state align in real terms. A number of conservative-leaning Local 594 members broke their allegiance to the governing right-wing Saskatchewan Party as a consequence of what they perceived to be a betrayal. Years of anti-labour rhetoric caught up to what would otherwise be a supportive segment of their base. Premier Scott Moe, the workers insisted, was situated squarely in the refinery's corner. While the dispute was littered with nuances that challenge this simplified understanding of how political officials advanced the employer's objectives, throughout the process, courts and the labour relations framework certainly advantaged FCL and the CRC. The municipal government's decision to secretly approve the replacement worker camp on land owned by the City of Regina exposed this alliance for many locked-out workers. Others commented on the lax environmental standards and enforcement regime as indicative of the state's complacency with this company's practices.

> Well, you can see that, definitely, Scott Moe was on the refinery's side. It seemed like he wasn't for the union workers at all. He was trying to, basically, get us to stop being in his way, I think was the feeling ... I think Scott Moe just wanted the oil and gas to keep flowing, especially for the farmers and his support base. (Worker 2)

Municipal government could have done more to try and end the dispute in a fair manner. But the fact of the matter is, Federated [FCL] was throwing a whole bunch of money at the city government. They were renting the land for the lockout camp for, I want to say it was something like $700,000 ... I mean, Federated's profits were massive in the years leading up to it, which is why I think they were so eager to go to a lockout situation because they were sitting with billions of dollars in capital assets in cash to be able to spend on this ... it shouldn't come as a surprise that Scott Moe and his Saskatchewan Party wouldn't do a thing for a working group, or a bunch of workers in this province. They care nothing for workers. (Worker 3)

Well they've slowly crept their way into labour laws over the [last] ten years, it's just been a slow tink, tink and change labour laws, and the fact that we have no anti-scab legislation in this province really murders any kind of unionized staff activity. (Worker 6)

Andrew [Scheer] [member of Parliament from Regina and former leader of the Conservative Party of Canada], he said he stands up for oil and gas workers and we didn't hear one word from him once, so. And I know ... he said with the election coming that he stands for oil and gas workers, and we can see that is false. He clearly stands for oil and gas employers, companies. (Worker 8)

I felt like we had pretty good representation from our municipal government. Not quite so much at the provincial level. We did have a very big political campaign with our Saskatchewan government, we had people go every day to sit in the house, right, and listen and, you know, try to talk to people, but there's just way too many times where my representative gave me some form letter and didn't care. (Worker 10)

Yeah, I think the municipal government at the time was a little too involved in the wrong ways. Again, they didn't show a lack of bias, it was pretty clear through building permits and temporary structure permits and grade permits ... and rezoning a huge chunk of land in order for them to build their scab camp. I think they were in the company's pockets for a lack of a better way to put that. (Worker 12)

Some of the intel that we had was, you know, when the Co-op finally gave us a final offer that it was [Minister of Labour and Workplace Safety] Morgan that phoned up [FCL CEO Scott] Banda and said, "Lookit, we're getting enough pressure that you may see a vote [on back-to-work legislation] in this sitting and we're instructing our people, we're going to instruct our people to vote the way they want."…The part that was the most frustrating was, every MLA knew what this was about, they knew that people were taking advantage of the laws, and they didn't care. (Worker 4)

I think the pressure of having six hundred people outside the leg[islature] every day honking, driving, rallies, like I said, it was an atmosphere like a ball tournament in small town Saskatchewan. People were flying all over the place, there was music playing, there was honking going on. When those MLAs got out of their cars it was complete chaos from the time they opened the door to the time they went in the door. And they couldn't not talk to five or six people along the way from their cars to the doors. And I think you know the NDP brought it up, and the NDP was really good, you know we kind of held them off 'cause our worry was if it was an NDP idea that the Sask Party wasn't going to do it. 'Cause they literally would phone us every day and say "are you ready, can we do something?" and they did really well. They brought it up every day. (Worker 4)

"JUST TRANSITION" AND THE FUTURE OF THE CRC

The future of fossil fuels and fossil fuel work is a difficult question. But rather than a set of responses that aligned with the conventional narrative that oil and gas workers want nothing but to prolong the life of their carbon-emitting industries, Local 594 members accepted that a transition is inevitable. It would just be a question of how and when. Many felt that the transition is far off (2045 or beyond) and that technologies to replace fossil fuels are not yet viable in Saskatchewan. Nevertheless, they suggested that governments and workers need to be prepared for the coming regulatory and technological changes.

> If there's just such [a] slow down, why are they [FCL and the Co-op system] still building gas stations at every corner and why are they still sending so much fuel out, and why are they still making so much product? Like, it just doesn't add up from their lovely little advertisements, to what we actually know is going on within the plant. (Worker 9)

> I mean I think it's ... inevitable. I worry about maybe what replaces it ... not fuel cells but like batteries, okay are we trading off, you know, burning, are we trading off CO_2 and the GHGs for just this battery waste ... or nuclear waste? Are we just trading one problem for another? But obviously there's, there will be a point where fossil fuels, yeah, are no longer, probably, no longer sustainable. (Worker 1)

> I'm looking at 2040, I'm probably going to see, like, a lot of Saskatchewan residents who are just like, "Nope, I've always bought fuel, I'm always going to buy fuel, no point in buying one of those new Teslas." I guess maybe it'll just be, the convenience will still win over. (Worker 1)

> I do believe that it will happen. I don't think it's gonna happen as fast as people say. I think there's still a few situations where fossil fuels are still needed, like in airplanes.... So I think until those problems are gone, there will still be a demand for fossil fuels. But I do feel the demand is going to shrink a lot. (Worker 2)

> A lot of people at work are trying *not* to talk about climate change. But that demand change, like I said, the person who told me [about] the demand change was one of the engineers on the management side.... Like, that was actually [Scott Banda's] argument about the pension before we went on lockout, was to switch over cause it's probably better for you in the long run. So, like I said, we've always seen this demand curve disappearing. (Worker 2)

Well, I sincerely hope [the refinery] is still there, for a number of reasons. I think it's a tremendous value-added facility, it pumps a tremendous amount of money into the Regina and Saskatchewan economy, as a whole. Not only in the individuals who are employed there, but jobs throughout the community itself. (Worker 3)

There's things that they can be doing even when this shuts down, right, when they're doing the cleanup, they can have them building windmills or working on the new grid, there's gotta be an improvement to the electrical grid. There's lots of things that they can do, there's lots of things that have to be done, and they can transition to that. But honestly, a lot of these guys don't even want to hear it, they just want to continue doing what they've always done. (Worker 6)

They're [FCL/CRC] using this as an excuse to do what they're doing. And to me what … FCL wants to do with the refinery, they want to get rid of the employees, the permanent people, they don't want that liability right, and to do that the union has put so many obstacles to them. (Worker 7)

I don't know if we're at the spot in the next twenty years to generate the needs of our residents for power. Or that people are willing to actually curtail what they use in order to make that change. 'Cause we could totally rely on solar and wind here, but it's just people would have to be used to not using as much energy, right? Or not taking that car trip, do you need to go, right? But I think over time there will be that shift, though, because I think there will have to be that shift, but I don't know if it'll happen in the next twenty years. (Worker 10)

So that's the rhetoric at work is that "we don't have much time left to refine oil. You know, things are just getting tougher, that darn Liberal government is just putting in those carbon [taxes]." Who would've ever thought that we would have to limit the amount of shit we put in the air, right? Don't think, you're just like boo on the government, can't believe this is happening to us, poor us. (Worker 10)

Managing the Energy Transition

Despite FCL's stated commitment to achieving net-zero carbon emissions at the CRC by 2050, workers questioned the future viability of what is ultimately an emissions-producing facility. So, what happens when demand for fossil fuels sharply declines? The workers talked about the need for education and retraining, but recognized that the new jobs produced are unlikely to match existing pay and benefits at the refinery. Local 594 workers reflected on the role they saw for employers, government and their union in the coming energy transition.

The Role of Employers and Industry

> I guess for a wind down, I would hope that the employer at least environmentally is able to remediate or clean up whatever site that they're leaving. I know things like abandoned wells and things like that exist…. I have no doubt at the end of it the accountants and the lawyers for Co-op, when things do wind down, they'll be like, "well, there's no more money." (Worker 1)

> Well, I would hope that they would be looking at assisting employees that were going to lose their job to find other meaningful, significant employment, in either a similar industry or a new skill or education to assist those individuals. Rather than just throwing them to the wayside and saying, well, we're done with you now so you're off our plate. To me, that would be the ethical thing for any business to do if they're going to downsize and close out their business. (Worker 3)

> Right now, that's not even being discussed on either side…. But the companies [are] not willing to go that step, the government's not willing to help; they're just going to throw them out, you figure it out, it's retraining, it's an issue of retraining. (Worker 6)

> Or you offer a retraining program of whatever kind of timeline, and that should be money that is saved and put away, and maybe that's a little bit on both, maybe workers put away some, maybe the company puts away some, and you do some kind of shared program to make sure that that money is there

when you need it. And it's not like EI doesn't pay for that stuff, it's just that EI pays you 55 percent and eventually it runs out. (Worker 10)

Some obligation on [the employer's] part to retrain or update some training so that people are able to get employment in whatever the next similar types of industries are. Whether it's, you know, biodiesel hydrotreater or carbon capture plant or a new hydrogen reformer. If we could get them to try to help with the transition of the workforce. But I don't know that we would ever be successful at that. But something like that would be fantastic. (Worker 12)

The Role of Government

Local 594 workers saw a role for the provincial and federal governments in helping workers transition to other jobs, especially through education and retraining.

We're gonna have these programs or have this money available, for these people so we can transition them into something else and we recognize that as being good for the economy, you know, because we're keeping these people working, we're keeping them as active members of the economy. Setting up that kind of thing, I guess, depending on how that's best set up, whether that's money spent from carbon tax revenue or whatever else. (Worker 1)

I think government has to offer … some means or incentive for workers to re-educate, retrain, because their initial position simply isn't going to be there because of a change in technology or a change in society. So, I think governments will need to assist, it can't all be on the backs of an employer. (Worker 3)

And the government, it's in their best interest to make sure there is a just transition. I get it, the Sask Party wants a smaller government, they want [that], right? But you cannot tell anybody that it's good economics, or good for the economy if all of a sudden you take a whole bunch of jobs that make $130,000 a year and pay them $70,000 a year. You tell me how that's going to drive the economy. So in a province of a million people, and you take your highest paid workers, and you now cut their wage in half? They should be the ones championing it, because it's in everyone's best interest that this next generation of power is driven by paying the employees the proper wage that drives the economy. (Worker 4)

Well, I'd like to see the government have spots available for these people at, whether its Sask Polytech or the university or something, right? Like there's got to be something available for them and the financial assistance to be able to do it, it's not just "here's a course." These people have bills, they've got kids, they've got lives, so it's, you can't just offer them a course; you've got to have logistics, too, to be able to do that. So the government has got to be able to step up for these people too. They can find billions of dollars for an irrigation project to help farmers, I'm pretty sure they can do this. (Worker 6)

I have already kind of thought of doing more education anyways. So, if there was some kind of help like that, maybe, say, become an engineer and get into some kind of water treatment, then I would definitely take that up. 'Cause it would be hard to just get kicked to the street for sure. (Worker 8)

I don't know if this would be a thing, but if they were able to partner with another company outside of FCL and be like, "okay, our refinery is now changing to XYZ but we have employees who don't want to stay here," or they're choosing, I don't know, they're at the point where they've worked here long enough that they can't retire but they don't really want to learn anything new. Like, I am pulling stuff out of the top of my hat, Nutrien [a multinational potash company with operations in Saskatchewan], can they go to Nutrien and work there as a trade, can they, you know, help people job shop in that area too, right? So, yeah, I think there's lots of opportunities and lots of options, they would just have to think more outside the box than just be like, "you're either staying or you're going" kind of attitude. (Worker 9)

> I would like to see some kinds of programs or things implemented to support workers who are having their jobs phased out through this and helping to retrain and identify similar alternative work where this is mostly, you know, skilled labour, skilled jobs, so where those skills could still be utilized. Different types of power generation, whatever that may be, lots of trade work. (Worker 12)

> I think the role they would play would be trying to examine alternatives to employment, alternatives to education or training for individuals. Ensuring that companies actually invest some money in ensuring that the people they are getting rid of still can maintain a decent quality of life and that their families can maintain a level of activity and security that is necessary for the society to continue to move forward. (Worker 1)

The Role of Unions

Local 594 members reflected on the difficult role of unions in negotiating a just transition. On the one hand, no union wants to contemplate negotiating protections for the anticipated end to its industry. On the other, if fossil fuel work as we know it is going to be wound down, workers and their unions want to be at the table and have a meaningful say in their collective future.

> [T]he unions are the only voice we [workers] have, if we don't have Unifor or PSAC, or SGEU or somebody, we're on our own 'cause these governments and these companies aren't going to step up and do anything without being forced. Without that kind of a hammer and that voice we're lost. It was funny 'cause in the infancy of some of these policies that Unifor National has, we actually had some pretty big disagreements with the direction we were going. And you can just imagine where all of sudden you get to a convention and there's a motion to put a moratorium on, you know, oil and gas in the West, and it's like, oh my god, right? (Worker 6)

> I think [Local] 594, they'll be okay, they're in good hands. But I think that you are going to see a lot of energy workers in Saskatchewan that, after they've lost their job, and then you go

back and ask them about [a] just transition and they're going to be like, "ah, I wish I paid more attention." So you need to be involved, but you need to be able to frame it so your members have some buy in, 'cause if you don't go that extra step, you're just, you're politically dead in the water. (Worker 4)

Saskatchewan is a tough place for unionized workers, and you know those oil and gas workers that aren't unionized? They aren't listening to the unionized people, I'll tell ya that, right? So it comes back to, unless you have a strategy to get in their heads, or find a way into their realm, it'll be too late before you actually can do that. But I think you just need to stay relevant and you just need to keep talking about it, and I think if you stop talking about it, you're dead. (Worker 4)

So, you need to somehow grasp that mentality and put it into your speakers, your people that are representing the unionized people because the non-unionized people think "don't worry about it, I'll be fine," right? And get that message starting to resonate a little bit outward, in through the families, in through the communities, and before you know it, everybody is talking just transition, it may be too late because that is a slow drip of messaging for sure. (Worker 4)

[The union] can only do so much too, right? And when you have an unwilling dance partner, it's pretty tough to get anything done, and [the union] doesn't have a dance partner that wants to go out on the floor. (Worker 6)

There [are] a lot of things we could do to be better. But if there was a just transition to completely closing the doors, I don't know if the union would fight for that 'cause I don't think anyone would actually want that right now. But for the union's involvement, I think everyone sees the writing on the wall, but I think, yeah, [the union] should get involved. (Worker 8)

[W]e need to try to bargain, like bargain a letter that says what happens. Like this is where I think we should go as a Local, [have] a letter that says the company needs to put away some cash in a legacy fund because you yourself have said that we're

> going to transition. So, what are those jobs going to look like, can we give people work in, like, we're a vast corporation, a vast co-operative, right? We've got jobs all over, we've got an ethanol plant, right? We've got fertilizer plants, we've got all kinds of stuff. (Worker 10)

> I would say it has more to do with the CBA [collective bargaining agreement] and the contract we have with the company. So, we have job protection language, we have layoff language, talks about severance, talks about who can be laid off…. You can't … be contracting people out to do work that any of our laid-off members would customarily perform. (Worker 12)

THE LOCKOUT AND CO-OPERATIVE VALUES

Current and former Local 594 members reflected on how the dispute shattered their faith in co-operatives and any belief in the company's adherence to co-operative values. Even though the principles of co-operation were outlined in their collective agreement, FCL and CRC, they insisted, functioned like any other large private sector employer in the industry. Of course, even co-op members have little to no direct influence over the function of the parent company, FCL, and by association how the refinery is managed and run. This structure enabled a top-down transformation of the entire co-operative enterprise.

FCL's takeover of the refinery is part of the transition toward a more conventional corporate model, workers surmised, from a genuine farmer-owned co-operative to a profit-seeking corporation determined to reduce labour costs, cut jobs, eliminate in-scope positions, subcontract work, and use profits to cross-subsidize retail operations. This is consistent with then FCL CEO Scott Banda's own reflections on the culture shift he led (see Chapter 1).

> To this day I cannot buy Co-op gas simply because of who's running the company. I can't shop at a Co-op, I just, I can't go in the doors. (Worker 3)

> That's actually what opened my eyes the most, just how they so quickly turned on you, kind of victimized you, went to the media and all of a sudden you have the whole province of

Saskatchewan that hates you for them taking stuff from you, right? (Worker 8)

But I think I work for one of the worst employers, and I'll just say that broadly, CRC and FCL and together they really strayed from what they're trying to say the co-op values are. And they used every level of their business to do that. We were getting hate mail and letters telling us Bittman's [the 594 president during the lockout] an idiot and you guys are never getting a deal, just accept the deal from Co-op retail presidents from across Canada. (Worker 10)

And when I came … I think FCL had taken over, they had bought the government's portion, I think, recently at that time, and it was a significant … it had been a significant change, in how bargaining had gone, and stuff like that … I think that was, again, the start of the transition from "this is a co-operative" to "we're going to start running this like a business and we're going to start benchmarking against other for-profit companies," Shell and whatever else. So you saw a lot of that, there's always been a huge disconnect between Saskatoon, FCL, and the refinery. (Worker 1)

So, like, in 2019, I did spend probably $6,000 in the co-op system. And last year, the only money I did spend was the hundred dollars for the gift card they gave us at the end of the lockout, basically…. I made changes and started going to Superstore and a closer gas station because it was easier. I actually went out of my way to go to the co-op, which is a bit more of a drive. But I don't think I'll be shopping back there for a while anyways. (Worker 2)

No, it feels very, it feels like a privatized company but even more, but with no accountability. It definitely does not feel like a co-op — clearly, as a co-operative, we own the company and you're supposed to care for your employees and it's not [being] in it as much for the bottom line. But right now it's all cost-cutting measures, it's all bottom line. (Worker 8)

> Yeah, so I said I don't think that we're sticking to our co-operative values as the Co-op. But I don't know, maybe there's a way to get back there, there are some grassroots movements that we've seen, you know, Co-op Members for Fairness [in Saskatoon] had a huge win this year, so maybe there is part of that work that can be done from outside of a workplace, where that's more at a board level, right, where you start to influence. (Worker 10)

> It definitely changed my perspective of [the] Co-op refinery. And when I first started there in [the 1990s], you know, you couldn't find a better place to work. Everybody was a family, everybody pitched in. I remember there was freeze-ups on Christmas eve and people left their families to get the refinery running again…. And then when they locked us out and actually started to fly helicopters over, day three over our line, people really understood that Co-op really doesn't care about you, and it doesn't care about your family, they only care about one thing. So I think there was a big shift and for me, it was, you know, at the end of the lockout I didn't want to work for somebody that didn't value me as an employee, so I had a decision to make, and my wife was adamant that I was never going to go back in there. (Worker 4)

> I think a lot of guys had a wakeup after this lockout that this might not be where they end up retiring, that things may be changing. A lot of guys may be thinking what their next move is, and I've been through this before, right? (Worker 6)

GAINS AND LOSSES

Finally, workers shared their reflections on what they thought was ultimately gained and lost during the lockout.

> So, we lost in the contract negotiations but keeping everybody solid is enabling the fights that are coming now, with them talking about layoffs and everything else. The membership, you know, they tried every trick in the book to try and divide amongst the groups or divide amongst the demographics, and nothing's really worked for them. (Worker 4)

I would say we gained a lot of solidarity. I would say often that it was the biggest teambuilding event Unifor 594 has ever participated in, 'cause it was, I know so much more of the membership. I am close to so much more of the membership, and people from other unions, labour activists in general in this area. We gained some notoriety, good or bad. But solidarity, it was big for us, we showed how strong we can be. (Worker 12)

I think we definitely lost that one-team atmosphere that the Co-op used to have, but on the other hand, for us, we gained a harder core union team. (Worker 10)

Well, they certainly took losses on the pension, absolutely they did, monetary losses for sure, not only the Local but the individual workers took a big hit. (Worker 3)

Well, what Unifor gained, they still do have their DB [defined benefit pension] plan in place to some extent, they've got a lot of the language still in place. So, they haven't, they really didn't lose as much as they had stood to, kind of stood to lose. But they weren't going to gain anything out of this, it was trying to hold on to what they had. (Worker 6)

When it comes to negotiations, we, uh, I think we definitely won keeping the DB … I'm just halfway through my career you know, I think I would be okay starting over but it just, I want to keep my compensation package. And we definitely lost some things, right, like we lost our maintenance complement, which was a huge blow and that will just continue to erode our maintenance department. (Worker 10)

But then we lost obviously in our CBA, so [the] savings plan was closed to new hires, the two-tiered pension from the contract before, so that stuff. We pay into it now, we lost [pension] indexing, so some of those monetary things out of our CBA. And we did lose, at least in the time being towards the end and for now, maybe some willingness to fight. (Worker 12)

I don't know, I guess, you know, it's a weird way to say it, but I gained the, I don't know how to word this — not the knowledge, that's not the right word — but for lack of a better word,

> I'll say the knowledge of really realizing that my job is just a job. (Worker 4)

> That is building the playbook, dismantling the unions in this province, if any employer after this is able to just delete any job position out of the CBA, that's a disaster for labour in this province and maybe beyond this province. But I do believe it boils down to union busting. (Worker 10)

MANAGING THE JUST TRANSITION

At its core, a "just transition" is necessarily a workers' rights–centred environmental movement, one that balances ecological well-being with the interests of labour. Chapters 8 and 9 of this collection explore these transition pathways in depth. Workers interviewed here spoke about the importance of creating good jobs as part of an energy transition away from fossil fuels. But this is a transition workers see as a matter of when, not if. Left to their own interests, interviewees remind us, energy corporations will work to achieve their financial objectives at the expense of workers — and in this case, their hard-fought pension. Interview participants insisted that unions, rank-and-file workers, and governments must collaborate to ensure that a move toward eliminating the use of fossil fuels is indeed "just." Part of the strategy, in the CRC case, requires a "takeover" of the co-operative structure and values. Regina's refinery was never meant to be a reflection of conventional oil firms, but rather a company premised on co-operative principles. Ostensibly, co-operatives *could* be uniquely positioned to advance a "just transition" that balances community and economic interests. However, the CRC's (and, by association, FCL's) appeal to the state, the judiciary, and the police to effectively criminalize picketing workers represents a very different trend. In a politically conservative province like Saskatchewan, where oil and gas are sacred, fossil fuel workers like those represented by Unifor Local 594 could play a critical role in leading a labour-centred transition.

Endnotes

1. Local 594 workers signed a non-disclosure agreement (NDA) as a condition of employment at the CRC.
2. Steve Early, *Refinery Town: Big Oil, Big Money and the Remaking of an American City* (Boston: Beacon Press, 1992).
3. Rick Fantasia, *Cultures of Solidarity* (Los Angeles: University of California Press, 1988), 11.
4. *Unifor Canada Local 594 v. Consumers' Co-operative Refineries Limited*, LRB File No. 173-20, October 17, 2022.
5. Mitchell Thompson, "The Strike-breakers Playbook," *Briarpatch Magazine*, May 3, 2021, <briarpatchmagazine.com/articles/view/the-strike-breakers-playbook>.

4

CLASS POWER AND LEGAL COERCION
Refinery Workers Confront the Limits of the "Right to Strike"

Charles Smith and Lisa Wanlin

ON DECEMBER 3, 2019, THE Co-op Refinery Complex in Regina, Saskatchewan, notified the members of Unifor Local 594 of an impending lockout after receiving a strike notice from the union. During the six-month dispute, the employer undermined the union's bargaining power through the aggressive use of scab labour while using court injunctions to restrict workers' ability to effectively picket.[1] Despite Supreme Court of Canada rulings recognizing the rights of workers to freely picket and strike as fundamental freedoms of expression and association, the injunctions severely limited these freedoms and stoked intense picket-line skirmishes.[2] These encounters intensified when union members blockaded traffic, prompting confrontations with truckers and scab workers trying to cross the picket line. The union blockade resulted in charges of mischief and injunction violations, leading to the arrest of several picketers, including Unifor's national president Jerry Dias and his executive assistant and chief negotiator, Scott Doherty. While picketing continued after these charges were laid by police, state intervention in the lockout — through direct government action (and sometimes inaction), state-appointed mediators, administrative and judicial interpretation of the law, and police enforcement of those laws — increasingly worked to the advantage of the employer. In the end, Local 594 was forced to concede on many of its core demands, resulting in significant losses for the workers.

Over the course of the lockout, there were twelve conflicts that brought the coercive force of the state into the lockout, allowing it to shape the dispute in various and sometimes contradictory ways, and it ultimately diminished worker power on the picket line. To defend this position, we have organized our analysis of these cases according to those that occurred in the Court of Queen's Bench and the Saskatchewan Court of Appeals, but we also considered as "legal disputes" several labour board hearings and a decision from the provincial privacy commissioner, as all of these institutions applied laws that shaped the outcome of the lockout.

To be sure, not every one of these legal cases worked against the union. Several months after the conclusion of the dispute, the Saskatchewan Labour Relations Board (SLRB) ruled that the CRC had committed an unfair labour practice when it unilaterally eliminated the most skilled job classification in Local 594's bargaining unit, that of the master operator (MO).[3] The board's remedy was not insignificant: the employer had to continue the MO position while protecting workers who had seniority in the role. Examining the lockout in its totality, however, the interpretation and enforcement of the laws regarding labour relations acted, in the words of labour historian Bryan Palmer, as a "constraint, both imposed and internalized [and] as a wall of silence and an articulation of the political economy's material and hierarchical ordering of society around its concepts of property and propriety."[4] Reflecting the current balance of class forces, the law fortified and deepened CRC's material, political, social power and led to major worker concessions and, ultimately, the union's defeat. Throughout the dispute, state actors and private media outlets legitimized the legal restrictions imposed on the union by appealing to the law's nominal liberal commitments to neutrality, public order, and fairness. However, in this dispute, the law was neither neutral nor free of class bias.

This case demonstrates how the law acts to reinforce class power, albeit in contradictory and uneven ways. In the linkage between capitalism and the law, legal institutions simultaneously defend long-held union freedoms while clearly working to undermine workers' abilities to effectively challenge employers during legal strikes and lockouts (to say nothing of illegal job action), however inconsistently. Although the CRC is a co-operative organization (in name) and therefore does not fit perfectly within the mould of a traditional capitalist organization, its actions throughout the lockout and how it treated its workers before, during, and after the strike do not in any way distinguish it from private capitalist actors. Regarding worker relations, the CRC is clearly a capitalist actor, as it used numerous legal and political tools to weaken the effectiveness of Local 594's picket line. Moreover, in the events surrounding these legal challenges and decisions, both the local and national union's legal gains only tangentially stifled employer anti-union strategies, while employer court victories legitimized the refinery's use of scab labour and created a weak and ineffective picket line. It is difficult to not conclude that the interpretation and enforcement of the law during the lockout highlights the limitations of Canada's industrial relations system. In particular, the significant limitations of the constitutional freedoms of association and expression to address class power in Canada are glaring.

THE LAW, THE STATE, AND CANADA'S INDUSTRIAL RELATIONS SYSTEM: A VERY BRIEF INTRODUCTION

It is neither original nor controversial to acknowledge that law — while a complex series of social, political, and economic institutions — reflects and preserves social power imbalances in capitalist societies.[5] It is impossible to ignore that throughout history, law has never acted in a manner that treats individuals or groups as equals, nor has it valued the collective actions that marginalized and dispossessed peoples use to challenge those with political or economic power. While law can be deployed to expand rights to historically marginalized peoples, it does so within the constraints of state and ruling class power. In this regard, the law is both constructed and interpreted in ways that are not autonomous from the power relations embedded in capitalist societies.

In their groundbreaking analyses on law and labour in Canada, Judy Fudge and Eric Tucker recognize that legal regimes are the products of class struggles. Thus, they are not preordained but are crafted in ways where "coercive and accommodative elements operate synchronously, in a variety of combinations, and diachronically, as new laws do not neatly supersede older ones, but often supplement them, producing a complex legal regime." Sustained class struggle and the power of Canada's industrial working class during World War II altered the political, economic, and (eventual) legal terrain in which workers and employers interacted. As Fudge and Tucker term it, after World War II, "industrial pluralism" emerged, in which the liberal state recognized certain workers' associational freedoms. Workers won the right to organize in bona fide labour unions and be legally recognized by an employer to then engage in good faith collective bargaining. However, the rights (and ability) to strike remained highly regulated and only legal under very specific circumstances. The "quid pro quo" was that workers gave up their unfettered ability to strike except under very narrow legal circumstances after a breakdown in negotiations and at the conclusion of a collective agreement.[6] From this point forward, industrial conflict in the form of union-initiated strikes or employer-imposed lockouts were weighed against the legitimacy of "legality."[7]

Industrial pluralism has proven remarkably stable since its codification in the late 1940s. In fact, when the Supreme Court of Canada ruled, in a series of cases between 2001 and 2015, that the Charter of Rights and Freedoms protected workers' rights to collectively bargain and strike, it seemed to further embed the system of industrial pluralism in the minds of Canadian unions. Those constitutional decisions, which include aligning union picket lines with freedoms of expression (RWDSU v. Pepsi 2001) and the ability of union workers to freely withdraw their labour (SFL v. Saskatchewan 2015), took on great significance during the CRC lockout.[8] In RWDSU v. Pepsi 2001, the Supreme Court recognized that workers have a constitutional right during a lawful lockout or strike to communicate with the public about the dispute, outside the workplace or at secondary locations. In short, unions have the right to show solidarity and strength of numbers on a picket line at the site of direct conflict or at other locations at the local and national level. In arriving at this decision, the court accepted that a picket line "is not a tea party,"[9] but also concluded that normal civil remedies (torts) could prevent any egregious behaviour by picketers. While the court confirmed that union constitutional rights were to be weighed against any expression of collective action that pushed against the rights of property (the "wrongful action model"), the extension of picketing rights to primary and secondary locations was certainly a victory for workers.[10] The court's observation about the legitimacy of workers' expression recognized that picket lines are designed to publicize the striking workers' labour dispute and to demonstrate workers' solidarity.

In the 2015 case *Saskatchewan Federation of Labour v. Saskatchewan*, the Supreme Court further acknowledged that strikes are not only a powerful form of economic pressure, but they also serve to maintain industrial and socioeconomic peace. To be sure, labour disputes may have broad economic implications and significant costs for the involved parties and the public. However, the court accepted that Canadian governments have justified such costs through achieving the higher policy goals of resolving labour disputes and maintaining economic and social stability.[11]

The purpose of a strike is to shut down the employer's operation or to at least make it difficult to maintain business functions. This is accomplished through dissuading various groups and individuals from engaging with the employer. In contrast, there are few statutory restrictions on the employers' use of replacement labour ("scabs") during legal strikes or lockouts. In the province of Saskatchewan, the long reign of the conservative Saskatchewan Party has included a series of labour law changes that have increasingly restricted workers' ability to successfully unionize or to wage successful strikes.[12] It is significant that the government continues to allow employers to maintain their operations during a legal strike or lockout, which gives them a natural advantage during any labour dispute. Notwithstanding this immediate legal advantage, Saskatchewan courts have long interpreted the employer's legal property rights and the constitutional rights to picket-line expression as equal.[13] Yet when legal remedies such as economic injunctions are readily obtained to limit picket-line activity, the employer has a clear advantage to weaken and defeat workers exercising their legal and constitutional freedoms. This economic and legal reality can allow labour disputes to fester for months since employers have less incentive to settle an agreement, as the CRC case demonstrates.

UNDERMINING WORKERS' RIGHTS IN THE CO-OP LOCKOUT

The CRC lockout began because the employer was seeking significant concessions to the workers' defined benefit (DB) pension plans (see Chapter 3).[14] The Co-op's attack on worker pensions followed the neoliberal realignment of the 1990s and 2000s, which witnessed employers shifting more and more of the onus and responsibility of pension funding and management onto individual workers.[15] In 2017, the union agreed to some of these concessions, accepting a two-tiered pension structure at the refinery. Under this reformed plan, new hires were placed into a defined contribution (DC) pension scheme while existing workers remained in the much more dependable DB plan. While such two-tiered compensation schemes certainly undermine workplace solidarity between younger and older workers, the union concession on this issue came with a verbal guarantee from CRC vice-president Vic Huard that the company would not target the existing contribution plan in future rounds of bargaining. In 2019, however, that guarantee was abandoned.

Defined benefit plans are generally preferred by workers and unions because they provide economic security in retirement. Under these plans, workers may or may not contribute to the fund, but employers guarantee workers an income upon retirement. These plans may be funded or unfunded, the latter of which means the future of the fund is dependent on contributions from the existing workforce, company performance, or market returns to the fund. The more common type of private retirement plan — the one employers prefer — is the DC plan. Under DC plans, workers and employers contribute equal sums, but the risk is ultimately shouldered by the worker. Upon retirement the company no longer guarantees retirement income. In other words, workers are left with the combined sum contributed (and invested) over the course of a career.[16]

Notwithstanding the fact that the company reported a record $1.1 billion in profits in 2018 and $959 million in 2019, CRC stated that the market was moving away from oil and gas, making future earnings unpredictable.[17] Ironically given CRC's legacy as a prairie co-operative, the company also claimed that the co-op model demanded profit redistribution to smaller regional co-operatives, which were to be bankrolled by cuts to labour and benefit costs at the co-operative's leading profit centre — the refinery. According to the company, both economic realities made the existing pension plan unsustainable.

The company was well prepared for the union's rejection of its pension proposals. When negotiations broke down on September 26, 2019, the employer was already laying the groundwork for a scab labour camp next to the refinery on land leased from the City of Regina.[18] The use of scab labour was a central point of contention during the dispute. When the lockout began on December 5, 2019, the employer paid the cost of flying replacement workers over the picket line and trucking additional labour into the plant. In public statements, the employer claimed that such actions were necessary to prevent scabs from being harassed by Unifor members.[19] The union countered these arguments by stating that the CRC's pre-emptive use of scabs was contributing to unsafe operations at the refinery, where serious accidents had occurred, such as the devastating 2011 plant explosion when fifty-two workers were injured (six seriously).[20] The union was also clear that using the helicopter was driving anger on the picket line, which had been peaceful to that point.[21] Co-op's incendiary actions led Unifor Local 594 president Kevin Bittman to point out an obvious truth about employer use of scab labour:

> When the company can bring in scab labour and, you know, put it in a camp. And we're not allowed to do anything on the picket lines it definitely makes everything a little jaded and on the side of the company.[22]

Canadian labour history shows a direct link between employer use of replacement workers and picket-line violence.[23] And in this case, the daily transportation of scabs across the line led to union rebuttals that included longer than normal delays at the refinery entry gates, general frustration over anti-union attitudes among some truckers, and increased striker anger at employer surveillance over activity on the line. Placed in this context, the union's attempt to tighten the line and delay fuel shipments makes sense, but such actions conflict with management's belief that it has a legal right to the unfettered continuation of its business operations. While the employer was free to fly replacement labour over the lines, the union was limited to what it could obstruct at the point of entry. When workers sought to expand their picket lines by exercising their rights to make shipping fuel more cumbersome through secondary picketing and a blockade at one of the gates, it inevitably ran contrary to the employer's legal freedoms to use their property for economic purposes.

As these events transpired, the dispute moved to the courtroom when the employer applied for an injunction banning all picketing within five metres of company property and limiting the stopping of vehicles entering the facility to five minutes.[24] The company's demand for a total picketing ban led Local 594's legal counsel, Rick Engel, to conclude that the company really thought that "they've got a law-given right to carry on business without interruption."[25] Although the constitutional landscape regarding workers' freedom to picket had expanded since the Supreme Court's decision in RWDSU v. *Pepsi*, the company's belief that its business operations should not be impeded by union picketing clearly influenced the judge.[26] The injunction from the Saskatchewan Court of Queen's Bench arrived in two parts. On December 17, Justice McMurtry issued an interim order granting the company's request for an interlocutory injunction. An injunction of this type is traditionally used by courts to bring the parties back to a "status quo," usually by ordering certain activities to cease.[27]

On December 24, Justice McMurtry released her final ruling on the injunction, granting the company's request, although she did not acquiesce to the company's call for a total picketing ban. Rather, she attempted to weave a complex legal thread between workers' rights to "communicate with the public, including replacement workers and out of scope employees, about the labour dispute" (the core expressive right to communicate information) and the company's demand to continue its operation unimpeded by the picket line.[28] McMurtry accepted the company's arguments that workers were pushing against tortious and criminal actions.[29] But while she recognized that both parties played roles in heightening tensions on the picket line, the permanent injunction fell squarely on the union. The judge ordered a restraint on "Unifor from impeding, obstructing, or interfering with the ingress or egress to or from the applicant's property, except for the purpose of conveying information and/or soliciting support and the restriction of access to or exit from the said premises, *shall only last as long as necessary to provide info, or a max of 10 minutes, or until the recipient of the info indicates a desire to proceed, whichever comes first*" (our emphasis).[30] The latter aspect of this decision — the ten-minute delay or "until the recipient ... indicates a desire to proceed" — became widely known as the "drivers' exemption" on the picket line. Put simply, in allowing drivers to bypass the picket line by indicating a desire to proceed, the rule significantly weakened the picket line's power to stop or even delay crossing trucks. Not surprisingly, this became a contentious focal point both on the line and later when the union challenged the constitutionality of the injunction in court.

While McMurtry's injunction aligned with long-held judicial hostility to workers' expressive action that did anything but inform the public about the dispute, the restrictiveness of the drivers' exemption took many observers by surprise. Labour had anticipated that judges might be less willing to grant such obstructive injunctions (following *Pepsi*), especially ones that allowed for breaking the integrity of the union's picket line. Surely, workers' freedom of expression rights had shifted the power relations in labour disputes by placing a heavier burden on employers who try to use the injunction to weaken a legal picket line? Indeed, the *Pepsi* decision made clear that applicants had to prove a strong prima facie case of tortious or criminal wrongdoing in addition to the previously existing requirement that the courts must find a serious issue to be tried.[31] Yet in court, the judge had found the CRC's limited evidence to establish that the "manner of picketing in the first week and a half of the lockout was unlawful as the apparent purpose of some of the picketing was not to disseminate information to the public, or to solicit support of the public, but to intimidate replacement workers and others from entering CRC facilities."[32]

In our view, the court's rationale is simplistic and does not reflect an understanding of labour relations, picket-line activity, or union democracy. To justify an injunction, economic harm must be severe. In cases such as this, the "balance of convenience" test is often used to determine whether to issue a preliminary injunction to stop the defendant's allegedly tortious or criminal practices. Here the court must weigh the benefit to the plaintiff and the public against the burden on the defendant.[33] The defendant's actions do not necessarily need to be criminal but must be proven to cause serious nuisance or inconvenience to the plaintiff. In simple terms, a delicate balance must be maintained between the union's right to picket and the employer's right to protect its premises. In terms of balance of convenience, granting the drivers' exemption was far more debilitating in its position on the labour dispute. Moreover, the union was locked out by the employer after a significant majority of union members voted for strike action. The union was facing a recalcitrant employer and simply exercising its basic freedoms of expression and association.

At the same time, there was no evidence that damages to the employer were irreparable. To be sure, long delays, such as those suffered by CRC employees, scabs, and contractors, caused tensions to rise to levels that might provoke additional confrontation and potentially violence. Yet whether the court was aware of it or not, this level of worker expression will inevitably cause delay, which is the entire point of a picket line. The injunction simply aimed to deal with the *potential* for damage rather than to provide a full hearing on the events that had occurred or to explore the actual reasons for their occurrence. In short, the injunction granted the employer a legal hammer and justified it based on broader, but highly contested, questions about the actual threats to public peace or to potential tortious or criminal behaviour by the union.

The CRC's use of the dual legal weapons of scab labour and the injunction severely tempered the effectiveness of the picket line and handed the employer two powerful legal tools to challenge the union's objectives. From this point, the injunction became the focus of the conflict, and every other picket-line activity was weighed against the question of legality as determined by the injunction. Picketers' responses to the injunction (and the drivers' exemption in particular) were predictable. The union had to strengthen the line or face defeat. Local 594, therefore, doubled down on reinforcing the picket line and engaged in various militant actions, including refusing CRC managers access to or exit from the refinery. On multiple occasions, picketers prevented buses full of management and replacement labour from entering the refinery or, in other cases, stalling the worker transport for several hours.[34] The union also built several barricades at picketing gates, including several secondary locations.[35] These actions led to further court intervention. A civil case was launched by the CRC and heard by Justice Keene of the provincial Court of Queen's Bench, who concluded that the union "intentionally and deliberately disobeyed the [injunction] order" and fined the union $100,000 for the violation.[36]

While Justice Keene financially punished the union for delaying several busloads of management and scab labour, police intervention threatened to permanently weaken the union's position through directly enforcing the injunction. The calls for police action had been growing louder in January, as both FCL CEO Scott Banda and Premier Scott Moe had been privately and publicly urging the police to act.[37] The premier's comments were particularly odd as he seemed to be directing police action, something even the Regina Police Service (RPS) leadership deemed a violation of its independence.[38] Nevertheless, on January 20, 2020, the police — who had insisted throughout that they did not "take sides in a labour dispute"[39] — arrested numerous Unifor members, including Unifor's national president, Jerry Dias. Their efforts to fully dismantle the barricades were frustrated by the scale of the crowd, although Unifor insisted that the barricades would come down once the employer agreed to return to the bargaining table. The police justified their actions by appealing to their duty to enforce the court-ordered injunction. They equated the arrests to "restoring the balance" they believed existed in the dispute, because while the union had the fundamental right to "lawful protest," the "company also has a right to do business."[40] Even though the company had never stopped exercising its right to "do business," the police action allowed the company to continue operations without the cumbersome delays that are traditionally associated with a labour dispute, thereby blunting the union's principled means of inflicting economic harm on the employer. Moreover, the police's defence of their actions added further legitimacy to the company's actions and further shifted the narrative of illegality squarely onto the shoulders of the union. In this portrayal, only the union's collective actions were capable of being scrutinized by the law and that scrutiny always sought to further limit workers' collective freedoms.

Shortly after the police raid, the CRC filed a second civil contempt complaint against the union for again violating the injunction, asking for jail time and a $1 million fine to the union.[41] On February 12, 2020, Justice Robertson determined that the injunction was indeed being violated; he fined the union an additional $250,000 and found Local 594 member Lance Holowachuk guilty of contempt for not respecting the drivers' exemption. Company lawyers went further by taking aim at Local 594 president Kevin Bittman, claiming that several of his picket-line speeches encouraged workers to breach the injunction. The CRC argued that these speeches were the equivalent of criminal contempt and they demanded Bittman be jailed.[42] The union's clever legal retort, that the injunction only applied to the local union and not the national body, was unsuccessful.

However, the court determined that the employer's arguments equating civil contempt with criminal contempt during labour disputes raised a high legal bar. While speech that incites violence could be equated with criminal contempt, in this case such an interpretation would be overly detrimental to workers' ability to seek public support during labour disputes. Citing earlier court decisions, the judge determined that if the court were to follow CRC's arguments that a simple speech rallying support during a strike or lockout was evidence of criminal contempt, Charter values risked being severely compromised.[43] Notwithstanding those so-called values, the court decision on April 15, 2020, stretched the power of the criminal law to limit National President Dias from being within fifty metres of the CRC gates.[44] These events serve as defining features of the lockout: once the law restricted the ability of workers to picket, the company was able to weaponize criminal law to defeat the union.

As the various legal disputes weakened the effectiveness of Unifor's picket line, bargaining became entirely one-sided as the company pushed for even further concessions while Unifor made a public request for the provincial government to appoint a special mediator with the power to impose a new agreement. Up to this point, the provincial government had remained largely in the background, although some reports suggested that CRC CEO Scott Banda and the minister of corrections and policing, Christine Tell, had been in discussion about the role of the police intervening on the picket line and gave at least some acknowledgement that if the RPS did not act, the province would "engage."[45] While the relationship between the company and the province was certainly enough to raise questions about its neutrality, Don Morgan, the minister of labour relations and workplace safety, did eventually appoint special mediators Vince Ready and Amanda Rogers on February 12, 2020, although he did not go so far as to empower the mediators to make their recommendations legally binding. Morgan maintained that enforcing Ready and Rogers' recommendations would require consent from both parties, in addition to legislative intervention — something the government was not willing to do.

To be sure, arbitration is always a risky proposition for a union, as it takes the final dispute out of the hands of the parties. It is thus difficult to interpret Unifor's demands for binding arbitration as anything but defensive, given the weakening of the line due to court injunctions and the sharp decline in demand for fuel amid the pandemic. At this point, momentum had entirely shifted to the CRC. Moreover, the condition of the labour minister and the premier — that mediation would only occur when Unifor had ceased "all illegal activity," which included "removing unlawful barricades" — indicates that the province saw the union as the antagonist in this dispute.[46] Rogers and Ready's March 19, 2020, recommendations attempted to broker a compromise between the two parties by establishing a potential resolution to the pension plan impasse, among other contentious issues.[47] The union endorsed the report, but the CRC rejected it. The employer then sent a counterproposal to the union, which demanded further concessions; however, that was rejected by 89 percent of Local 594 members in a labour-board-certified vote requested by the employer.

The membership's rejection of the proposal led to further picketing, including at secondary locations across Regina, Moose Jaw, and even into Alberta. All these secondary pickets were stifled by police intervention.[48] The police made very public statements at these secondary locations that Unifor's actions justified arresting the picketers for mischief, leading local labour lawyer Ronni Nordal to question whether there was actually a right to picket in Saskatchewan.[49] In the meantime, the COVID-19 pandemic descended on the province, leading to even greater pressure on the union and the employer as the March public health lockdown of the province made picketing even more complicated.

In what proved to be a whimper at the end of a tense dispute, in June 2020, the union accepted a contract offer from the CRC that mimicked the original "final" offer the employer had attempted to impose on March 30, 2020. This new offer was a seven-year agreement that included modest wage bumps, but also — and importantly for the employer — the weakening of the DB plan. There was also a return-to-work plan, although the company continued to insist on disciplining some workers' activities on the picket line, which included several firings.[50] Disputes over company investigations and the privacy of those targeted for disciplinary measures ended up in arbitration and later before the labour board, as the union filed a series of unfair labour practice allegations against the CRC for violating the return-to-work order.[51] In a final show of force, the CRC announced a hundred temporary layoffs on June 28, only weeks after Unifor members began to return to work. This announcement certainly left an increasingly bitter taste in the mouths of workers and union officials, which only worsened when the company confirmed, on October 5, that thirty-nine master operator layoffs were now permanent.[52] The company's decision to push forward with these dismissals and eliminate the MO position in March 2021, even after the union accepted the new contract, led to a bitter labour board struggle between Local 594 and the CRC. When the board released its decision on October 17, 2022 — a staggering two years after the dispute ended — it found that the company had indeed acted in bad faith by misleading the union in bargaining, and it ordered the workers reinstated.[53] In other words, the employer had attempted to advance its objective of eliminating the MO after the lockout and despite its failure to achieve this through bargaining. While that was a victory for the union, it did not erase the fact that the employer had won significant concessions in the new contract and came out well after the dispute had concluded.

THE CONTINUING EROSION OF WORKERS' RIGHTS

The CRC's contract victory over Local 594 was certainly a defeat for these workers. Local 594 president Kevin Bittman recognized this in his post-lockout press conference, stating that the union was squeezed, won little, and was the victim of an employer "that was trying to break us."[54] At the national level, Unifor lost several high-profile disputes between 2018 and 2020 in Saskatchewan, weakening an already beleaguered movement in the small conservative province. While it would be unfair to place the blame entirely on Unifor, the fight for guaranteed and DB pension benefits seems to be all but lost for workers. The struggle also suggested that the consumer co-operative model of business organization does not extend to its workforce. Throughout the lockout, CRC management acted in a manner that was as callous and merciless against its workers as any private sector employer in recent Canadian labour history. Within the workplace itself, the CRC's layoff of over a hundred workers after the labour dispute, and the continuing quarrel over company discipline for actions on the picket line, continued to plague relations at the refinery.[55]

These disputes and larger political issues, however, were not the final bookend of the lockout. On March 9, 2021, the Saskatchewan Court of Appeal released its final decision on the constitutionality of the labour injunction, which Unifor lawyers had appealed immediately after the December 2020 decision.[56] At the centre of this appeal was the question of the "drivers' exemption" and whether it violated the Charter of Rights' protection of workers to express themselves through picketing. The court determined that the question about the constitutionality of the "drivers' exemption" needed to be heard, and it interpreted its role as one of umpire between two equal parties who had "two competing rights," which "involves establishing a protocol which interferes with both rights to the least extent possible."[57] These competing rights — one a constitutional human right and the other an economic common law protection of property — hardly seem to exist on the same moral plane, but in capitalist democracies they stand as legal equals. Weighing all these "rights," the court determined that the original decision on the injunction was reasonable and that the "drivers' exception rule was designed, as a whole, to keep the peace and to prevent unlawful conduct."[58]

While courts in Saskatchewan have allowed picketers to "delay access" to an employer's property, it has generally been associated with time constraints. Moreover, for the courts, the reasons for delays matter. A picket line is not an absolute barrier but an act of expression. And sections 7 and 9 of the Charter recognize that the rights of the listener (security of persons and the right not to be arbitrarily detained) also need to be considered. While none of these sections were necessarily triggered in this dispute, they imply a right to not listen to the union's message and an economic right to access property.[59] For the court, this "right" to decline to listen to communication is supported "by a significant line of authority both in labour relations context and otherwise. This line of authority provides … a principled basis to impose, where necessary, a drivers' exception provision."[60] This reasoning suggests that workers' ability to strike and to picket is not absolute and will always be weighed against other private economic activity.

Having recognized that there are multiple peoples with "rights" in a labour dispute and that they are weighed against capitalist economic activity, the court concluded that it would be "highly problematic" to constitutionalize the right to delay people seeking access to business property. Thus, the court's job, in this case, is to determine the legitimacy of the "drivers' delay,"[61] considering, among other things, "the degree of obstruction, its duration on each occasion and the length of time the obstruction has occurred."[62] In so doing, the court began to weigh the rights of workers to picket, the right of drivers to refuse to hear picketers' information, the economic right of third parties, and the right of the CRC to do business. Coming to that conclusion, the court dismissed Unifor's constitutional case.

The Saskatchewan Court of Appeal's decision on the constitutionality of the injunction put the final stamp on a series of legal institutions that undermined Unifor Local 594's ability to run a successful picket line. The labour code allowed for scab workers to replace striking workers, and the premier and Cabinet aligned their actions and messaging to support the company. Deferring to the law, the police intervened to protect "public order" and to protect the "right of the company to do business," while detaining several important union figures for simply attempting to picket. The court's decision to grant an injunction based on a narrow understanding of expression and picket line activity at the beginning of the dispute almost immediately impaired the union's ability to challenge the CRC's total control of the plant. In the end, the law reinforced and deepened an already imbalanced relationship between workers and employers. The legal rights that workers had long championed — including rights to protest and picket, as well as for freedom of speech — were always secondary to the legal right of employers to do business.

Ultimately, the power imbalance that was reflected in the application and interpretation of the law throughout this disputes demonstrates that it will place workers at a significant disadvantage as the industry begins its transition away from oil and gas extraction into renewable energy resources. The workers in plants like the Co-operative Oil Refinery will be forced to make difficult decisions with regard to training and jobs. What the CRC lockout demonstrates is that without strong worker input, transitions away oil and gas refining (whether in co-operative or private facilities) will be done entirely on terms dictated by employers. Workers and unions must fight to change these laws if they are to benefit from these transitions.

Endnotes

1. There is some controversy about the terms *scab* and *replacement worker*. *Scab* originates from the labour movement and has its origins in the nineteenth-century radical union organizing of so-called non-skilled workers. The term is designed to shame and to challenge employer power and those who undermine collective efforts for individual gain. The term *replacement worker* has no known origin but is a management term that became popularized in the 1950s. Such a term legitimizes employer action to undermine union solidarity because it seeks to normalize the use of scab labour without the stigma associated with the action.
2. On these constitutional cases, see Larry Savage and Charles Smith, *Unions in Court: Organized Labour and the Charter of Rights and Freedoms* (Vancouver: UBC Press, 2007).
3. *Unifor Canada Local 594 v. Consumers' Co-operative Refineries Limited* [hereafter CCRL], LRB File No. 173-20, October 17, 2022.
4. Bryan Palmer, "What's Law Got to Do With It? Historical Considerations on Class Struggle, Boundaries of Constraint, and Capitalist Authority," *Osgoode Hall Law Journal* 41 (2003), 466.
5. Bob Fine, *Democracy and the Rule of Law: Liberal Ideals and Marxist Critiques* (London: Pluto, 1984). See also Palmer, "What's Law Got to Do With It?" and

Maureen Cain and Alan Hunt, *Marx and Engels on Law* (New York: Academic Press, 1979).
6 Judy Fudge and Eric Tucker, "The Freedom to Strike in Canada: A Brief Legal History," *Canadian Labour and Employment Law Journal* 15 (2010), 335.
7 Judy Fudge and Eric Tucker, *Labour Before the Law: The Regulation of Workers' Collective Action in Canada, 1900–1948* (Toronto: Oxford, 2001), 1–9.
8 See *RWDSU, Local 558 v. Pepsi-Cola Canada Beverages (West) Ltd.* [2002] 1 SCR 156; *Saskatchewan Federation of Labour v. Saskatchewan* [2015] 1 SCR 245. For an overview, see Savage and Smith, *Unions in Court*.
9 CCRL *v. Unifor Canada, Local 594*, QBG 3302, 2019, para 17.
10 For an overview, see Charles Smith, "'We Didn't Want To Totally Break the Law': Industrial Legality, the Pepsi Strike, and Workers' Collective Rights in Canada," *Labour/Le Travail* (2014), 74.
11 Savage and Smith, *Unions in Court*.
12 On the history of the Saskatchewan Party's restrictive labour legislation, see Andrew Stevens and Charles Smith, "The Architecture of Modern Anti-Unionism in Canada: Class Struggle and the Erosion of Workers' Collective Freedoms," *Capital and Class* 43 (2018), 3.
13 CCRL *v. Unifor Canada, Local 594*, QBG 3302, 2019.
14 Arthur White-Crummey, "Unifor v. Co-op: What is the CRC Dispute Really About?" *Regina Leader-Post*, January 20, 2020.
15 See Sirvan Karimi, *Beyond the Welfare State: Postwar Social Settlement and Public Pension Policy in Canada and Australia* (Toronto: University of Toronto Press, 2016).
16 See Karimi, Beyond the Welfare State.
17 David Giles, "FCL Reports Record Profit of $1.1B in 2018," Global News, December 20, 2018, <globalnews.ca/news/4781169/fcl-record-profit-2018/>; Andrea Hill, "FCL Posts Second-Highest Earnings in 2019," *StarPhoenix*, December 20, 2019.
18 CCRL used this same tactic in 2017 when negotiations reached an impasse. In that round of bargaining, a concession agreement at the last minute averted the dispute. See Andrew Stevens and Doug Nesbitt, "Refinery Town in the Petro-State: Organized Labour Confronts the Oil Patch in Western Canada," *Studies in Political Economy* 104 (2023), 1.
19 Jonathan Guignard, "Co-op Refinery Using Helicopters to Transport Staff, Supplies into Regina Plant," Global News, December 9, 2019, <globalnews.ca/news/6272132/co-op-refinery-helicopters-staff-supplies-regina/>.
20 See Tucker, this volume.
21 Jennifer Ackerman, "Locked Out Refinery Workers Union Calls for Nation-Wide Boycott of All Things Co-op," *Regina-Leader Post*, December 17, 2019; Mickey Djuric, "Locked Out Employees of Co-op Refinery Concerned About Safety of Community," Global News, December 6, 2019 <globalnews.ca/news/6266170/unifor-refinery-health-and-safety-regina/>.
22 CBC, "Co-op Refinery Complex, Union Sign Deal to End Labour Dispute," June 22, 2020, <cbc.ca/news/canada/saskatchewan/labour-co-op-refinery-unifor-local-594-regina-deal-signed-1.5622636>.
23 See Larry Savage and Jonah Butovsky, "A Federal Anti-Scab Law for Canada: The Debate Over Bill C-257," *Just Labour* 13 (2009). More broadly, see David Doorey and Alison Braley-Ratti, *Canadian Labour Relations: Law, Policy, and Practice*, 2nd

ed. (Toronto: Irwin, 2020). When an employer uses the law as a weapon to challenge the legitimacy of any delays on the picket line, it seeks to redefine the struggle as one where the union is incapable of challenging its basic business operations. The Saskatchewan Labour Relations Board recognized this in its famous *Pepsi* ruling in 1997, where anti-scab restrictions were read into the Trade Union Act. See, *Pepsi v. RWDSU, 1997*, Saskatchewan LRBR (No. 166-97).

24 Barb Pacholik, "Regina Judge Puts Limits on Unifor Pickets Tin Refinery Labour Dispute," *Regina Leader-Post*, December 18, 2019 <leaderpost.com/news/local-news/regina-judge-puts-limits-on-unifor-pickets-in-refinery-labour-dispute>.

25 CCRL Draft Order, QBG, CCRL *v. Unifor Canada, Local 594 and Kevin Bittman*, 2020, 4. See also Stephanie Taylor, "Company Seeks Injunction, Co-op, Union in Court over Pickets at Regina Refinery," Global News, December 23, 2019, <globalnews.ca/news/6332407/company-seeks-injunction-co-op-union-in-court-over-pickets-at-regina-refinery/>.

26 On the history of employer uses of injunctions to crush union organizing drives and strikes, see Fudge and Tucker, *Labour Before the Law*. See also, Judy Fudge and Eric Tucker, "Forging Responsible Unions: Metal Workers and the Rise of the Labour Injunction in Canada," *Labour/Le Travail* 37 (1996); Smith, "We Didn't Want To"; Joan Sangster, "'We No Longer Respect the Law': The Tilco Strike, Labour Injunctions, and the State," *Labour/Le Travail* 53 (2004).

27 *Unifor Canada Local 594 v. Consumers' Co-operative Refineries Limited*, QBG 3302 of 2019 JCR (Interim Order), December 17, 2019.

28 CCRL *v. Unifor Local 594, Decision on Interim Injunction*, QBG 3302 of 2019, December 24, 2019, para 11.

29 CCRL *v. Unifor Local 594, Decision on Interim Injunction*, paras 16, 26.

30 CCRL *v. Unifor Local 594, Decision on Interim Injunction*, para 41.

31 Chris Rootham, Sean McGee, Steve Waller, and Annie Berthiaume, "The Expanded Scope of Union Protection under the Charter," *Canadian Labour & Employment Law Journal* 10 (2003), 171.

32 CCRL *v. Unifor Local 594, Decision on Interim Injunction*, para 36.

33 Rootham et al. "The Expanded Scope," 172.

34 CCRL *v. Unifor Local 594 and Kevin Bittman*, 2020 SKQB 19, January 22, 2020, paras 13–14.

35 CJME *News*. 2020. "Unifor Blockades Sherwood Co-op Home Centre," January 16, <cjme.com/2020/01/16/unifor-blockades-sherwood-co-op-home-centre/>.

36 CCRL *v. Unifor Local 594 and Kevin Bittman*, 2020 SKQB 19, paras 30–33.

37 Coop Refinery Press Release, "The Law Must Be Enforced," Twitter, February 3, 2020, 2:20 p.m., <twitter.com/CoopRefinery/status/1224412383675809792/photo/1>. Also see *PressProgress*, "An Oil Company Was Angry Police Would Not Stop Picketing Workers. The CEO Claims Scott Moe's People Offered to Help," October 20, 2020, <pressprogress.ca/an-oil-company-was-angry-police-would-not-stop-picketing-workers-the-ceo-claims-scott-moes-people-offered-to-help/>.

38 Regina Police Service, *News Release*. February 3, 2020, <reginapolice.ca/2020/02/regina-police-service-role/>.

39 CBC Saskatchewan, "Van Attempting to Cross Picket Lines Creates Tension at Co-op Refinery," December 9, 2019, <cbc.ca/news/canada/saskatchewan/van-job-action-1.5390296?cmp=rss>.

40 Alec Salloum, Alec, "Unifor National President Jerry Dias Taken into Custody at

Refinery Picket Line," *Regina Leader-Post*, January 21, 2020.
41 Arthur White-Crummey, "CRC Asks for 'Historic' Fine against Unifor 594, Threat of Jail for 2 Leaders," *Regina-Leader* Post, February 6, 2020.
42 CCRL *v. Unifor Canada, Local 594*, 2020 SKQB 38, paras 51–67.
43 CCRL *v. Unifor Canada Local 594*, paras 63–67.
44 R. *v. Dias and Doherty*, 2020 SKPC 18, April 15.
45 *PressProgress*, "An Oil Company."
46 Arthur White-Crummey, "Premier Offers Special Mediator if Refinery Blockades Come Down; Emissary to have Larger Powers to Get Sides Back to Bargaining," *Regina Leader-Post*, February 4, 2020.
47 *In the Matter of A Special Mediation Pursuant to the Saskatchewan Employment Act*, 2013, c.S15.1, CCRL and Unifor Local 595, *Report of Special Mediators Vincent Ready and Amanda Rogers*, March 19, 2020.
48 The RCMP were very aggressive when workers exercised their freedom of expression. See labour lawyer Ronni Nordal's blog post on this issue: "RCMP Tramples on Right to Picket on Behalf of Consumers Co-op Refinery in Saskatchewan." June 2, 2020 <lawofwork.ca/rcmp-coop/>. See also Jonathan Guigenard, "Unifor Sets Up Blockade at Co-op Bulk Storage Facility near Moose Jaw, Sask," Global News, February 10, 2020, <globalnews.ca/news/6531015/unifor-sets-up-blockade-at-co-op-bulk-storage-facility-near-moose-jaw/>. Police intervention was hardly consistent in this dispute. On February 18, 2020, local police did not disclose to workers that a bomb threat had been made against picketers. See Creeden Martell, "Unifor President Livid with Policy, Union Not Told about Bomb Threat Later Deemed Non-credible," CBC, May 19, 2020, <cbc.ca/news/canada/saskatchewan/unifor-president-livid-after-police-investigation-finds-bomb-threat-non-credible-1.5575891>.
49 Roni Nodal, "Saskatchewan: The Long Arms of the Law Still Denying Unifor Local 594 Members the Ability to Obtain a Collective Agreement," *Law of Work*, 2020, <lawofwork.ca/saskatchewan-the-long-arms-of-the-law-still-denying-unifor-local-594-members-the-ability-to-obtain-a-collective-agreement/>; Ronnie Nodal, "Is There a Meaningful Right to Picket in Saskatchewan?" *Law of Work*, March 2020 <lawofwork.ca/elementor-11888/>.
50 Those workers would eventually get their jobs back after the union grieved the decision.
51 *Unifor Canada, Local 594 v. Consumers' Co-operative Refineries Ltd.*, LRB File No. 126-20; August 31, 2020.
52 Alec Salloum, "Co-op Refinery to Lay Off 54 Unionized Employees," *StarPhoenix*, October 5, 2021.
53 *Unifor Canada Local 594 v. Consumers' Co-operative Refineries Lt.*, LRB File No. 173-20, October 17, 2022.
54 CBC Saskatchewan, "Unifor Holds News Conference at Saskatchewan Legislature," June 18, 2020, <pscp.tv/w/1DXxyAwqkbRxM>.
55 *Unifor Canada Local 594 v. CCRL*, SLRB 126-20, August 31, 2020.
56 *Unifor Canada Local 594 v. Consumers' Co-operative Refineries Ltd.* 2021 SKCA 34.
57 *Unifor Canada Local 594 v. Consumers' Co-operative Refineries Ltd.*, para 89, citing *Ideal Railings Ltd. v. Laborer's International Union of North America*, 2013 ONSC 701, para 66.
58 *Unifor Canada Local 594 v. Consumers' Co-operative Refineries Ltd.*, para 157.

59 *Unifor Canada Local 594 v. Consumers' Co-operative Refineries Ltd.*, 106.
60 *Unifor Canada Local 594 v. Consumers' Co-operative Refineries Ltd.*, paras 107–15.
61 *Unifor Canada Local 594 v. Consumers' Co-operative Refineries Ltd.*, 97.
62 *Unifor Canada Local 594 v. Consumers' Co-operative Refineries Ltd.*, para 89.

5

UNGOVERNABLE
How a Refinery Became "Too Big to Fail" — and What it Means to the People of Saskatchewan[1]

Patricia W. Elliott *(with files from Kaitlyn Schropp and Julia Peterson)*

THE SECRET BOX

IN THE ARCHIVES OF SASKATCHEWAN'S Court of Queen's Bench in Regina sits a brown cardboard box sealed with clear packing tape. A clue to its contents is revealed in red felt pen lettering on one side: "Files sealed as per order of Keene, J. on October 13, 2016 … Co-operators vs. City of Regina." From court records we know the box contains details of a Major Hazards Risk Assessment Report, commissioned in 2012 by the Co-operative Refinery Complex at the request of the City of Regina.[2] From a released executive summary, we know it contains details of smokestack plumes that drift over residential areas.[3] We also know the City of Regina was agreeable to publicly releasing the full report in response to a journalist's freedom of information (FOI) request. And we know that the refinery's legal counsel objected strenuously enough to ensure this would never happen.[4] As for what major risks might have been revealed, that part is sealed.

For the city, its residents, and the refinery, the secret box is bound by codependencies as sticky as packing tape. If you peel back a piece, something might tear. In this light, the CRC presents a governance challenge that municipal and provincial authorities struggle to surmount. Official records suggest the refinery has been left to largely self-monitor its pollutant emissions with limited regulatory involvement or major penalties for transgressions, beyond cost compensation for stressing the municipal wastewater system. This reflects a wider picture of Saskatchewan's oil and gas sector, where direct provincial oversight of environmental impacts has been gradually reduced in favour of industry self-regulation that, in the words of a Ministry of Environment presentation, invites "environmental management aligned with a growing economy."[5]

The refinery has successfully propagated a general consensus that its operations are too crucial to the local economy to suffer any hinderance. "You can't survive without me" is the mantra of domination in a relationship. It is how secrets and transgressions accumulate unaddressed. What does this mean for the promise of a just transition? When it comes to the health of citizens, this is a crucial question to consider.

WHAT'S AT STAKE

James Whittingham lives 1.6 kilometres northwest of the refinery as the crow flies. Some homes in his neighbourhood are within three hundred metres of the plant. There are other industrial sites nearby, including a steel plant and a pipeline, but Whittingham says he can readily recognize the refinery's distinct odours and the particular wind conditions that bring them. "You sort of get accustomed to it and you don't react very much when it's at a lower level. But when it's really strong and you've got a sore throat or irritated eyes, then you get very concerned," he says in an interview. Sometimes he awakens in the night to strong chemical odours and a sore throat. After shutting the windows, it can take an hour for the air to clear inside. As well, fumes have seeped through his car vents, strong enough to make him gag: "You wonder if you can breathe, it's that bad sometimes, or if you should be breathing it."

Whittingham notes that Enbridge goes door-to-door to inform residents of upcoming work being done on their pipeline site. He'd like the CRC to similarly visit residents following refinery explosions or during planned releases, so they know when to close their windows. He would also like to know if cancer rates are higher in his neighbourhood, and if there are things he should be doing to protect himself. He wonders what the situation is for neighbourhoods to the south that are more often in the path of prevailing winds. In any case, he and his family love their home and plan to stay.

Whether or not the fumes scraping Wittingham's throat can be conclusively attributed to the CRC, it's a fact that living near any refinery carries risk of exposure to toxins. The CRC emits over fifty distinct substances that Environment Canada recognizes as potentially harmful to human health and/or the environment; the list includes toxic gases such as hydrogen sulfide (H_2S) and heavy metals such as arsenic and mercury.[6] Refineries are required to track and report toxic releases annually to the federal National Pollutant Release Inventory (NPRI). Among sixteen reporting refineries in 2019, the CRC ranked sixth in production capacity at 130,000 barrels per day (bbl),[7] but stood fourth in total pollutant emissions, releasing 19,058 tonnes of toxins.[8] In 2020, the CRC's production dipped to as low as 90,000 barrels daily during the pandemic downturn,[9] yet still the refinery emitted 17,373 tonnes of toxins.[10] By 2021, the most recent year of complete data, emissions bounced back up to pre-pandemic levels, registering 19,216 tonnes.[11]

Ideally, such emissions are treated, stored, or recycled rather than released. The CRC captured and injected 48 percent of its emissions underground in 2021. Less ideally, refinery waste is released into the atmosphere through flaring and stack emissions, creating a cloud of CO_2 and particulate matter known as smog. Thirty-four percent of the CRC's air emissions went up the stack in 2021, standing fifth as a percentage of total Canadian refinery stack emissions. Smog contributes to global warming and, at a local level, can harm the health of nearby humans, animals, crops, and backyard gardens. Particulate matter in refinery smog includes liquid and solid particles that carry pollutants. The Co-op released 423 tonnes of particulate matter into the air in 2021.[12] Of this amount, 177 tonnes were fine particulate matter, meaning 2.5 microns or less in width, which Health Canada warns "poses a risk to your health because, when inhaled, it can travel deeply into your lungs."[13]

Least ideal of all, pollutants can escape through unplanned leaks and spills. The CRC has long held Canada's top spot in refinery fugitive emissions, meaning releases of pressurized gas into the atmosphere through faulty equipment or operational errors.[14] In 2021, among 3,688 tonnes of fugitive refinery emissions released nationally, the

CRC contributed 1,772 tonnes, or 48 percent, an enormously outsized contribution.[15] For comparison, the next highest was Shell's Corunna refinery, at 332 tonnes, or 9 percent.[16] It is possible the CRC simply has better detection and reporting protocols than other refineries; however, this is immaterial at the local level, where 1,772 tonnes of fugitive toxins are still 1,722 tonnes, no matter what the neighbour's report card says.

Beyond unintended releases, the CRC is a top-level emitter generally, particularly in the category of volatile organic compounds (VOCs). While *organic* seems a friendly word, VOCs are anything but. They are one of the most prevalent factors in outdoor air pollutant–related cancers, representing between 35 and 55 percent of all cases.[17] The CRC led Canadian VOCs refinery emissions every year from 2011 to 2021; of 98,181 tonnes, no less than 35,019 tonnes — or 36 percent — emanated from the CRC over the decade. This far exceeded the next-highest contributor, Edmonton's Suncor refinery, responsible for just 8 percent of emissions.[18]

Refinery-produced VOCs contain a roster of particularly hazardous substances.[19] N-hexane, for example, can induce throat irritation and neurological symptoms such as headaches and vertigo at acute levels, while long-term chronic exposure has been related to damage to peripheral nerves in humans, causing weakness and numbness in the limbs, as well as reproductive damage in mice.[20] In 2021, the CRC alone was responsible for half of Canada's total n-hexane refinery emissions, at a staggering 203 tonnes; its competitors averaged 12.6 tonnes. The Co-op also led the pack in total overall emissions of toluene, releasing 58 tonnes of the neurotoxin,[21] and emitted 11 tonnes of benzene, a VOC that can lead to leukemia in humans subjected to long-term airborne exposure.[22]

Altogether, the CRC emitted 2,708 tonnes of VOCs in 2021, of which 51 percent were fugitive emissions. For comparison, the next-highest VOC emitter, Suncor's Edmonton refinery, released 801 tonnes — despite being a higher-capacity refinery at 142,000 barrels per day — and just 3.7 percent were accidental.[23] The CRC's 1,393 tonnes of fugitive VOC emissions included 191 tonnes of fugitive n-hexane (highest in Canada); thirty-seven tonnes of ethylbenzene (highest in Canada); eleven tonnes of naphthalene (highest in Canada); 4.75 tonnes of cyclohexane (highest in Canada), eleven tonnes of toluene (second highest in Canada); and two tonnes of benzene (second highest).[24]

Workers inside the complex are aware of lapses but feel constrained from speaking about them because of a stringent non-disclosure agreement and, in the words of one employee, there's "so much negativity about telling the truth." Outside the gates, average citizens hear reassuring messages that all is well, but they have limited access to the information behind these messages. The public can read reports on the CRC's website about how sustainability targets are being met, while hard data on pollutant exceedances and accident details are sequestered in annual environmental reports obtainable only in redacted format via the protracted process of formal FOI requests to the Ministry of Environment. The CRC has defended this practice before Saskatchewan's Information and Privacy Commissioner on the grounds that its environmental reports are "prepared and presented to the Ministry of Environment in a manner which anticipated that such information was to be used internally only by the Ministry of Environment and not in a manner which anticipated further disclosure."[25] Federally, the NPRI maintains a higher standard of public disclosure by providing an accessible online data portal on emissions from all industries. However, the data is very dense, requiring time and advanced research skills for citizens to extract relevant information. This leaves a large measure of public trust to the company's word, which can be a scarce commodity. For example, the CRC did not respond to my requests for comment on information contained in this chapter.

Marriage Vows

Deference to industry and capital has deep roots in Regina. The small prairie city's location was chosen not for proximity to natural bounties but for railway access and the ease with which the area could be depopulated of its original inhabitants and then divided and subdivided in an endless game of land speculation that drives the city to this day. Hence, the primary source of potable water is fifty-seven kilometres distant, drawn from Buffalo Pound Lake, which has now fully replaced the city's relatively meagre underground aquifers.[26] The burden of washing away all the city's effluent is given to tiny Wascana Creek, one of Saskatchewan's smallest watersheds, which winds toward the Qu'Appelle River system and Pasqua Lake.[27] Like a family in an overcrowded home, these physical limitations factor into the relationship between the city and refinery.

As with most marriages, things began well enough. In early January 1935, the newly formed Consumers' Co-operative Refineries Limited (CCRL) presented to Regina's city council a plan to set up shop on a plot of rural land just past Winnipeg Street on the Canadian National Railway branch line.[28] It would be the first co-operative refinery in Canada and today remains the world's only co-operative oil refinery.[29] Regina's founders had imagined a Chicago-sized hub city, but the Dust Bowl had dimmed visions of residential growth beyond the city's Eastern Annex, which stopped short of the Co-op's planned site. Although not on city land, the new refinery was intimately connected to Regina. The very first construction activity was to drill into Regina's aquifer for water to cool the facility.[30] In the midst of crushing drought, it was the same year Regina householders protested high utility charges for scarce water.[31] But the refinery brought economic benefits to a deeply depressed economy, particularly for its 632 shareholding members,[32] who held between them eight thousand shares at $25 each[33] ($480 per share in 2021 dollars).[34] Within its first eight months of operation, the new oil and gas refinery had generated jobs and a healthy $28,000 surplus.[35]

In March 1936, the provincial legislature considered a private member's bill to register the enterprise as a co-op, not a company, thereby exempting it from provincial income and corporate taxes. British American Oil objected, arguing the co-op structure was a mere tax dodge and that the refinery was in fact a joint stock company "in the fullest sense."[36] Liberal premier James Patterson responded, "The onus should be on the company to show that the 'savings' are not 'profits.'"[37] Patterson's bar was apparently met: on April 1, 1936, the Act to Incorporate Consumers' Co-operative Refineries Limited was passed, providing tax-free leave to "to buy, sell and otherwise deal in crude petroleum oil and other oils, greases and products thereof," as well as "to sink oil wells, to erect, acquire, buy, purchase, lease or otherwise maintain and operate oil refineries or plants."[38] It was a vote of confidence not just in the refinery itself, but in the idea that co-operatives delivered a common good deserving of public support via tax-free status.

From that moment, the refinery was on a growth path. Within ten years, successive expansions increased capacity from 500 to 2,400 barrels per day. In 1944, it joined forces with co-operative wholesalers across western Canada under the banner of Federated Co-operatives Limited (FCL). In 1951, cheering crowds celebrated a major addition that leaped capacity forward to six thousand barrels per day. The outdoor event featured a rousing speech by Co-operative Commonwealth Federation premier Tommy Douglas, who dedicated the new addition "to the glory of the pioneers who conceived the refinery, to the memory of those who laboured to produce it and to the benefit of the people of the prairies who belong to the great world brotherhood of co-operatives."[39]

Representing the city as deputy mayor, Art Riddell's remarks were somewhat less effusive, offering congratulations for "a great milestone of progress."[40] Within a year, the refinery was bent on doubling production to twelve thousand barrels per day, a project that depended on the city's agreement to extend water and sewer service to the growing complex. The sewer pipes needed to handle one thousand gallons per minute of refinery wastewater, which was to contain no oil. The refinery also required 850 gallons-per-minute capacity of clean water piped from the new Buffalo Pound Water Treatment Plant then under construction. At the same time, residents in the rural municipality of North Regina had been told they could not access the city's piped drinking water due to lack of lift pumps. The question of why neighbouring householders didn't have equal access was deferred; the refinery's provision of two hundred jobs and its favourable prospects as a paying water customer sealed the deal.[41]

Tying the Knot

While tapping into the water system and other services, the refinery was not a tax-paying resident of the City of Regina. In 1951, the city pushed its limits further east but skirted the complex's land holdings. The public school board cried foul, claiming that out of 125 employees' children who attended the refinery's Christmas party, all but three attended Regina schools. It would take another two years of school board pressure for city council to reconsider annexing the land, with the refinery's reported agreement to not object.[42] On January 1, 1954, the Co-op parcels were annexed, though it took additional time for the school board to secure expanded boundaries through the courts, following objections from two impacted rural boards. The urban board claimed during this time that it had to construct several new north-end schools, put twenty-six classrooms on double-shift to ease congestion, and pay for extra school buses to accommodate refinery families.[43]

Meanwhile, CCLR grew beyond refinery ownership, expanding into oil drilling. Competitors complained the Co-op received unfair "plums" from the province in 1958 with a deal to drill on Crown lands outside a competitive bid process.[44] Expansion of the refinery itself laddered upward, with a $1.3 million addition in 1957,[45] a $1.25 million addition in 1961,[46] a $30 million addition in 1978,[47] and a $25 million addition in 1982 financed by a Saskatchewan Economic Development Corporation loan.[48] Then in 1988, a heavy oil upgrader was grafted onto the existing works, a highly complex $700 million undertaking to turn heavy prairie crude into lighter petroleum products such as gasoline and diesel fuel. Typically high in gases that corrode equipment and present safety hazards, Saskatchewan crude is notoriously difficult to handle. "Other crudes are worse than ours, but then no one has built a facility specifically to refine these inferior crudes," noted the company's senior vice-president of refining.[49]

In November 1988, the City of Regina and the refinery signed an agreement that waste would be sequestered in holding ponds until it had been cleaned to meet agreed-on maximum thresholds for oil, sulphides, heavy metals, and other contaminants before entering the sewage system.[50] On the Co-op's side, hopes for an environmentally clean operation were high. A new company, New Grade Energy, was formed to assess impacts.[51] "Using one of the most severely contaminated oils in the world, we'll end up without any residue," project director Ivan Donald enthused in an advertising supplement published in the *Regina Leader-Post*.[52]

However, the first year of operation was plagued by fires, spills, and emissions, including a twenty-minute H_2S (sour gas) leak on February 27, 1989, that caused children at a nearby school to be overcome with nausea. Sour gas is one of the oil industry's most feared emissions, capable of causing near-instant death in enclosed spaces at high concentration. Moderate levels bring sore throats, stinging eyes, and severe nausea. Long-term low-level exposure may contribute to low blood pressure, headaches, eye inflammation, a staggered gait, and neurological symptoms, including psychological disorders. Further, "chronic exposure may be more serious for children because of their potential longer latency period," raising additional concerns for schools and daycares near refineries.[53]

In another incident, residents complained of oil droplets landing on homes and cars up to two kilometres away. While the Co-op accepted that the H_2S leak was concerning and should have been reported to the Ministry of Environment sooner than it was, the oil spray incident was "blown out of proportion," according to refinery manager Bud Dalhstrom. "We created a helluva nuisance and it shouldn't have happened. But we don't really think we created a hazard," he told local media.[54] Despite the company's assurance of air safety, one resident told the media that inhaling the oily mist caused her throat to become sore and numb, while another reported a severe asthma attack.[55]

Later that year, employees at an adjacent greenhouse fled in terror when a fiery explosion rocked the plant. The greenhouse, which was heated by the refinery, had a gas detector installed but never enabled. Afterwards, the workers and some local businesses requested an early-warning system to alert them when gases inside the plant were reaching dangerous levels. In response, refinery spokesperson Ivan Donald stressed that the fire had presented no danger to the public and argued an alert system would do more harm than good, saying, "If we set it off without knowing for sure there's a problem, it will become a case of crying wolf. The best situation is the one we've got."[56]

Toxic Relations

As the humble refinery co-operative grew into today's sprawling Co-op Refinery Complex, each expansion brought new employment but also new stresses to the City of Regina. Containing wastewater in the refinery's sewage lagoon emerged as an ongoing problem. In 1992, spilled fuel was discovered floating in an aquifer that lay directly above the Regina aquifer, which supplied 10 percent of the city's drinking water at the time (it is no longer used today). "Any refinery/upgrader is going to have the odd spill," stated refinery co-chair Harold Empey. He added, "Show me some other site with this type of industry. All the other refineries have pulled out of the province."[57] The implication was that the refinery was doing Saskatchewan a favour by forsaking greener pastures elsewhere.

In 1992 it was also revealed that the refinery was flushing considerable amounts of oil and grease through the sewer system and had been doing so at least since 1989. The city had set fifteen milligrams as the acceptable upper limit but found seventy-four samples above that limit in 1992, with nine discharges registering one hundred to two hundred milligrams. A refinery spokesperson acknowledged the problem but took issue with the fifteen-milligram limit, describing it as an arbitrary measure that allowed the City to exaggerate the contamination.[58] Yet the original 1951 sewer access request included an understanding there would be no oil at all. At a works and utilities committee meeting, a councillor called for denial of sewer access or revocation of the refinery's operations licence if the discharge wasn't cleaned up. However, the earlier "greener pastures" message had seemingly been heard; another councillor expressed fear the simple requirement to not flush oil and grease into the sewer could somehow shut down the whole operation, endangering 450 jobs. In the end, sewer access continued uninterrupted, despite a city report that warned continued discharges could damage the sewer lines and the wastewater treatment plant.[59]

The warning did not stop contaminants from finding their way into the city's sewage services; in fact, the problem has been even worse in some years. According to a 2019 environmental report obtained through an FOI request, the refinery's oil and grease discharges exceeded the City of Regina fifteen milligram-per-litre limit on 174 days, with a yearly average of 18.9 milligrams per litre. As well, refinery discharges exceeded the city's limits for manganese in 148 of 151 of samples.[60] A beneficial mineral when occurring naturally in small amounts, manganese nonetheless poses risks when present in water in higher concentrations as a result of industrial processes. The environmental report for 2020 shows elevated manganese in 294 samples, fifty-two over-the-limit oil and grease samples, as well as five days of zinc exceedances and one day when cyanide was detected at four times over the limit.[61] In May 2020, oil and grease spiked at six hundred milligrams per litre, dramatically eclipsing the allowable fifteen milligrams per litre.[62] Just four Canadian refineries discharged pollutants to municipal sewage systems in 2020: the Edmonton refinery discharged four kilograms; the Moose Jaw's refinery 250 kilograms; Burnaby's, 3.08 tonnes; and the CRC at a comparatively towering 12.1 tonnes.[63] The 2021 amount was 7.6 tonnes — a reduction, but still far greater than any other Canadian refinery.[64] At stake is the health of Wascana Creek, which joins the Qu'Appelle River, flowing toward Pasqua Lake and the Qu'Appelle Lakes chain, then following the Assiniboine and Red Rivers to Lake Winnipeg and Hudson Bay. Also at stake is the efficiency of a new multibillion-dollar public-private-partnership (P3) wastewater treatment plant operated by

EPCOR. An internal report estimates more than $15 million in upgrades could be required if current levels of industrial contamination are not curtailed.⁶⁵

In 2016, the CRC announced construction of a system to clean and recycle 100 percent of its wastewater. The project received a recognition award from *Global Water Intelligence* magazine in 2017⁶⁶ and in 2019 was honoured with a Resource Revolution Award from Suez Water Technologies & Solutions (now Veolia) — the same company that designed and installed the system.⁶⁷ Less heralded are wastewater breaches. In May 2020, EPCOR employees discovered that a tarlike substance had clogged pumping station equipment and was drifting toward the plant. They were able to divert sixty thousand litres of oily water into a separate lagoon, narrowly avoiding major damage to the plant and the prospect of untreated, hydrocarbon-laced sewage spilling into Wascana Creek.⁶⁸ An investigation by the Saskatchewan Water Security Agency later found the contaminated water originated in a Co-op refinery storage pond. Although both the city and the refinery were aware of the release, there was no public notice and the Chief of Pasqua First Nation was not informed until one week after the incident. Instead, a concerned city councillor and attentive journalists brought the matter to public attention.⁶⁹

In response to an FOI request for documents pertaining to the spill, I received 1,774 fully redacted pages, on the grounds of solicitor-client privilege and potential prejudice to legal proceedings and contractual negotiations.⁷⁰ Thus, each page was its own secret box in the form of large grey squares placed over content labelled as remediation reports, sampling results, cost estimates, photographs, and other spill-related information.

On May 6, 2022, the city registered a claim for $4.6 million from CCLR, citing the company's "wanton disregard" for safe handling of toxic waste and "egregious, oppressive, high-handed, reckless, destructive, [and] pervasive" conduct.⁷¹ The refinery responded with a statement of defence denying liability for "frivolous and baseless" claims.⁷²

Frustration had been simmering for some time. EPCOR had observed foaming in its lagoons repeatedly since 2015, the year the company took on a P3 contract with the city. This generally indicates something has gone awry with the microbial balance needed to break down wastes. There had also been repeated springtime E. coli spikes dating back to

2011, according to an investigation report obtained through FOI request. By early 2019, the plant was fully online and "operating in stable condition, without chemicals" — until April, when the water suddenly began to froth again. Following a second occurrence in May 2019, EPCOR launched an investigation that correlated foaming to elevated levels of vanadium, a heavy metal that occurs naturally in crude oil, as well as molybdenum, a metal used as a catalyst in refining heavy oil. The metals harmed the microbes that clean wastewater, causing some to die off and others to go into defensive overdrive, opening the door to E. coli. During the investigation, a review of historical data found "significant increases" of additional metals, including mercury and lead, at approximately the same time every spring, as well as in October 2018. The situation abated after ECPOR contacted the city, and the city in turn communicated with "an external party in relation to the event." [73] In its final report, EPCOR estimated the cost to restore its system would reach $1 million.

Although naturally occurring and not normally harmful, high concentrations of vanadium from industrial processes are considered toxic by Health Canada, capable of causing cancer and damage to internal organs.[74] On June 28, 2020, above-standard levels of vanadium appeared again, revealed in test results returned to the plant on July 10. This time the substance was found not just in the influent, but in discharged treated water. Downstream users were informed by the City of Regina in a communiqué that stated:

> The Water Security Agency was notified and has confirmed the metal released is low risk. The wastewater effluent leaving the City of Regina's Wastewater Treatment Plant had the elevated metal for a short time period and long term exposure is not applicable for this situation.[75]

Perhaps these words offered some small comfort to people who used the water during a twelve-day time lag between test sample and result. Downstream uses include watering livestock, fishing, irrigation, and potash mining.[76] Speaking to the media, a refinery spokesperson said the source water had been segregated and was being hauled offsite, and he assured the public that vanadium discharge was part of routine maintenance and not usually present in high amounts.[77]

Statistical data presents a much different picture. In 2020, the Co-op reported 162 tonnes of vanadium waste, eclipsing all other refineries in Canada (in comparison, the next highest, Quebec's Raffinerie Jean-Gaulin, created just three tonnes). Of that, 157 tonnes were shipped to the Miller Environmental Corporation in Manitoba for treatment and disposal. However, the sheer volume of material left a significant amount dealt with on site, including 1.92 tonnes "transfer[red] to municipal sewage treatment plant," nearly double the amount in 2019.[78]

Vanadium's presence in refining depends on both the nature of the crude oil and the combustion process; Regina's refinery appears to present a perfect storm. There is a green opportunity in this scenario, however: if recovered instead of disposed or dispersed, vanadium is in increasingly high demand for wind and solar power batteries.[79] For example, in 2019 Regina's EVRAZ steel plant recycled 19,334 tonnes of vanadium from its steel slagging process for use in strengthening steel alloys and manufacturing vanadium redox batteries for renewable energy production.[80] Burnaby's refinery reported three of its total four tonnes of vanadium were recycled in 2019, with none discharged into the municipal sewage system. The CRC, meanwhile, reported just 20 kilograms transferred for recycling in 2019, and it was the only Canadian refinery to send vanadium to a municipal wastewater plant, discharging one tonne into the sewage system.[81] The refinery was more successful in reducing its stack emissions, from 4.6 tonnes to 1.3 tonnes by 2020, notable because airborne vanadium binds strongly to particulate matter and can travel far into the surrounding environment.[82] However, sewer releases remained stubbornly high, at 1.28 tonnes. [83]

Breaking with history, the city held fast with its legal claim, winning a $4.6 million settlement.[84] This display of backbone was accompanied by a marked reduction in sewage system releases to 290 kilograms in 2021.[85] However, stack emissions rose 25 percent that year.[86] While EPCOR's plant was protected, citizens faced increased risk.

Conditioned Tolerance

Resident James Whittingham has never complained to the CRC. Once, when the smell seemed different, he called Enbridge, which owns the main pipeline running through the neighbourhood, and found them very responsive about checking their line. As for the refinery, it's just the way things are in Regina, a familiar odour. "I think I read somewhere that you can phone a number and complain, but that seemed absurd to me," Whittingham says. "A very large complex like that, that one person ... would get them to shut down. It just didn't seem logical to me." Further, he doesn't think he'd be able to prove the source. Given the history of publicly downplayed incidents, it's perhaps not surprising citizens have been conditioned to accept that the onus of proof is on them, not the company.

Also, jobs are on the line; Whittingham agreed to be quoted only after a relative stopped working at the refinery. Similarly, an oilfield worker whose H_2S personal safety alarm went off while driving past the plant did not want to say anything publicly. In Saskatchewan's tightly networked economy, word gets around about people who complain about the bread and butter. Indeed, the records show the refinery fielded just five public complaints regarding chemical odours, dust, and ash in 2020, and four in 2019, although, as demonstrated above, the records show unplanned leaks are significant.[87]

The problems are well known on the inside. In interviews with University of Regina researchers, past and current employees pointed to a combination of faulty equipment, underqualified operators, and inattentive management. As one worker explained, "There's all kinds of emissions out there; they're so far behind on maintenance that you pretty much have to get a pump seal to the point where it's on fire before they're going to do anything." Another stated:

> It's kind of the employer who has to really take charge if they want to make those changes ... if you know something's not running as efficiently as it should be or something's slowly leaking a little bit, like we should take charge as an employee and fix that if we can. But realistically some of the equipment is old and ... there's really not much you can do anyways.

One employee described persistent issues with airborne coker dust, which can cause severe heart and lung damage through prolonged exposure. Three employees raised questions about the much-heralded wastewater recycling project's efficiency, saying the system has never worked properly. "They received their award before it ever came online, and it still to this day has recycled almost nothing. They'd be better to sell the equipment and ship the water down the sewer like they always did," said one worker. Another employee said fear of speaking up contributes to an already underinformed public:

I think the information about hydrocarbons in the air, the spills, I think it's very poorly communicated to Regina and surrounding areas as a whole. I think the public should have more knowledge of what's actually going on up there, for their own safety, and when they're deciding where to live in the city.

Several expressed confusion about why they did not see provincial inspectors visiting the refinery on a regular basis or holding management to account for faulty equipment. This observation coincided with regulatory changes brought in by the Saskatchewan Party government.

INDUSTRY, POLICE THYSELF

In June 1989, following a series of refinery accidents, a Conservative-led provincial government increased maximum environmental fines from $5,000 to $1 million and vowed to get tough on the refinery.[88] But as oil and gas gained primacy, the opposite occurred. In 2013, Saskatchewan's provincial auditor examined air quality enforcement and found that "since February 2011, the Ministry [of Environment] has not followed the existing law regarding the issuance of permits under the [Saskatchewan] Clean Air Act."[89] Rather than step up efforts to enforce the Act, the governing Saskatchewan Party instead chose to repeal it, effective November 2015. As part of the move, the government piggy-backed air quality responsibility onto a national network of primarily industry-funded non-profit associations run by volunteer boards. Seven years later, the ministry's website describes "a successful program built on consensus-based decision-making and partnerships."[90] However, the system appears far from robust: of six designated air zones, just three have active volunteer associations. The Great Plains Air Zone (GPAZ), encompassing Regina, has three monitoring stations to cover forty thousand square kilometres. Although the GPAZ website features a picture of the refinery, the association has no technical or regulatory capacity to track down specific sources of pollution or issue fines, and it makes no claims beyond a mandate to raise awareness of air quality issues. A Ministry slide presentation titled "Transitioning from Facility Based Monitoring to Airzone Management" specifically clarifies the associations are in place "to reflect general air quality in an area, rather than monitor facility emissions."[91]

As for facility emissions, under the Clean Air Act companies had to apply for operations permits that could be revoked for non-compliance.

But now the Act itself has been revoked, rather than industry permits. The province has instead put in place a consolidated Saskatchewan Environmental Code that lays out minimum standards. To meet these standards, regulated industries were invited to create and monitor their own Environmental Protection Plans (EPPs) under the Environmental Management and Protection Act. Annual progress reports replaced the permit system, which, according to a ministry presentation, had presented "a barrier to economic growth and innovation."[92] Four years later, the refinery submitted two EPPs to the province, one for emissions and one for discharges. The discharges plan was brief, stating spills would be addressed immediately and reported to provincial authorities, with the exclusion that "CCRL will not report fugitive emissions resulting from commissioning, operating, or decommissioning works."[93] The air EPP included a commitment to work toward reduced emissions, along with a pledge to conduct air quality assessments every ten years starting in 2020 and to conduct a human health risk assessment "following the completion of the air quality assessment."[94] The assessments are commissioned and paid for by the company, relieving the ministry of costs and staff time. This model has been adopted elsewhere within the neoliberal framework of ever-thinner governance. As for the downside, Ontario's provincial auditor pointed out the implications of industries performing their own environmental impacts analyses:

> "This means that spillers are left to police themselves and ensure effective environmental remediation, with little risk of Environment Ministry enforcement action."[95]

WHAT WE DON'T KNOW WILL PROBABLY HURT US

In 2007, CRC embarked on a five-year, $2.7 billion expansion to boost capacity to 130,000–145,000 barrels per day (bbl) and handle Alberta oilsands production.[96] "The additional staff required for construction and operation of the Expansion Project and supporting industries will positively affect the City's tax base," the project proposal promised. "During the construction phase there will be a major increase in cash flow throughout the city." As for emissions risks, the proposal stated that its commissioned study found "potential for minor reductions in air quality due to the Expansion Project; however, the modelled increase in emissions is expected to be small."[97] Others saw the data differently.

Environment Canada and Saskatchewan Ministry of Environment officials noted that H_2S, benzene, toluene, and xylene were predicted to "substantially" exceed air quality guidelines, while overall CO_2 production was expected to increase 23 percent.[98] A report dispatched to CRC's corporate entity, CCRL, on February 4, 2008, stated that "[i]nternal reviewers have raised concerns regarding predicted increases in levels of certain materials, lack of evaluation of the implications of these emissions and the lack of proposed mitigation to deal with the concerns."[99] The City of Regina followed up with its own objections on February 22, writing, "The refinery emissions impact zone of benzene and hydrogen sulfide into Regina residential areas … is of significant concern."[100] Confronted with divergent views of the same data, Saskatchewan's Ministry of Environment sent the report out for peer review. The results were, as one ministry official put it in an internal email, "less than stellar."[101]

The refinery's human health risk study was "not consistent with the current state of scientific knowledge and standard risk assessment protocols as required for similar projects in other Canadian jurisdictions," the review report stated. The review further noted that modelled elevations in H_2S, toluene, and benzene were in excess of air quality standards, concluding:

> the analysis is not appropriate to support the conclusions reached, that "human health risks are deemed negligible" for all chemicals except [particulate matter], benzene, toluene, and H_2S. Insufficient data is presented to conclude that "it is unlikely that human health effects due to H_2S exposure would arise at any of the assessed locations."[102]

CCRL replied that the review was "disappointing and unfortunate" because it "erroneously challenged" the refinery's risk assessment by widening the research scope beyond what the ministry had previously agreed needed to be done.[103] A far bigger elephant in the room showed itself in a June technical panel review meeting, reported in a memo to Environment officials:

> The most adamant "objectors" [to the expansion] were Min. of Health, the Health District and the City. Their focus seemed to be on the cumulative health effects on people (all sources) but I believe they recognized that the existing facility was by far the bigger emissions source.[104]

In other words, the refinery already presented a problem, expansion or no. Concerns were raised about what emergency plan was in place to protect residents if there were a major accident. "Apparently the CCLR has such a plan but it is not widely known or understood," the memo stated. Among the city's list of demands in its February 22, 2008, email was a Major Hazards Risk Assessment — the document that now resides in a sealed box at the provincial courthouse.

In September 2008, Environment Minister Nancy Heppner settled the debate with a decision in favour of expansion. Her decision communiqué stated a study that had been peer-reviewed predicted increases in health-adverse emissions would be confined to the refinery's property and would occur whether there was an expansion or not. On this basis, she wrote the project "does not pose any significant environmental or health risk."[105]

Construction began, marred by a 2011 explosion that injured fifty-two workers, six seriously. To follow up on the city's air quality concerns, between July 2012 and August 2013 the Ministry of Environment conducted a study of twenty-five locations in city limits; just three were in residential areas adjacent to the refinery. Taken together, the results from all locations presented a clean bill of health, with the exception of some elevated H_2S levels attributed to a municipal sewage lagoon. This report has been foundational in decision making to the present day.

In 2013, city council reviewed city planning amendments to accommodate a new neighbourhood, Somerset, seven hundred metres north of the refinery. The Ministry of Environment and Regina-Qu'Appelle Health Region raised objections to the plan, joined by the CRC itself "due to the proximity and possibility of complaints."[106] The city planning office responded that "the City does not have policies defining what is an acceptable level of nuisance, and this issue tends to be viewed subjectively."[107] The mayor was solidly behind the proposed neighbourhood, along with the majority of councillors. There were already homes much closer to the refinery than seven hundred metres, argued the area's councillor, who added that concerns about air quality were "a little bit of a scare tactic."[108] The Environment Ministry air study was not complete at the time, but the undisclosed Major Hazards Risk Assessment prepared for the refinery expansion indicated no major problems, the planning office reported. The development was approved but ultimately Somerset never made it past the drawing board.

On Christmas Eve 2013, another major explosion was heard across the city, the second in just over two years. In media interviews, nearby residents seemed fatalistic about potential future explosions. "If it's big, then I'm the first to go and I won't have to worry about it," remarked one. Another said she "loved" the neighbourhood and added, "If it's my time, it's my time."[109]

No Warnings

In contrast to Regina's reliance on air samples taken a decade ago, refinery-adjacent residents of Sarnia and Aamjiwnaang First Nation in Ontario have ten continuously operating air monitors in their streets and school grounds. Residents can view hourly-refreshed data on a public website. An eleventh air monitor is planned near a daycare in Aamjiwnaang.[110] Residents are also participating in major study into airborne refinery pollutants and health outcomes led by the Ontario Ministry of Environment. Further, in the event of toxic accidents, there are fifteen community-embedded sirens that alert people to "head indoors, close all windows and exterior doors, and turn off heating and cooling equipment."[111] While the system has been criticized as inadequate, it provides a measure of public information and safety at a level so far unknown — perhaps even undreamt of — in Regina.

No sirens sounded, for example, when 1.1 tonnes of sulfur dioxide (SO_2) were accidentally released up the refinery stack on March 16, 2020, in the midst of the CRC's lockout of its employees.[112] In addition to irritating the nose and throat, short-term sulfur dioxide spikes can trigger asthma attacks and cause breathing difficulties for children and seniors.[113] When asked about a public alert, a Ministry of Environment official responded, "Based on information collected at the time of the event a decision was made to not notify residents in the surrounding area as there was no health based concern to warrant notification."[114] The communication did not elaborate on who was responsible for making the decision, only that it "was made."[115] It is possible to ferret out a few sparse details of such releases, after the fact, in an online database of incidents reported to the Ministry of Environment. However, exceedances are recorded only if it is an uncontrolled discharge: when air standards are breached as part of "normal operations," there is no such reporting requirement.[116]

The CRC employs two onsite fenceline air monitors as part of its internal alert system. However, stack pollution tends to move up and outwards before settling to ground level, sometimes several kilometres away. Outside the refinery, a lone GPAZ monitor in Regina's east end captures some pollution spikes at a distance, such as twelve H_2S exceedances detected in 2022.[117] Monitoring specific residential areas is beyond the instrument's scope. The closest thing to a public alarm system like Sarnia's is a city-operated phone app, launched in 2015 with a three-year $320,000 donation from the CRC, a funding partnership that expired in 2020. "notifynow" alerts its 96,000 subscribers via text message about emergencies such as storms. Without neighbourhood-level air monitoring, the system lacks a trigger to automatically sound the alert on airborne toxins. "If a discharge or air emission event occurs, industry is required to notify the City," a city spokesperson explained via email in response to my inquiry. As for how often this happens: "Since NotifyNow was initiated, there have been no public alerts issued concerning industrial air emissions or spills."[118]

Perhaps a Sarnia-style independent monitoring system would have repeatedly sounded the alarm on the CRC's twelve tonnes of fugitive H_2S emissions recorded in 2019.[119] After the CRC brought a sulphur degasification project online, H_2S exceedances dropped to thirty-three incidents in 2020, as detected by the company's two fenceline monitors.[120] Nonetheless, NPRI data indicates H_2S fugitive emissions continued unchanged at twelve tonnes in 2020 and again in 2021, accounting for nearly 60 percent of all uncontrolled refinery H_2S discharges in Canada. While the long-term impacts of living amid frequent H_2S emissions are not conclusively known, the Canadian Centre for Occupational Health and Safety advises that "[s]ymptoms may include restlessness, reduced ability to think, muscle tremors, memory loss and personality changes. May harm the respiratory system."[121] Despite this, the provincial Ministry of Environment states that H_2S air quality standards "are intended to prevent detectable odours from impacting neighboring property, and are not a health-based standard."[122] The conception of H_2S as primarily a nuisance odour outside the CRC's gates is compounded by repeated use of the neighbourhood samples collected across the city in 2012–2014. For example, ten years later, a consultant hired by the CRC to predict the degasification project's benefits drew on this data to conclude the new installation would improve what was no more than an unpleasant odour issue without serious health risks. On this basis, the consultant's risk assessment recommended developing a plan to curtail H_2S emissions "to the extent practicable to reduce odour complaints."[123] Given how few citizens actually contact the refinery when they smell strange odours, this does not seem a heavy lift.

TOO BIG TO FAIL

Over nearly ninety years of operation, the Co-op Refinery Complex has expanded considerably, today occupying eight hundred acres of land and employing just over a thousand workers.[124] The City of Regina has expanded as well, with homes and business sprouting in the refinery's shadow. As the two entities have aged together, their interactions have been fraught with tensions and risks and have lacked the guidance of higher authorities to step in where needed. From this has arisen a social consensus to get along as best possible, in a relationship defined as more codependent than co-operative.

On the near horizon is energy transition on a global scale. In January 2022, Federated Co-operatives Limited, in partnership with pulse crop producer AGT Foods, announced construction of a canola crushing plant near the Co-op Refinery Complex that will include renewable diesel production, "a hydrocarbon produced most often by hydrotreating and also via gasification, pyrolysis, and other biochemical and thermochemical technologies."[125] In public statements, FCL has presented the project in the context of replacing conventional fuel production over time, although the specifics are vague. For now, the anticipated biofuel capacity is 15,000 barrels per day (bbl), a fraction of the CRC's conventional oil 130,000 bbl capacity, and the promise of transition is overshadowed by a long-standing power imbalance. While the industrial product may change over time, relationships tend to hold their shape. History suggests the biodiesel plant will bring a new array of municipal water requirements and waste management challenges, which the city will struggle to contain amid light-handed provincial environmental regulations. However, the biodiesel project promises $2 billion in investment, 2,500 construction jobs and 150 permanent jobs.[126] Like the refinery itself, the project is already too big to fail and therefore very likely too big to govern.

As for conventional refinery operations, in May 2020 Ottawa stepped in where Saskatchewan dare not tread, drafting a suite of new regulations to control VOCs under the Canadian Environmental Protection Act. Not yet fully in force, the regulations focus on fixing leaky valves, plugging open-ended pipes, standardizing fenceline monitoring, conducting regular inspections, and submitting reports on leaks and repairs. According to the new rules, seals, valves, pumps, and storage vessels are to be inventoried and annually inspected by personnel trained in leak detection. Faulty equipment is to be repaired within fifteen days or, if it can't be done that quickly, flagged to repair within sixty days. Leaky valves face three strikes, you're out: any valve that has a significant leak three times in two years must be replaced with a certified low-leaking valve. The rules are being brought in slowly, the first step being a compliance audit of the past two years, due in 2024, that will presumably set baselines for improvement. The definition of a "significant" VOC leak as one thousand parts per million volume (ppmv) — down from the current ten thousand ppmv — does not come into force until 2026. Beginning in 2028, the audit period will be extended to every four years. [127]

None of the safeguards seem beyond the pale of what a member of the public might reasonably expect for a highly polluting industrial process. Neither do the additions overreach the national Environmental Protection Act's declaration that "the protection of the environment is essential to the well-being of Canadians."[128] Yet it seems inevitable these new regulations will be just as difficult to enforce as previous efforts. Indeed, the Canadian Fuels Association is already crying foul, arguing before a Senate committee that the VOC regulations, alongside other climate-focused initiatives, will contribute to the potential shutdown of up to five refineries and a 44 percent reduction in capacity.[129]

While this is the most extreme scenario, the Co-op Refinery will doubtless face particularly difficult compliance challenges, given the facility's age and history of leaks and accidents. There are some "outs" already baked into the regulations, such as the ability to propose an alternative fenceline monitoring program rather than adopting the federal standard, as well as an option to forgo inspection of a piece equipment as long as a reason is listed in the report. Further, the refineries are given a large measure of responsibility to police themselves; if lapses are discovered, they trigger not fines and penalties but rather a corrective action plan, in which the refinery self-authors its cleanup plan and self-reports on its success. In short, Ottawa's underlying enforcement mechanism echoes provincial oversight mechanisms that have so clearly failed to reduce emissions and accidents over the years.

The City of Regina has committed to net-zero carbon emissions by 2050. At the same time, a refinery sits within city limits, releasing thousands of tonnes of greenhouse gasses annually. The Co-op's net-zero commitment places its eggs in the basket of transporting captured emissions to Whitecap Resource's Weyburn carbon capture, utilization, and storage (CCUS) project, a facility that has generated its own record of mishaps — such as a two-hundred-million-litre CO_2 leak from a failed valve in 2017 — while pursuing a not-uncontroversial technology.[130] Indeed, a 2021 peer-reviewed independent study of 236 carbon capture initiatives found "most CCUS projects initiated in the past three decades have failed."[131] Further confounding net-zero pronouncements, the Weyburn unit transfers sequestered gases to the oil patch for the purpose of forcing out more hard-to-reach fossil fuel. Then there is the matter of what isn't captured, namely the refinery's ongoing high level of fugitive emissions. Such emissions have been flagged by the Global Observatory on Non-State Climate Action flags as "a blind spot" in the climate change picture:

> Fugitive emissions represent a significant proportion of anthropogenic greenhouse gas emissions and their assessment, let alone reduction, is still in its infancy. Often overlooked by climate policies and institutional mechanisms, actions in this area rely primarily on the emitters themselves, pushed by civil society and local stakeholders.[132]

This statement encapsulates the situation in Regina, where pollution regulators at all levels — municipal, provincial, and federal — have long been backed into a corner by the refinery's status as a major employer. This weak position places workers and residents at risk from exposure to toxic substances and the planet at risk from greenhouse gas emissions. One wonders at what point the refinery's management, through lockouts and layoffs, will cross the boundary of its social licence. For now, as a refinery employee review on a popular jobs website states, "Just gotta put on a happy face and pretend everything is ok until you can go home."[133]

Endnotes

1. This chapter was prepared as part of the Price of Oil Journalism Project, a national consortium of student and faculty researchers. Research was supported in part by the Corporate Mapping Project, funded by the Saskatchewan Social Sciences and Humanities Research Council. The author wishes to acknowledge the invaluable assistance of Price of Oil project coordinator Patti Sonntag and student research assistants Kaitlyn Schropp and Julia Peterson. Research interviews with employees quoted in this chapter were conducted by Emily Eaton, Sean Tucker, and Andrew Stevens.
2. *Consumers' Co-operative Refineries Limited (CCRL) v. Regina (City)*, SKQB 335 (CanLII) (Saskatchewan Court of Queen's Bench, October 13, 2016) <canlii.ca/t/gvbpw>.
3. Barb Pacholik, "Portion of Co-op Refinery's Major Hazards Risk Assessment Report Released," *Regina Leader-Post*, November 21, 2016 <leaderpost.com/news/local-news/portion-of-co-op-refinerys-major-hazards-risk-assessment-report-released>.
4. CCRL *v. Regina*.
5. Saskatchewan Ministry of Environment, *Changing How We Do Business: An Introduction to Results-based Regulations and the Saskatchewan Environmental Code* (Regina: Government of Saskatchewan, 2014), 1.
6. National Pollutant Release Inventory (NPRI), *Single Year Data Tables by Facility — Releases, Transfers and Disposals —* 2020 data (Ottawa: Environment and Natural Resources Canada, 2022) <open.canada.ca/data/en/dataset/1fb7d8d4-7713-4ec6-b957-4a882a84fed3>.
7. Canadian Fuels Association, "Refining Sites and Capacity." <canadianfuels.ca/our-industry/fuel-production/>.
8. NPRI, *Single Year Data Tables*, 2019 data.
9. Arthur White-Crummey, "Co-op Refinery Production to 90,000 Barrels Per Day." *Regina Leader-Post*, April 16, 2020 <leaderpost.com/news/saskatchewan/co-op-refinery-cuts-production-to-90000-barrels-per-day>.
10. NPRI, *Single Year Data Tables*, 2020 data.
11. NPRI, *Single Year Data Tables*, 2021 data.
12. NPRI, *Single Year Data Tables*, 2021 data.
13. Health Canada. *What is Fine Particulate Matter (PM2.5)?* (Ottawa: Government of Canada, 2021) <canada.ca/en/health-canada/services/publications/healthy-living/infographic-fine-particulate-matter.html>.
14. Thibault Laconde, "Fugitive Emissions: A Blind Spot in the Fight Against Climate Change." *Climate Change 2018 Annual Report* (Global Observatory on Non-State Climate Action, 2018), 106–16.
15. NPRI, *Single Year Data Tables*, 2021 data.
16. NPRI, *Single Year Data Tables*, 2021data.
17. Alberta Environment. Air and Water Branch. Science and Standards Division, *Approaches to a Total (or Grouped)* VOC *Guideline: Final Report* (Edmonton: Government of Alberta, 2002).
18. NPRI dashboard search: Substance: (NA–M16) Volatile Organic Compounds (Total) and (Industry 324110) Petroleum Refineries, 2011–2021 (Ottawa: Environment and Natural Resources Canada, 2022) <canada.ca/en/environment-climate-change/

services/national-pollutant-release-inventory/tools-resources-data/all-year-dashboard.html>.
19 Alberta Environment, *Approaches to a Total*.
20 Cantox Environmental, *Assessment Report on Hexane for Developing Ambient Air Quality Objectives*. Prepared by Cantox Environmental Inc. in conjunction with RWDI West Inc. for Alberta Environment (Edmonton: Alberta Environment, 2004).
21 Alberta Ministry of Environment, *Alberta Ambient Air Quality Objectives: Toluene* (Edmonton: Government of Alberta, 2005).
22 Centers for Disease Control and Prevention, *Facts about Benzene* (Washington, DC: US Department of Health and Human Services, 2018).
23 NPRI, *Single Year Data Tables*, 2020 data.
24 NPRI, *Single Year Data Tables*, 2020 data.
25 Saskatchewan Information and Privacy Commissioner, *Review Report 043-2015*, May 25, 2015.
26 Environment Canada and Health Canada, *Screening Assessment for the Challenge: Vanadium Oxide (Vanadium Pentoxide)*, Chemical Abstracts Service Registry Number 1314-62-1 (Ottawa: Government of Canada, 2010) <ec.gc.ca/ese-ees/62A2DBA9-0636-4217-8D9B-36AFEB878179/batch9_1314-62-1_en.pdf>.
27 Wascana Upper Qu'Appelle Watershed Association Taking Responsibility (WUQWATR), *Wascana Riparian Health Assessment Interim Report 2013* (Regina: WUQWATR, 2013).
28 *Regina Leader-Post*, "Refinery Site East of City," January 9, 1935, 3 <news.google.com/newspapers?nid=w9EjUEod0xMC&dat=19350109&printsec=frontpage&hl=en>.
29 *Regina Leader-Post*, "New Refinery Produces 500 Barrels Daily," June 15, 1935, 9.
30 *Regina Leader-Post*, "Drilling Well for Refinery," January 12, 1935, 3.
31 *Regina Leader-Post*, "Dispute Over Water Charge May Be Issue," March 19, 1935, 3.
32 *Regina Leader-Post*, "100 Percent Surplus First Year Record of Co-operative Plant," December 9, 1936, 6.
33 *An Act to Incorporate Consumers' Co-operative Refineries Limited, SS 1936, c. 124* <canlii.ca/t/54lfp>.
34 Bank of Canada, *Inflation Calculator* <bankofcanada.ca/rates/related/inflation-calculator>.
35 *Regina Leader-Post*, "100 Percent Surplus."
36 *Regina Leader-Post*, "Objections to Pleas to Free from Taxation," March 3, 1936, 3.
37 Cited by *Regina Leader-Post*, "Objections to Pleas."
38 *Act to Incorporate CCRL*, 1936.
39 Cited by Jack McArthur, "Co-op Refinery Opens Huge Addition to Plant, "*Regina Leader-Post*, August 25, 1951, 20.
40 Cited by McArthur, "Co-op Refinery."
41 *Regina Leader-Post*, "City Approves Water, Sewer for Refinery," August 29, 1952, 8.
42 *Regina Leader-Post*, "Refinery Annexation Suggested," January 28, 1953, 3.
43 *Regina Leader-Post*, "Regina Public School Ask Refinery Assessment," October 12, 1954, 8.
44 *Regina Leader-Post*, "Behind Closed Doors Deal is Denounced," 26 March 26, 1958, 1.
45 *Regina Leader-Post*, "$1,300,000 Addition for Co-op Refinery," October 29, 1957, 1.

46 *Regina Leader-Post*, "$1,250,000 to be Spent, Beginning this Year: Co-op Refineries to Boost Capacity," March 4, 1961, 1.
47 *Regina Leader-Post*, "Co-op Refinery in $30 million Expansions," June 21, 1978, 31.
48 *Regina Leader-Post*, "SEDCO Loans $25 to Co-op Refinery," March 5, 1982, A11.
49 Bud Dahlstrom, cited by New Grade Energy, "Mega-projects Involve Mega-challenges," *Energy. Jobs. A Future: The Co-op Upgrader*, Regina Leader-Post advertising supplement, January 15, 1988, 7.
50 *Agreement Between the City of Regina and Consumers' Co-operative Refinery Limited and New Grade Energy Inc.*, November 18, 1988.
51 W.H. Smith, "The Co-op Upgrader: A Step Forward," paper presented at the Technical Meeting/Petroleum Conference of the South Saskatchewan section, Regina, October 1987 <doi.org/10.2118/SS-87-20>.
52 New Grade Energy, "Environmental Safety a Top Priority at Upgrader," *Energy. Jobs. A Future: The Co-op Upgrader. Regina Leader-Post* advertising supplement, January 15, 1988, 18.
53 United States Agency for Toxic Substances and Disease Registry, "Medical Management Guidelines for Hydrogen Sulfide," *Toxic Substances Portal*, 2014 <wwwn.cdc.gov/TSP/MMG/MMGDetails.aspx?mmgid=385&toxid=67>.
54 Cited by Bruce Johnstone, "Dahlstrom Says Only Few Problems Serious," *Regina Leader-Post*, April 24, 1989, B1.
55 Therese Macdonald, "Oil-belching Refinery Facing Charges," *Regina Leader-Post*, April 5, 1989, A1.
56 Cited by Donella Hoffman, "Nearby Businesses Want Alarm System," *Regina Leader-Post*, June 27, 1989, A3.
57 Cited by Gord Brock, "Regina Water in No Danger," *Regina Leader-Post*, September 2, 1992, A1.
58 Brock, "Regina Water in No Danger."
59 Neil Scott, "Upgrader's Discharges Above Limit," *Regina Leader-Post*, October 14, 1992, A3.
60 Consumers' Co-operative Refineries Ltd. (CCRL), *Co-op Refinery Complex 2020 Annual Environmental Report* (Regina: CCRL, 2021).
61 CCRL, *2020 Annual Environmental Report*.
62 City of Regina, *Statement of Claim*, Court of Queen's Bench, May 6, 2022.
63 NPRI, *Single Year Data Tables*, 2020 data.
64 NPRI, *Single Year Data Tables*, 2021 data.
65 EPCOR, *Spring 2019 Metals Investigation Report* (Regina: EPCOR, 2019), 12.
66 Federated Co-operatives, Ltd., "Refinery Wins Global Water Award," *News & Reports*, May 1, 2017 <fcl.crs/news-reports/news/article/refinery-wins-global-water-award>.
67 Callum O'Reilly, "Co-op Refinery Complex Wins SUEZ Award," *Hydrocarbon Engineering*, Februrary 1, 2019 <hydrocarbonengineering.com/refining/01022019/co-op-refinery-complex-wins-suez-award/>.
68 City of Regina, *Statement of Claim*, Court of Queen's Bench, May 6, 2022.
69 Alec Salloum, "Questions Linger about Notification, Impact of Refinery's Oil Spill," *Regina Leader-Post*, June 1, 2020 <leaderpost.com/news/local-news/questions-linger-about-notification-impact-of-refinerys-oil-spill>.
70 Sections 14(a)(d), 17(1)(d), and 21(a) of *The Local Authority Freedom of Information and Protection of Privacy Act* were cited on all redactions.

71 City of Regina, *Statement of Claim*, Court of Queen's Bench, May 6, 2022, 12.
72 *Consumers' Co-operative Refineries Limited and City of Regina*, Court of Queen's Bench, 8 September 2022.
73 EPCOR, *City of Regina Wastewater Treatment Plant Annual Operating Report 2018* (EPCOR, 2019), 10 <open.regina.ca/dataset/annual-report-wsa-foi-2020-014/resource/0a7f3a5f-4ac8-4f8a-8a81-57943bdb3d34>.
74 Environment and Natural Resources, *Toxic Substances List: Vanadium Pentoxide*, n.d. (Ottawa: Government of Canada) <canada.ca/en/environment-climate-change/services/management-toxic-substances/list-canadian-environmental-protection-act/vanadium-pentoxide.html>.
75 Rural Municipality of Sherwood, "City of Regina Waste Water Treatment Plant — Notice to Downstream Users," July 10, 2020 <rmofsherwood.ca/city-of-regina-waste-water-treatment-plant-notice-to-downstream-users/>.
76 Suren Kulshretha, Cecil Nagy and Ana Bogdan, *Present and Future Water Demand in the Qu'Appelle River Basin* (University of Saskatchewan: Department of Bioresource Policy, Business and Economics), 2012, 7–12.
77 Roberta Bell, "Heavy Metal Used by Co-op Refinery Detected in Regina Wastewater," Global News, July 10, 2020 <globalnews.ca/news/7163972/heavy-metal-co-op-refinery-regina-wastewater/>.
78 NPRI, *Single Year Data Tables*, 2020 and 2019 data.
79 Simon Constable, "Shell and AMG Planning Clean Tech Project with Chinese Oil Giant Shandong." *Forbes*, October 26, 2020 <forbes.com/sites/simonconstable/2020/10/26/shell-and-amg-planning-clean-tech-project-with-chinese-oil-giant-shandong/?sh=4c522b7866ca>.
80 EVRAZ, *Our Approach to Climate Change*, 2019, 4, 6. <evraz.com/upload/iblock/ce1/ce1e55ad49856e0fe2563b0599e3f073.pdf>.
81 NPRI, *Single Year Data Tables*, 2019 data.
82 Environment Canada and Health Canada, *Screening Assessment for the Challenge: Vanadium Oxide (Vanadium Pentoxide)* (Ottawa: Government of Canada: 2010) <ec.gc.ca/ese-ees/62A2DBA9-0636-4217-8D9B-36AFEB878179/batch9_1314-62-1_en.pdf>.
83 NPRI, *Substance Detail 2020*. Database search: CRC, Vanadium (and its compounds).
84 Alec Salloum, "Co-op Refinery Pays City of Regina $4.6M for 2020 'effluent' spill." *Regina Leader-Post*, January 18, 2023; NPRI, *Single Year Data Tables*, 2021.
85 NPRI, *Single Year Data Tables*, 2021 data.
86 Environment Canada and Health Canada. *Screening Assessment*.
87 CCRL, *2020 Annual Environmental Report*.
88 *Regina Leader-Post*, "Swan Says Fines Will Remedy Problem," June 27, 1989, A3.
89 Provincial Auditor of Saskatchewan, *2013 Report — Volume 1* (Regina: Office of the Provincial Auditor, 2013), 275.
90 Environment, Health and Public Safety, *Air Zone Management* (Regina: Government of Saskatchewan) <saskatchewan.ca/residents/environment-public-health-and-safety/environmental-health/outdoor-air-quality/air-zones>.
91 Alison Tucker, *Air Quality Management in Saskatchewan — Transitioning From Facility Based Monitoring to Air Zone Management* [slide presentation] (Saskatchewan Ministry of Environment, n.d), slide 18.
92 Saskatchewan Ministry of Environment, *Saskatchewan Environmental Code: Moving Forward in Partnership*, SUMA Convention education session presentation,

January 29, 2012, slide 2.
93   CCRL, *Co-op Refinery Complex: Discharge Environmental Protection Plan* (Regina: CCRL, 2019), 4.
94   CCRL, *Co-op Refinery Complex: Air Environmental Protection Plan* (Regina: CCRL, 2019), 3.
95   Auditor General of Ontario, *Value for Money Audit: Hazardous Spills*, 2021, 35 <auditor.on.ca/en/content/annualreports/arreports/en21/ENV_HazardousSpills_en21.pdf>.
96   Reuters, "UPDATE 1 — Canada's Federated Finishes $2.7 bln Refinery Expansion," October 26, 2012 <reuters.com/article/consumers-refinery-idIN-L1E8LQERB20121026>.
97   CCRL, *Project Proposal for Expansion Project: Section V & Revamps* (Regina: CCRL, 2007), 32 <environment.gov.sk.ca/2007-184EIA%28ProjectProposal%29>.
98   Email correspondence re. "CCRL Expansion," G. Mutch to H. Seguin, Saskatchewan Ministry of Environment, February 4, 2008.
99   Saskatchewan Ministry of Environment, "Towards TRC for CCRL Expansion — for discussion February 4, 2008," unpublished memo, February 4, 2022, 1.
100 Email correspondence, "Comments on the Co-op Refinery Expansion Review," G. Neiman, City of Regina to G. Mutch, Saskatchewan Ministry of Environment, February 22, 2008.
101 Email correspondence, "Technical Review Panel Meeting — CCRL," R. Seguin to L. Quarshie and D. Phillips, June 27, 2008.
102 Intrinsik Review, cited in *Response to the Human Health Risk Assessment Peer Review*, unpublished report to Saskatchewan Ministry of Environment, July 2008, 51.
103 *Response*, July 2008, 52.
104 "Towards TRC for CCRL Expansion," 1.
105 Nancy Heppner, "Reasons for Decision: Ministerial Decisions Under the Environmental Assessment Act: Expansion of the Consumers' Co-operative Refineries Limited Oil Refinery in Regina" (Regina: Ministry of Environment, September 8, 2008), 8. <environment.gov.sk.ca/2007-184ReasonsForDecision>.
106 City of Regina, *Minutes of the Planning Commission*, February 13, 2013, 10.
107 City of Regina, *Minutes*, 10.
108 Jerry Flegel cited by Emma Graney, "Somerset Set for Council Despite Air Quality Concerns," *Regina Leader-Post*, November 14, 2013, A1.
109 Cited by Aaron Stuckel, "North Regina Residents Worry Little about Refinery Explosions," *Regina Leader-Post*, December 30, 2013.
110 Clean Air Sarnia and Area, CASA *Air Monitoring Network Reporting* [web portal] <reporting.cleanairsarniaandarea.com/>.
111 Troy Shantz, "About Those Warning Sirens that Blare Every Monday," *The Sarnia Journal*, April 9, 2019 <thesarniajournal.ca/about-those-warning-sirens-that-blare-every-monday/>.
112 Saskatchewan Ministry of Environment, *Discharge Cases Database*, Saskatchewan GeoHub, Case ID 2020-03-16T18:04:53.
113 Health Canada, *Human Health Risk Assessment for Sulphur Dioxide* (Ottawa: Government of Canada, 2016).
114 Wes Kotyk, assistant deputy minister, Saskatchewan Ministry of Environment, letter to Sean Tucker, University of Regina, June 18, 2020, 3.
115 Kotyk letter, 4.

116 Kotyk letter, 4.
117 Great Plains Air Zone, *Air Monitoring Annual Report 2021* (Saskatoon: Saskatchewan Research Council), 10.
118 Wayne Gibson, City of Regina Strategic Communications, email to Patricia Elliott, July 11, 2022.
119 NPRI, *Single Year Data Tables*, 2019 data.
120 CCRL, *2020 Annual Environmental Report*, 50.
121 Canadian Centre for Occupational Health and Safety. *Chemical Profiles: Hydrogen Sulfide*. 2017 <ccohs.ca/oshanswers/chemicals/chem_profiles/hydrogen_sulfide.html>.
122 Kotyk letter, 4.
123 CCRL, *2020 Annual Environmental Report*: 71.
124 Federated Co-operatives Limited, *Co-op Refinery Complex*, n.d. <https://www.fcl.crs/our-business/refinery>.
125 United States Department of Energy, "Alternative Fuels Data Centre," n.d. <afdc.energy.gov/fuels/emerging_hydrocarbon.html>.
126 Saskatchewan Trade and Export Development, "Major Value-Added Agriculture Investment Announced in Saskatchewan," *media release*, January 17, 2022.
127 *Reduction in the Release of Volatile Organic Compounds Regulations (Petroleum Sector)*, SOR/2020-231, <https://canlii.ca/t/55c67>.
128 *Canadian Environmental Protection Act, 1999*, SC 1999, c 33 <canlii.ca/t/54tsw>.
129 Canadian Fuels Association, *Refinery Competitivenes and Climate Change Policies* [slide presentation], May 2018 <sencanada.ca/content/sen/committee/421/ENEV/Briefs/May1_CndFuelsAssociation_e.pdf>.
130 Saskatchewan Agriculture, Natural Resources and Industry, *Saskatchewan Upstream Oil and Gas* IRIS *Incident Report, Incident #19399*.
131 Nan Wang, Keigo Akimoto, and Gregory Nemet, "What Went Wrong? Learning From Three Decades of Carbon Capture, Utilization and Sequestration (CCUS) Pilot and Demonstration Projects," *Energy Policy*, 158 (2021).
132 Thibault Laconde, "Fugitive Emissions," 106.
133 Process Operator, "Caustic Work Environment," August 29, 2020 <ca.indeed.com>.

6

"YOU'RE NOT BOILING MILK"
Health and Safety at the Co-op Refinery

Sean Tucker

> I work at a refinery; I'm not living until I'm 80 or 90. It would be nice to hit 80, but it's more important that I would be able to take care of my wife when I'm not here, and that pension that we currently have would have done that. (Daryl Watch, Local 594 member)[1]

DARYL WATCH'S MATTER-OF-FACT STATEMENT SPEAKS to the bargain many Co-op Refinery Complex workers make between their health and livelihood. Working at an oil refinery can expose workers to a number of potentially deadly hazards, from known carcinogens to fires and explosions. Between 2011 and 2019, there were two major explosions and several fires at the CRC. But refining oil is not only a threat to the health and safety of refinery workers, it also poses a hazard to adjacent communities. Uniting around a healthy future for workers and communities involves planning a safe and orderly transition away from the production of fossil fuels.

Community and occupational health and safety (OHS) has been and continues to be a major issue at the CRC. In 2015, Scott Banda, CEO of Federated Co-operatives Limited (FCL, the parent company of the CRC), claimed, "Our culture of safety is top-notch and we work to improve it all the time.… We have an 80 year history in this city and over those 80 years I would put our record up against anyone's in the industry."[2] However, in reality the refinery has a tendency to treat safety as a problem of public relations. During the lockout, the CRC strategically framed its workers' union, Unifor Local 594, and some individual workers as unsafe and dangerous in order win public support and distract attention from both safety inside the plant and the demand of locked-out workers to maintain their pension. A critical understanding of related health and safety events is crucial in assessing the narratives advanced during the lockout by both Local 594 and the CRC. My interest in health and safety at the CRC began in 2014 when a local journalist asked to interview me for a follow-up story about a large explosion at the CRC. As is my practice when preparing for a media interview, I called the CRC for information on presumed improvements implemented since the explosion. Within minutes, the CRC's public relations official made it clear that my inquiry was unwelcome. What would normally be a ten-minute phone call in preparation for a media interview turned into a multi-year research project on health and safety at the refinery. My analysis here is informed by interviews and conversations with individuals who possess intimate knowledge of refinery operations but must remain anonymous in order to prevent any possible reprisals that impact their personal and professional lives.

REFINERY WORK IS DANGEROUS WORK

One of the central issues in the dispute was the CRC's demand for concessions from the workers on their pension plan. Refinery workers are exposed to chemicals and incidents that put them at greater risk of certain types of occupational disease and early death than other workers. The refinery's pension guaranteed a good retirement and supported workers and their loved ones should their lives be shortened by occupational disease or a catastrophic event.

Many hazards at oil refineries are similar to those found in large industrial plants, including falls from heights, electrocution, burns from exposure to heat, hearing loss, and illness from exposure to chemicals and other substances, to name a few. An important part of injury prevention in any workplace is controlling hazards. Perry Feltham, a now-retired Steelworker (Local 9316) who worked at Newfoundland's only refinery, characterized oil refining to me this way: "We all know the oil refinery business is dangerous. You're boiling oil, you're not boiling milk."[3] The refining process involves converting crude oil into fuel and other by-products using various processing units connected by a vast network of piping. It is essential that this infrastructure is effectively monitored and maintained and that workers are adequately trained and experienced in their roles. The Canadian Fuels Association, which represents most refiners in Canada, acknowledges that a high commitment to process safety is key to the efficient and safe operation of refineries.[4]

The most visible and unique risks of working in a refinery are explosions and fires. As Feltham told me, "You want to keep all your product and your fuel inside the piping, not outside. If you get vapours outside, vapour clouds and a source of ignition, you know what you've got, kaboom."[5] There have been several high-profile cases of uncontrolled gas releases that have led to explosions that killed and seriously injured workers throughout North American refineries. In 2005, an explosion at British Petroleum's Texas City refinery killed fifteen workers and injured 180 others.[6] In 2010, an explosion at the Tesoro Refinery in Washington State killed seven workers.[7] More recently, in 2022, an explosion at the refinery in Come By Chance, Newfoundland and Labrador, led to one death and five workers being hospitalized with serious injuries.[8]

In relative terms, fires are more common than explosions at refineries. Unfortunately, information about the occurrence and severity of fires is not publicly available in Canada despite the fact that workers who are exposed to fires and explosions can experience respiratory illnesses due to exposure to noxious fumes, as well as tracer burns, hearing loss, PTSD, and other injuries. There are other risks associated with refinery work that are less apparent to the public. In refineries with older infrastructure, like parts of the CRC, asbestos was commonly used to insulate pressurized vessels, pipes, and other equipment. Inhaling asbestos fibres can cause mesothelioma (most commonly), asbestosis, and other respiratory cancers, which can appear decades after initial exposure.[9] Those who are diagnosed with asbestos-related illnesses typically pass away within a few months.

The results of a recent meta-analysis of thirty-six high-quality studies of cancer rates among refinery workers found that risk of mesothelioma is three times higher among refinery workers and four times higher among refinery maintenance workers than other workers.[10] A large-sample follow-up study of 25,000 workers at a large Canadian petrochemical plant concluded: "There is a continuing excess of mesothelioma.... This excess is mostly attributable to men who died in their 50s and 60s and who worked in the refining."[11] Over the years, I have received numerous credible accounts of workers who claim they were exposed to asbestos at the CRC. In one, written minutes from a September 2019 CRC joint worker-management occupational health committee meeting noted the need for further investigation into a significant asbestos exposure event in 2017 that affected a number of workers.[12]

Refineries can also expose operators, maintenance workers, and other employees to on-site gases and chemicals that are known to be harmful to health. CAREX Canada (CARcinogen EXposure) profiles numerous known carcinogens that workers are exposed to if proper controls, training, and personal protective equipment are not effectively implemented. The organization notes that refinery workers may be exposed to a variety of hazardous chemicals, such as butadiene, benzene, carbon tetrachloride ethylbenzene, gasoline, diesel exhaust, and trichloroethylene.[13] Benzene is a colourless and odorless gas that can be lethal with even limited exposure. There is also the potential to be exposed to deadly hydrogen sulphide (H_2S or sour gas). Benzene and H_2S can lead to a range of illness, from headaches to death, depending on the duration of exposure, interactions with other chemicals, and other factors. Sources at the refinery have divulged that historically CRC workers have been exposed to both gases.

Unfortunately, the public does not have the full picture of the number and severity of injuries at the CRC.[14] In 2015, a lawyer representing injured contract workers at the CRC was able to obtain information from the Saskatchewan Workers' Compensation Board showing that there were five accepted occupational disease fatality claims between 2000 and 2014.[15]

Taken together, the research evidence supports what Daryl Watch and others know about the potential consequences of refinery work on both their health and life expectancy. An open letter posted on social media from the wife of a CRC refinery worker near the beginning of the 2019–2020 lockout speaks to the worry about occupational cancer: "Facing the fear every year when he goes to have the recommended chest X-ray to check for signs of Asbestosis. Or Mesothelioma. Looking back now, the risks far outweigh the benefits."[16] A comprehensive review of health and safety at Regina's refinery should be pursued, if only to capture the human cost of work in FCL's leading profit centre in Saskatchewan.

HEALTH AND SAFETY AT THE PLANT (2011–2019)

To understand safety incidents at the CRC, I drew on information from media reports, court documents, interviews with current and former unionized and non-unionized CRC employees and other confidential sources with knowledge of the refinery, information obtained through freedom of information requests, and publicly available sources.[17] The CRC has chosen to share very little health and safety information with the community. CRC employees are required to sign a non-disclosure agreement (NDA) as a condition of employment, further limiting what is known about health and safety within the plant and potential risks to the public.[18]

Banda's 2015 characterization of the CRC's safety culture as "top notch" is at odds with the evidence from the past decade and indeed with public statements made by refinery managers. Four years prior to the CEO's claim, on October 6, 2011, the CRC was rocked by a massive explosion that left fifty-two contract workers injured, including six with severe burns and PTSD.[19] The cause of the explosion was a leak in a corroded processing unit pipe. The CRC faced several charges under Saskatchewan's OHS legislation. Eventually, in 2015, the company pled guilty and was fined $200,000 plus an $80,000 victim surcharge. Submissions to the court indicated numerous problems in the lead up to the incident, including concerns about gas smells, disconnected alarms, and complaints being ignored by management.[20] In court, lawyers for the CRC argued that an incorrect pipe had been installed in the 1960s, while the Crown prosecutor argued that the CRC failed to properly track pipe corrosion and could have prevented the explosion through effective maintenance and monitoring.

In a letter to one of the workers who was seriously injured by the explosion, Banda stated: "We do place the safety of our workers and the public ahead of everything we do at the refinery. When despite our best efforts people are injured, we will use every effort to find out what happened and take whatever steps we can to ensure nothing like it happens again."[21] Following the 2011 explosion and two subsequent fires, FCL VP Vic Huard, in 2013, "conced[ed] that their safety record used to be among the best in the industry but he admits he 'can't say that now.'"[22]

Nine months later, on December 24, 2013, another large explosion at the plant shook windows throughout the city and was heard twenty kilometres away.²³ Fortunately, the plant was operating with limited staff and there were no reported injuries. However, many workers and their spouses have told me that this explosion was traumatic for those who work close to where the incident occurred. By sheer luck they were not on site at the time of the blast. In the aftermath of the explosion, CRC manager Dan McMurtry said, "I'll tell you, one is one too many and we've had a number. It's a serious concern for us at this point in time."²⁴ An investigation by the Technical Safety Authority of Saskatchewan (TSASK), the regulator responsible for overseeing compliance with regulations for pressurized vessels and other equipment in Saskatchewan, determined that water had frozen and ruptured a bypass line. As the water in the bypass line thawed, hydrocarbons leaked from the ruptured portion of the line and ignited. The report noted: "A similar pipe rupture due to freezing occurred in December 2008, where the resulting vapour cloud did not ignite. Effective corrective actions were not implemented."²⁵ Between 2014 and 2019, there were three publicly reported leaks and at least two more fires at the refinery.²⁶

Outwardly, health and safety began to improve after about 2015. There were several changes including new senior leadership, engagement with outside process safety consultants, and additional investments in safety systems. However, even after 2015, there were incidents and at least one serious injury at the CRC. In one case, the Occupational Safety Division at the Saskatchewan Ministry of Labour Relations and Workplace Safety and the Saskatchewan Labour Relations Board found that the CRC had failed to report a serious injury in 2017 that involved a worker who was hospitalized when their neck, face, and ear were seriously burned from being sprayed with hot diesel gas oil.²⁷ And in 2017, the refinery attempted to remove the most experienced, skilled, and safety-sensitive job from bargaining unit — the master operator (MO). These attempts continued throughout the 2019–2020 negotiations despite the union making it clear that the MO was "crucial to maintaining the safe operation of the refinery."²⁸

SAFETY AS PUBLIC RELATIONS

During the lockout, safety was front and centre. Yet the company's communications continued a pattern of treating safety as public relations exercise. Several sources indicated to me that before 2000, the CRC went about its business near the city limits without too much concern for community relations.²⁹ This was due to the fact that, in 1935, the plant was established on the open prairie, at the time relatively far from the City of Regina. Over the decades both the refinery and city's footprint grew with light industrial development and, to the west, a residential community known as Uplands, adjacent to the refinery site.

Although uncommon, publicly reported incidents at the refinery have impacted neighbouring communities and businesses. Shortly after the refinery's heavy oil upgrader was brought online in 1989, a gas leak caused students to become ill at a school in Regina's Uplands neighbourhood, which borders the facility. A media report noted: "A plume of foul-smelling hydrogen sulphide gas wafted over a Regina school.... Gas levels measured inside the school, about three kilometres away from the refinery, were 50 times higher than provincial air-quality standards allow.... Dozens of children suffered nausea and headaches."³⁰ This event underscores the CRC's potential risk to public safety.

In 2013, when a developer sought approval to build another residential community near the refinery, the local health region and Ministry of the Environment opposed the proposal due to their concerns about the risk to public health. The then-VP of the refinery, Bud Van Iderstine, agreed, stating, "The CRC believes the city should not allow a residential development in this area of Regina, and establish a reasonably large setback for residential developments from industrial facilities."³¹ FCL VP Vic Huard said the city's interest in the development was "an ill-advised decision."³² Despite these warnings, Regina City Council approved the development, and by this time it was apparent that the CRC was now more mindful of the importance of community relations and the potential impact that incidents could have on residents who neighboured the facility. Unfortunately, the CRC's concern for community safety did not extend to replacement worker housing situated a few hundred metres away from the processing sections of the refinery during the 2019–1920 lockout — all of which was approved by the City of Regina.

The CRC has track record of responding to safety concerns with a coordinated public relations strategy. As noted in FCL's 2013 annual report: "Brand-specific research [conducted in 2013] included ... monitoring public opinion and support of the Co-op Refinery Complex as it operates in alignment with both FCL's values and values important to the public."³³ Beginning in about 2014, the CRC stepped up its public relations activities through more visible charitable donations, sponsorship, and media advertising (billboard, newspaper, radio, and television). Related messaging highlighted the refinery as a safe and generous community partner that produces a significant economic benefit to the community. This worked to strengthen the company's community acceptance, which it would deploy years later against Unifor 594. In 2016, the company even gave $320,000 to the City of Regina to fund an emergency alert system known as "notifynow." As Patricia Elliot notes in Chapter 5, "Since NotifyNow was initiated, there have been no public alerts issued concerning industrial air emissions or spills," despite the fact that spills and air emissions are a chronic problem at the refinery.[34]

Overall, the CRC's approach to public safety is consistent with the Canadian refining industry's philosophy of social licence. The Canadian Association of Petroleum Producers (CAPP) sees the obligation to safety in utilitarian terms; it is not just the right thing to do:

> Corporate responsibility as demonstrated in your process safety management program leads to a greater range of business flexibility. When you openly display responsibility through implementing an effective process safety program, your company can achieve greater freedom and self-determination.[35]

Announcement of "notifynow" emergency alert system. (Photo by Neil Cochrane/CBC Listening, reprinted with permission)

"Safety: We Refine it Daily" billboard at the CRC site. (Emily Leedham, Rankandfile.ca)

There is, however, a gap among the co-operative values espoused by FCL (in particular, integrity and responsibility to the community[36]), the CRC's carefully managed narrative about community and occupational safety, and its related actions. Of particular concern are misleading statements, coupled with a lack of transparency and openness with journalists and members of the public about potential health and safety risks and incidents.

Following the explosions and fires between 2011 and 2013, the CRC hired a new spokesperson to build the CRC brand and promote a positive narrative about the refinery. Subsequent inquiries about incidents at the plant have almost always been rebuffed and offer little insight into the causes of incidents and corrective actions. Reporting on an incident in 2017, one journalist noted: "When asked about the refinery's track record, [the CRC's public relations manager] repeated a line he delivered in November [2014], when the facility experienced another minor leak.... 'Obviously,' said the public relations manager, 'the refinery is a complex facility and with complexity comes challenges.... We are confident that we have the necessary procedures in place to detect these leaks and isolate the areas, because the Number 1 priority is safety of our people and our neighbours.'"[37]

A legal battle between a CBC Saskatchewan journalist, Geoff Leo, and the CRC is an example of the lack of transparency. Between 2014 and 2016, the refinery intervened to prevent any public disclosure of the 2012 third-party Major Hazards Risk Assessment Report (MHRA) that it had commissioned to explore the potential impacts of a "worse-case scenario" on neighbouring residents.[38] In 2014, Saskatchewan's Information and Privacy Commissioner recommended the city and province release part of the report to Leo. The CRC appealed the decision to the Court of Queen's Bench, but in 2016, the court ordered part of the report released to the public. At the end of the process, the refinery's spokesperson stated: "Public safety has always been our top priority, and this report validates that."[39]

During the 2017 round of collective bargaining between Unifor 594 and the CRC, which narrowly averted a work stoppage, the job title of the refinery's Director of Communications and Public Affairs temporarily changed in public communications to "Director of Communications *and Public Safety*" (emphasis added). To my knowledge, this individual has no public safety credentials or experience, and I suspect the change in job title was an attempt to influence the media and public perceptions about the credibility of safety-related messages from coming from its public affairs department.[40] Despite repeated claims that public safety is the CRC's "top priority," representatives of the refinery have declined to participate in public town hall forums related to community health and safety. Nor has the CRC initiated any public meetings of its own to discuss health and safety impacts of the plant on workers and the surrounding community.

In the decade leading up to the 2019–2020 lockout, the CRC was confronted with significant safety issues, including two large explosions and several fires. A change in senior leadership, a stronger public commitment to process safety, and other changes have led to fewer and less severe incidents, but there continues to be instances where workers are injured or exposed to dangerous substances. In the five years leading up to the lockout, there were also significant strategic investments in public relations that focused on situating the refinery as a safe community partner and driver of economic growth. However, the evidence shows that the refinery engages with the media and community members on its own terms, to carefully (and often successfully) control its message.

HEALTH AND SAFETY NARRATIVES AND REALITIES DURING THE 2019–2020 LOCKOUT

By November 2019, a prolonged strike or lockout at the refinery seemed inevitable. Bargaining had dragged on for months and state-sponsored mediation proved unsuccessful in bringing the parties together. For its part, the refinery was close to finishing construction on what it called a "first-class work camp" next to the plant on land leased from the City of Regina.[41] In the weeks leading to the work stoppage, separate union and company narratives took shape about the potential risks of such a stoppage to community safety.

Two weeks before the lockout, I invited both the CRC and 594 to participate in a public panel discussion at the University of Regina, but only a representative from Local 594 agreed to join.[42] My chief concern was the impact of inexperienced and under-trained replacement workers as well as fatigue. Ironically the latter concern was shared by Vic Huard, who said, in 2017, "when you're tired it's not a good time to be maybe operating heavy equipment or to be maintaining a highly sensitive … place like a refinery."[43] These words were conveniently sidelined during the dispute. Dan Josephson, a retired thirty-eight-year process operator represented Local 594 at the town hall. He characterized the risks of operating without union members this way: "having the plant run by untrained, under-qualified replacement workers is like a 12-year-old kid taking dad's car for a joy ride, he might be able to navigate that car for a little while down a straight road. But as soon as the curves start coming, and the traffic hits, there's going to be an accident."[44] The CRC's director of health, safety, security and environment, Lenita Knudsen, responded in a related media interview: "We are confident in our ability to safely and reliably operate."[45] In an effort to identify and manage community concerns, the CRC invited residents with questions to contact their office directly.[46]

On December 3, 2019, the CRC announced a forty-eight-hour lockout notice, which it claimed was "in the interest of public safety,"[47] following a strike vote by Local 594. Two days later FCL issued a press release, stating: "the only way we can ensure a safe operating environment is to lock the Union out and have our management team assume the safe operation of the Refinery. We simply can't run the risk of employees conducting rotating strikes and walking off the job in our safety-sensitive operating environment."[48]

At this time Unifor 594 wrote an open letter to FCL and the CRC, stating: "oil refining is a high hazard operation and continuing to run the CRC Refinery without members of Unifor 594 would be an unnecessary risk and, in our mind, a mistake."[49] They also offered to assist in any emergency response "while Unifor 594 is taking legal job action" on the condition that its members were covered by the benefits outlined in the collective bargaining agreement. Sources confirmed that the refinery did not reply to the invitation and presumably there was no plan for 594 members to have any involvement in a response to a large-scale incident.

At 5:30 p.m. on December 5, 2019, the CRC posted this message on its social media: "To ensure the safety and reliability of the Refinery, our highly skilled management team has assumed control of the refinery."[50] The lockout had begun. A couple of days later the refinery responded in writing to several questions I had emailed them about a range of issues related to their operational plans during the lockout. Spokespeople for the refinery stated in an email that the plant would operate at 85 percent capacity and that management was guided by a "maximum safety, not maximum output" philosophy. They claimed all workers had appropriate training and certifications and that managers "are among the very best our industry has to offer" and "we have total faith in their incredible capabilities." In terms of worker fatigue, the CRC stated: "We have been very deliberate in our shift rotations to ensure adequate rest time and days off." Furthermore, "We have designed our shift schedules to maximize down time. They will be encouraged to rest and relax in their downtime."[51]

Prior to the lockout, sources shared concerns with me about some of the replacement worker training and certification decisions. Other sources, with knowledge of operations, told me that one of the plant's sections was taken offline due to a lack of staff and that the plant in fact had been running at 60–70 percent capacity *before* the onset of the pandemic in March 2020. The role of replacement worker fatigue on operational safety was an important concern, as well. However, the refinery and FCL suggested that the actions of locked out unionized workers were the real threat to public safety. It was also noteworthy that the CRC stated to me that its VP of operations and its director of health, safety, security, and environment would handle the media's "technical questions" about health and safety. However, over time, health and safety reverted back to a public relations exercise, with the CRC's spokesperson handling most media interviews on the subject in 2020.

The refinery's communications strategy during the lockout focused on highlighting the alleged dangers of Unifor's tactics. While parts of some FCL media releases raised legitimate questions about safety, they primarily served to frame Unifor's tactics as being a threat to the safe operations of the plant (see also Chapters 1 and 4). For example, on December 7, 2019, the CRC justified using helicopters to transport replacement workers "due to the dangerous situation at the picket lines and the need to ensure the safe operation of our refinery."[52] On December 18, a CRC replacement worker alleged that he was harassed and assaulted by 594 workers.[53] However, a video of the incident later surfaced clearly showing there was no harassment or assault.[54] Justice Janet McMurtry's December 24, 2019, injunction about picketing addressed the CRC's allegations of union harassment on the picket line: "I am not satisfied that CCRL is entitled to an order responding to the intimidation that has occurred, as it has occurred on both sides."[55] Indeed, 594 members I spoke with cited several instances of harassment and intimidation by security staff hired by the CRC.[56]

The CRC also took the position that the picket line was a danger to truckers who risked working over their maximum regulated work hours due to waiting at 594 picket lines. In court, CRC lawyers reasoned that if truckers were delayed entering the plant, "safety could be at risk because needed people or supplies may be kept out [of the refinery]."[57]

About one month into the lockout, media reported cases of fuel trucks being vandalized. Some vehicles had punctured tires after driving over what were described as welding spikes. Chad Heibein, owner of Heibein's Transport, a company that transported fuel for FCL, said, "If you're going down the road and the steering tire comes off the rim, it basically results in you going in the ditch. It could result in a rollover, you know, we had 58,000 liters of gas on. Potentially that could be on the ground, start fires, explosions whatever; very dangerous."[58] In response, Local 594 president Kevin Bittman stated, "I don't know where it came from, but to me, people aren't going to put their jobs on the line vandalizing trucks. The truckers are in the middle of this, there's no reason for us to do any of that."[59] To date, there is no evidence to suggest that any of these incidents resulted in charges or were traced back to locked-out workers, but the suggestion that it was the work of Local 594 members influenced public perceptions of the union.

A blockade of the plant by Unifor National and Local 594, which began on January 9 and continued on and off until early February, elevated the level of attention and concern about safety. FCL declared Unifor's action a "threat to public safety."[60] Gil Le Dressay, VP of refinery operations, stated that the "union is cutting off emergency access to these facilities, and that should not be allowed."[61] Regina's fire marshal issued an order for Unifor to clear the barricades to allow access and egress from the CRC.[62] My sources with Unifor responded saying that it would quickly clear the gates in the event of an incident.

In late January 2020, negotiations resulted in an agreement to keep one gate open at the plant for emergency vehicles. Regina Police Service (RPS) chief Evan Bray issued a special video statement in which he stated: "We have an emergency gate that has been set aside; it is not blockaded, and should we need to get emergency vehicles onto the site we will be able to use that gate. I think that is absolutely essential in maintaining community safety and our community should feel better as a result of that information."[63] At that time I made several inquiries with reliable, independent sources with knowledge of the operations of the plant to better understand the level of risk posed by the other blockaded gates to emergency response. These sources told me that the situation would not negatively impact an emergency response. Overall, the refinery's messaging to the media and public exaggerated the risks of Unifor's actions on safety at the plant. This served a useful purpose in both maligning the union and distracting attention from working conditions within the plant. Understandably industrial conflict is visible, dramatic, and, indeed, newsworthy (see Chapter 7). What was less visible during the lockout was the state of safety within the plant.

Officially it was business as usual for the regulatory bodies responsible for overseeing and ensuring compliance with provincial health and safety regulations. These included the City of Regina, the Ministry of the Environment, the Ministry of Labour Relations and Workplace Safety (LRWS), and TSASK. However, it was not business as usual given the tension surrounding the dispute and importance of the refinery to the provincial economy. According to the minister of labour relations and workplace safety, Don Morgan, occupational health officers visited the plant four times during the lockout and found that the CRC was in compliance with relevant OHS laws and regulations.⁶⁴ Related records obtained from LRWS through a freedom of information request confirmed this. Other regulators were also monitoring the plant for compliance, but as Patricia Elliot points out in Chapter 5, industrial regulatory oversight is weak in Saskatchewan.⁶⁵ This included the City of Regina's oversight.

To the surprise of many, in March 2020, it was revealed that the CRC had leased land from the city for their replacement worker camp. Furthermore, the city had approved temporary occupancy of the camp days before the lockout. Documents obtained through access to information showed that discussions started in February 2017, shortly after an earlier round of bargaining nearly resulted in a work stoppage. At the time, a senior city planner stated in an email to FCL, "from a zoning perspective we had determined that there is enough flexibility to permit the use [of a work camp] on a temporary basis, providing any safety concerns that may be identified can be addressed."⁶⁶ In the lead up to the lockout in 2019, the city confirmed with FCL that it was permitted to construct a work camp with up to six hundred beds.⁶⁷ The city's only concern was that the camp be compliant with city zoning and building codes.⁶⁸ The fact that the camp was situated close to the refinery was not material and no additional independent risk assessment was required, a point driven home by Regina councillor Andrew Stevens:

> The refinery in 2013 had issued concerns around the development of the Somerset neighbourhood citing health. I was really puzzled as to why an employer didn't want a neighbourhood to be built far away, was all of a sudden okay with having a neighbourhood built right on its site where there are signs everywhere talking about health and safety and environmental hazards.⁶⁹

While the CRC mastered the safety narrative, similar concerns were not extended to Local 594 members, who were the target of an anonymous letter sent to the RPS, RCMP, and mayor of Regina, on February 18, 2020, claiming that a group of farmers had built an explosive device and were prepared to use it if the RPS didn't take down barricades at the plant.⁷⁰ The RPS investigated the letter and found the threat was not credible, in part because the blockades were removed at the time the letter was received. However, Unifor 594 was never notified of the bomb threat.⁷¹

A "TREMENDOUS" SAFETY RECORD ... AND A MAJOR SPILL

Two months into the lockout, on February 24, 2020, the CRC's spokesperson claimed, "Our safety record during the labour disruption has been tremendous."[72] Most of what is known about occupational and community safety during the lockout comes from observations outside the plant. In mid-January large flares were caught on video, which the CRC insisted were caused by power outages.[73] In February and March, cell phone videos showed unplanned releases from different sections of the plant.[74] The CRC did not acknowledge or explain these incidents. Videos circulated on social media of ambulances entering and leaving the plant on March 2, March 11, and May 21. The CRC offered no comment on any of these incidents.

On April 29, 2020, Le Dressay reiterated how well the plant was operating, signalling the company's capacity to operate with fewer staff and without its more experienced unionized workers: "Members of our management team as well as skilled industry personnel have operated the refinery safely, reliably and efficiently since the dispute began on December 5, 2019, and we're extremely confident they can continue to do so for an indefinite period of time, if necessary."[75]

Less than one month after Le Dressay's pronouncement, and while 594 workers were still locked out, the refinery spilled sixty thousand litres of oily sludge into the City of Regina's sewer system, causing damage to the municipal sewer treatment facility. Some quantity of the discharge leaked into Wascana Creek. The city wastewater treatment plant first became aware of the discharge but it was not until a week later that the public was informed via media reports.[76] Chief Todd Peigan of Pasqua First Nation, which is downstream from the treatment plant on Wascana Creek, said it was "an employee with EPCOR, which operates Regina's wastewater treatment facility, that contacted the band."[77] Despite multiple reassurances during the lockout that community safety was its number one priority, the CRC never notified the public about the spill. A CRC spokesperson told a journalist that "high wind gusts" were responsible for the spill even though the maximum wind speed on the day of the spill was just forty-eight kilometres per hour.[78]

In a surprise move, in August 2022, the City of Regina sued the refinery for $4.5 million for the costs of cleaning up the spill.[79] The city claimed that the refinery had told them that "a diesel pump was used in the holding ponds to discharge the wastewater but the pump had been improperly positioned."[80] The contributory cause(s) of the spill (e.g., worker inexperience, fatigue) will likely never be known, but publicly available data makes clear that the CRC continues to expel hydrocarbons and other harmful substances into the sewer system despite their stated claim to be improving their management of refinery waste.[81]

And what of the working and living conditions inside the plant during the lockout? Several sources I spoke with on the condition of anonymity, but who have knowledge of refinery operations, said that they were not aware of any serious incidents on site and that they never felt unsafe in the plant. When the lockout began there was a strong feeling among the managers and replacement workers to "show the union guys we can run the plant" and a belief that the dispute would be over in a few days or, at longest, a couple of months. Units were "spotless and clean" at the beginning of the lockout. A source said the upsets discussed above did not lead to higher risk, in part because people lived on site and could respond quickly. However, in terms of training, there was concern that some replacement workers would not have been able to respond appropriately if there had been an upset due to their lack of experience at the CRC. A number of people were "learning as they went." Nor did any of these sources believe that the Unifor picket lines posed a material threat to the refinery. I asked if the barricades made the plant unsafe and a source said, "The union wasn't going to let the plant burn down because that's their place of work. That's their livelihood. People on the picket line are thinking ahead and would not want to stop a fire truck."[82] The source did not recall hearing anyone inside the plant say it was unsafe because of the barricades.

The conditions of work facing replacement workers and managers living in the camp is also worth some examination. Initially managers and replacement workers were paid for their days off. Living in the camp was an adjustment for some who had not worked shift work before. One source confirmed that as the lockout dragged on into April and May 2020, FCL wanted the CRC to spend less and people were no longer being paid to stay on site. Moreover, managers and replacement workers were expected to cross the picket line to get to and from work instead of flying over the line in the helicopter. According to sources, Le Dressay and other senior managers said they expected 594 members to start crossing the line to return to work by April 2020, but that never materialized. These sources confirmed that over time apathy in the camp grew significantly. By May and June 2020, people needed time off and fatigue was fairly widely felt: "The shine comes off after a while," said one source.

A final footnote on health and safety in the aftermath of the lockout. The refinery negotiated hard to remove the MO position — a role critical to safety — from the bargaining unit. It failed to do so in 2020 but went ahead anyway the next year. Local 594 challenged the decision and, in 2022, the Saskatchewan Labour Relations Board found the company had engaged in bad faith bargaining and ordered the MO position reinstated. The board's written decision cited a public statement by FCL, on October 4, 2021, noting that the decision to eliminate of the MO was "made once the Company had undertaken the appropriate steps to ensure that any workforce reduction *would not* impact the safety and reliability of the Refinery" [emphasis added].[83] In reality an internal CRC report assessing the health and safety risks of proceeding with the layoffs was not completed for another two months. The board was especially critical of testimony of the refinery's superintendent of process safety. The board concluded that the superintendent "was not able to name anything that would have been a safety 'show stopper' to the Employer proceeding with the elimination of the positions" and concluded that "[the risk assessment process] was not a legitimate process."[84] Unfortunately, it seems the pattern of misrepresenting health and safety to the public continued after the lockout.

THE LEGACY OF THE LOCKOUT

> It's kind of a dangerous workplace, like we all know that it's an oil refinery. I personally have dealt with explosions, and it's not fun to be [there], so you kind of try to justify it, you always justify it: "well I have a good pension and the benefits are good." And so that's kind of why you're there. (Interview with Local 594 member)

For most 594 members, the lockout was a fight to keep a pension they had planned their working lives around. As Daryl Watch's quote at the beginning of this chapter, the open letter from a refinery worker's wife, and this quoted 594 member illustrate, many Local 594 members working in the plant accept occupational health hazards and other risks in part because their pension guaranteed them a comfortable retirement that provides for their families. However, the open letter from a refinery worker's wife ends with regret: "Looking back now, the risks far outweigh the benefits. Health is everything."

The next part of the CRC's health and safety journey has yet to be written. I have followed up with several trusted sources about the workplace culture after the lockout. They all said, that after the dispute had ended, the working environment was not conducive to a high-quality safety culture. One person stated: "However bad it was up prior to the lockout it is worse now. For eight months you [FCL/CRC] told people that you don't value them" and now people care less about their jobs. "Overall, it's probably less safe now due to the conflict at the plant. The CRC is spending so much time on human resource issues and operations.[85] If you're in constant conflict, I don't know how you can be laser focused on operations." Another source stated: "The old Co-op (e.g., catching up on family, having lunch together) isn't there anymore. Many long-term relationships have been severed and people tend to keep to themselves now." And, there are ongoing concerns about the implications of cutting staff and running lean. In a refinery where management has seemed preoccupied with efficiency and public perception of safety, it's uncertain if this reality will ever change.[86]

Looking ahead to 2040, it seems likely that some refineries will close and many others will shrink in size due to declining demand for fossil fuels. It is an open question whether the owners of these multibillion-dollar plants will prioritize investments in preventative maintenance during the energy transition — and in doing so protect the health of their workers and surrounding communities — or chose to squeeze every dollar of profit out of future stranded assets and in doing so put people at risk. What is clear is that our notions of "just transition" must be defined by safer workplaces, a meaningful regulatory environment that holds industry accountable, and attention to the well-being of surrounding communities negatively affected by the day-to-day operations of fossil fuel enterprises.

Endnotes

1. Adriana Christianson, "Pensions and Power: Local Co-op Workers Speak from the Picket Line," CJME News, January 24, 2020, <cjme.com/2020/01/24/pensions-and-power-local-co-op-workers-speak-from-the-picket-line/>.
2. Raquel Fletcher, "'Safety is Top-notch': CEO Responds to Fine for 2011 Refinery Explosion," Global News Regina, May 15, 2015, <globalnews.ca/news/1996951/safety-is-top-notch-ceo-responds-to-fine-for-2011-refinery-explosion/>.
3. Perry Feltham, interview with author in 2015.
4. In the United States, refinery safety is regulated by the Chemical Safety and Hazard Investigation Board (CSB), whereas in Canada refineries are provincially regulated. Due to the regulatory patchwork in Canada, statistics on incidents and injuries in the refining sector are not publicly available.
5. Feltham interview, 2015.
6. United States Chemical Safety and Hazard Investigation Board (CSB), "BP America Refinery Explosion," n.d., <csb.gov/bp-america-refinery-explosion/>.
7. United States Chemical Safety and Hazard Investigation Board (CSB), "Tesoro Refinery Fatal Explosion and Fire," n.d., <csb.gov/tesoro-refinery-fatal-explosion-and-fire/>.
8. Terry Roberts, "Union Demands Inquiry after Come By Chance Refinery Worker Dies Following Explosion," CBC News, October 17, 2022, <cbc.ca/news/canada/newfoundland-labrador/refinery-fatal-inquiry-1.6618816>.
9. CAREX, "Carcinogen Profiles & Estimates," <carexcanada.ca/carcinogen-profiles/>.
10. A. Robert Schnatter, Min Chen, Elizabeth A. DeVilbiss, R. Jeffrey Lewis, and Elizabeth M. Gallagher, "Systematic Review and Meta-analysis of Selected Cancers in Petroleum Refinery Workers," *Journal of Occupational and Environmental Medicine* 60, no. 7 (2018): e329–e342.
11. A. Robert Schnatter, Nancy C. Wojcik, and Gail Jorgensen, "Mortality Update of a Cohort of Canadian Petroleum Workers," *Journal of Occupational and Environmental Medicine* 61, no. 3 (2019): 225.
12. Sean Tucker, excerpts from CRC occupational health committee meeting minutes, September 2019, Twitter/X, December 16, 2019, <twitter.com/SeanTucker16/status/1206604406516371458>.
13. CAREX, "Carcinogen Profiles & Estimates."
14. Freedom of information legislation prevents the Saskatchewan Workers Compensation Board from sharing company-level injury, illness, and fatality data with the public.
15. This information was obtained from the Saskatchewan WCB by a lawyer representing injured workers and shared with me.
16. Sean Tucker, "An Open Letter from 'A Refinery Worker's Wife,'" Twitter/X, December 11, 2019, <twitter.com/SeanTucker16/status/1204947272074551296>.
17. These research-related interviews are covered under University of Regina Research Ethics Board approval REB 2015-149. Readers interested in more details may wish to watch related public lectures. I have facilitated four public lectures about safety at the CRC. Recordings of these events can be found here: <youtube.com/watch?v=l-NokqHifaso> (2015); <youtube.com/watch?v=FwkMpevCQxE> (2017); <youtube.com/watch?v=vLYrVCHsByQ> (2018); <youtube.com/watch?v=nwvSD6l77AU> (2019).

18 This silence extends to the refinery's propensity to keep quiet its hydrocarbon spills and airborne emissions, as Chapter 5 demonstrates.
19 Geoff Leo, "Victims of Refinery Explosion Fear Co-op Won't Be Held Accountable," CBC Saskatchewan, December 4, 2014, <cbc.ca/news/canada/saskatchewan/victims-of-refinery-explosion-fear-co-op-won-t-be-held-accountable-1.2859673>.
20 Court documents accessed by author.
21 Court documents accessed by author, letter dated October 12, 2011.
22 paNOW, "Co-op Confirms Another Refinery Fire in Regina Monday," February 11, 2013, <panow.com/2013/02/11/co-op-confirms-another-refinery-fire-in-regina-monday-morning/>.
23 Canadian Press, "Blast from Regina Refinery Fire Felt Downtown; No Injuries Reported," CTV News, December 24, 2013, <regina.ctvnews.ca/blast-from-regina-refinery-fire-felt-downtown-no-injuries-reported-1.1607194>.
24 PANow, "Explosion at Co-op Upgrader in Regina," December 25, 2013, <panow.com/2013/12/25/explosion-at-co-op-upgrader-in-regina>.
25 Technical Safety Authority of Saskatchewan, Co-op Refinery Complex Incident—December 24, 2013, October 2014.
26 Sean Tucker, "Safety at the Co-op Refinery," December 2015, public presentation.
27 Update with link to decision from LRB: Sean Tucker, "SK Lab. Relations Board upholds decision by LRWS...," Twitter/X, February 23, 2020, <twitter.com/SeanTucker16/status/1231719810712494080>.
28 Saskatchewan Labour Relations Board, "Unifor Canada, Local 594 and Consumers' Co-operative Refineries Ltd." (LRB file no. 173-20), October 17, 2022, 18, para. 68, <sasklabourrelationsboard.com/decisions/reasons-for-decision/2022>.
29 In 1935, the plant was established on the open prairie, at the time relatively far from the City of Regina. Over time both the refinery and city's footprint grew with light industrial development and, to the west, a residential community known as Uplands, adjacent to the refinery site.
30 "Flip-flop on Gas Leak," *Edmonton Journal*, March 10, 1989.
31 Vanessa Brown, "Housing Project Criticized; Said Too Close to Refinery," *Regina Leader-Post*, March 18, 2013.
32 Emma Graney, Cause of Blast Still Unknown; Another Refinery Explosion; Officials Continue Probe, *Regina Leader-Post*, December 26, 2013.
33 Federated Co-op Ltd., *2013 Annual Report*.
34 CBC News Saskatchewan, "Regina Launches Mass Emergency Notification System, notifynow," CBC News Saskatchewan, May 4, 2016, <cbc.ca/news/canada/saskatchewan/city-of-regina-launches-notifynow-system-for-emergencies-1.3565409>.
35 Canadian Association of Petroleum Producers, 2014.
36 FCL, *2021 Annual Report*, 9, <fcl.crs/wcm/connect/www.fcl.crs-14309/e07130cc-e413-4e1f-a71a-418d31e28b2e/2021+Annual+Report+Web.pdf?MOD=AJPERES&CVID=nYIyDQa>.
37 Natasha Lypny, "Minor Leak Causes Evacuation," *Regina Leader-Post*, September 15, 2015.
38 Geoff Leo, "Co-op Refinery Fights in Court to Keep Major Hazards Report Secret," CBC News Saskatchewan, September 14, 2015, <cbc.ca/news/canada/saskatchewan/co-op-refinery-fights-in-court-to-keep-major-hazards-report-secret-1.3225114>.
39 Barb Pacholik, "Portion of Co-op Refinery's Major Hazards Risk Assessment Report Released," *Regina Leader-Post*, November 21, 2016, <leaderpost.com/news/

local-news/portion-of-co-op-refinerys-major-hazards-risk-assessment-report-released>. The CRC-funded report concluded: "The study found that although the effects from fire, explosion and toxic gas release can leave the CRC refinery site, the probability to do so is low enough for these large events that the risk is acceptable according to accepted guidelines.… It is important to realize that the probabilities calculated are based on fatally injuring third party individuals outside of the CRC site. It does not calculate the probability of persons outside of the site being able to detect a release or even become very ill due to a release from the CRC, but not be fatally injured"; Marsh Risk Consulting, *Major Hazards Risk Assessment Report, 2012, Federated Co-operatives Limited Co-op Refinery Complex*, 51.
40 Sean Tucker, "Public Relations ≠Public safety,'" Twitter/X, April 4, 2020, <twitter.com/SeanTucker16/status/1246522728066060289>. In a statement to me, the CRC noted: "the press release you show in your slides indicating Brad DeLorey's title. Mr. DeLorey has never held the title of Director of Public Safety. His correct title is Director of Communications and Public Affairs."
41 CRC, correspondence with the author, December 8, 2019.
42 Sean Tucker, "Public Safety Implications of a Potential Lockout or Strike at the Co-op Refinery," November 21, 2019, <youtube.com/watch?v=nwvSD6l77AU>.
43 Vic Huard, interview on John Gormley Show, March 2017.
44 Arthur White-Crummey, "Refinery Risk: Prof, Union and Managers Debate Impact of Potential Job Action," *Regina Leader-Post*, November 20, 2019, <leaderpost.com/news/local-news/refinery-risk-prof-union-and-managers-debate-impact-of-potential-job-action>.
45 White-Crummey, "Refinery Risk."
46 CRC, CRC invites public to contact them with safety concerns, Twitter/X, November 20, 2019, <twitter.com/CoopRefinery/status/1197182747975938048>.
47 CRC, CRC lockout notice, Twitter/X, December 3, 2019, <twitter.com/CoopRefinery/status/1202007117810601989>.
48 FCL, "Lockout Ensures Safe Operation of the Co-op Refinery Complex," December 5, 2019, <fcl.crs/news-reports/news/article/lockout-ensures-safe-operation-of-coop-refinery-complex>.
49 Unifor 594, Letter to CRC about emergency response, Twitter/X, December 3, 2019, <twitter.com/SeanTucker16/status/1220739995415134209>.
50 CRC, public notice of lockout, Twitter/X, December 5, 2019, <twitter.com/CoopRefinery/status/1202731888986734593>.
51 CRC, Email response from CRC Public Affairs to occupational health and safety questions, Twitter/X, December 7, 2019, <twitter.com/SeanTucker16/status/1204947272074551296>.
52 FCL, "Steps Taken to Ensure Staff Safety and Fuel Supply," December 8, 2019, <fcl.crs/news-reports/news/article/steps-to-ensure-staff-safety-secure-fuel-supply>.
53 Marc Smith, "OHS Contractor Alleges Harassment, Assault, from Unifor 594 Members," CTV Regina, December 18, 2019, <regina.ctvnews.ca/ohs-contractor-alleges-harassment-assault-from-unifor-594-members-1.4735925>.
54 Larry posted a video. On January 9, 2020, the CRC responded to a video released by Unifor entitled "Meet the Scabs" which identified several replacement workers by name. The company slammed the union, stating: "We will ensure that we protect the safety and well-being of those individuals featured in the video."
55 In May 2020, RPS charged four union members for assault following a physical

altercation on the picket line involving one security guard being pushed over. RPS reported this individual had "minor abrasions." Alec Salloum, "Police Charge Locked Out Workers with Assault Traffic Violations," *Regina Leader-Post*, May 5, 2020, <leaderpost.com/news/local-news/police-charge-locked-out-workers-with-assault-traffic-violations/>.

56 Later in the dispute RPS investigated paint balling of a few managers' houses. Sarah Ashley-Hewitson, "Police Investigating Several Cases of Mischief at Homes of FCL Managers," CKRM News, February 5, 2020, <620ckrm.com/2020/02/05/police-investigating-several-cases-of-mischief/>. In an alleged unfair labour practice, Unifor said "external agents" hired by CRC were following 594 members, driving to their houses and recording. See also Sean Tucker, excerpts from Unifor 594 allegation of unfair labour practices, Twitter/X, March 30, 2020, <twitter.com/SeanTucker16/status/1244639453169061890>.

57 Lisa Schick, "Unifor, Co-op Refinery Await Decision after Arguments on Picketing Injunction," CJME News, December 23, 2019, <cjme.com/2019/12/23/unifor-co-op-refinery-await-decision-after-arguments-on-picketing-injunction/>.

58 Jonathan Guignard, Colton Praill, "Unifor Accused of Breaking Court Order, Vandalizing Trucks at Regina's Co-op Refinery," Global News Regina, January 8, 2020, <globalnews.ca/news/6355578/vandalism-regina-refinery-strike/>.

59 Marc Smith, "Trucking Company Accuses Unifor of Vandalizing Fuel Tankers," CTV News Regina, January 2, 2020, <regina.ctvnews.ca/trucking-company-accuses-unifor-of-vandalizing-fuel-tankers-1.4750753>.

60 FCL, "Unifor Blockade is Threat to Public Safety," January 10, 2020, <fcl.crs/news-reports/news/article/unifor-blockade-threat-to-public-safety>

61 FCL, "Unifor Blockade is Threat to Public Safety."

62 David Baxter, "14 Co-op Refinery Picketers Arrested as City Held Hostage: Regina Police Chief," Global News Regina, January 21, 2020, <globalnews.ca/news/6441876/14-co-op-picketers-charged-with-mischief-unifor-escalates-boycott/>.

63 Sean Tucker, excerpt from RPS Chief, Evan Bray's public statement, January 24, 2020, Twitter/X, January 26, 2020, <twitter.com/SeanTucker16/status/1221580919607156736>.

64 Sean Tucker, excerpt from Hansard regarding OHS inspections at the CRC, Twitter/X, June 16, 2020, <twitter.com/SeanTucker16/status/1272927809095098368>.

65 Global Regina, "A U of R professor is raising questions around the safety oversight at the Co-op Refinery," Twitter/X, February 23, 2020, <twitter.com/GlobalRegina/status/1231664087618215943>.

66 Sean Tucker, excerpts from correspondence between the City of Regina and FCL February 28, 2017, Twitter/X, February 25, 2020, <twitter.com/SeanTucker16/status/1232493887001751554>.

67 Sean Tucker, excerpts from correspondence between the City of Regina and FCL, August 22, 2019, Twitter/X, February 25, 2020, <twitter.com/SeanTucker16/status/1232499667247587328>.

68 Sean Tucker, excerpts from correspondence between the City of Regina and FCL, August 22, 2019, Twitter/X, February 25, 2020, <twitter.com/SeanTucker16/status/1232499667247587328>.

69 Jennifer Ackerman, "Councillor and Professor Concerned about Site of Refinery Worker Camp," *Regina Leader-Post*, February 26, 2020, <leaderpost.com/news/

local-news/councillor-and-professor-concerned-about-site-of-refinery-worker-camp>. Later, in March and April 2020, concerns were raised about the potential for COVID-19 spread in the camp. City council passed a motion asking the Saskatchewan Health Authority to conduct a review of the CRC's protocols. "Regina city council to ask SHA for health assessment of refinery work camp," *Regina Leader-Post*, March 22, 2020, <leaderpost.com/news/local-news/regina-city-council-to-ask-sha-for-health-assessment-of-refinery-work-camp>.

70 Sean Tucker, excerpts from letter to the Regina Police Service, February 18, 2020, Twitter/X, May 17, 2020, <twitter.com/SeanTucker16/status/1262088337885519872>.

71 Regina Police Service, "Regina Police Service investigation into anonymous letter and potential threat at the Co-op Refinery Complex," Twitter/X, May 19, 2020, <twitter.com/reginapolice/status/1262868669052248064>; Alec Salloum, "Regina Police Say Bomb Threat against Refinery Workers Not Credible," *Regina Leader-Post*, May 19, 2020, <leaderpost.com/news/local-news/regina-police-say-bomb-threat-against-refinery-workers-not-credible/wcm/78f3686b-196a-4569-9d55-8861dd4511d2/>.

72 Global Regina, "A U of R professor is raising questions around the safety oversight at the Co-op Refinery,'" Twitter/X, February 23, 2020, <twitter.com/GlobalRegina/status/1231664087618215943>.

73 CRC, Larger than normal flares at the Refinery, Twitter/X, January 21, 2020, <twitter.com/CoopRefinery/status/1219627205329711105>.

74 Sean Tucker, link to video of emissions from Section 5's fluid catalytic cracking unit,'" Twitter/X, February 2, 2020, <twitter.com/SeanTucker16/status/1224141455049887746>.

75 FCL, "The CRC Disappointed Unifor 594 Membership Votes to Reject Best and Final Offer," April 29, 2020, <fcl.crs/news-reports/news/article/the-crc-disappointed-unifor-594-votes-to-reject-offer>.

76 Marc Smith, "City of Regina Investigating Oil Spill from Co-op Refinery," CTV News Regina, June 2, 2020, <regina.ctvnews.ca/city-of-regina-investigating-oil-spill-from-co-op-refinery-1.4965553>.

77 Alec Salloum, "Questions Linger about Notification, Impact of Refinery's Oil Spill," *Regina Leader-Post*, June 1, 2020, <leaderpost.com/news/local-news/questions-linger-about-notification-impact-of-refinerys-oil-spill>.

78 Alec Salloum, "Unknown Quantity of Oil Spilled from Refinery into City Sewers," *Regina Leader-Post*, May 29, 2020, <leaderpost.com/news/local-news/unknown-quantity-of-oil-spilled-from-refinery-into-city-sewers>.

79 Alec Salloum, "City of Regina Sues Co-op Refinery for $4.5M from Spill," *Regina Leader-Post*, August 25, 2022, <leaderpost.com/news/crime/city-of-regina-sues-co-op-refinery-for-4-5m-from-spill>.

80 Salloum, "City of Regina sues Co-op refinery."

81 Alexander Quon, "Regina Attempts to Make its Reporting on Toxic Spills, Leaks More Transparent," CBC News, May 26 2022, <cbc.ca/news/canada/saskatchewan/regina-toxic-spills-data-1.6466680>.

82 Interview with author.

83 FCL. "The Co-op Refinery Complex to Proceed with Involuntary Separations," October 4, 2021, <fcl.crs/news-reports/news/article/The-Co-op-Refinery-Complex-to-Proceed-with-Involuntary-Separations>.

84 SLRB, para. 36 and 94.
85 In June 2023, Unifor Local 594's chief shop steward noted: "Since I took over the Chief Shop Steward role in 2014, the Union has filed 337 grievances and dealt with over 35 different labour relations professionals who have come and gone from the refinery. A significant reason for the insane number of grievances in that time span is due to their high turnover rate and every new face trying to read and interpret our storied collective agreement in their own way." <myemail.constantcontact.com/April-2023-Conciliator.html?soid=1132774298893&aid=DDDsifw2oWo>.
86 At the time of writing, in July 2023, there are signs of improving labour relations between Local 594 and the CRC. In the Union's public bulletin their chief shop steward noted the establishment of a joint "Grievance Backlog Project" and progress towards resolving 125 active grievances: <myemail.constantcontact.com/April-2023-Conciliator.html?soid=1132774298893&aid=DDDsifw2oWo>.

7

WHERE IS THE "LABOUR BEAT REPORTER"?

The Regina Refinery Lockout and the Many Crises of Journalism

Doug Nesbitt and Emily Leedham

ON JANUARY 20, 2020, NEWS outlets covered the Regina Police Service (RPS) arrests of Unifor president Jerry Dias and six other Unifor members, who were plucked from the picket line. While it is uncommon these days for Canada's traditional newsmedia to cover local labour disputes, reporters, photographers, and video crews all captured Dias being hauled into a police van. This event led other national and international news organizations to descend on Regina to subsequently witness the who's who of Canadian labour leaders rally to support locked-out members of Unifor Local 594.

January 20, however, was just one day in the six-month lockout. Following the arrests, most of the newsmedia lost interest in the dispute as it overlapped with the beginning of the COVID-19 pandemic. Nevertheless, local and regional newspapers and TV and radio stations played an important role in shaping public opinion throughout the lockout. Both the union and management recognized that advancing their message through the media was critical for their respective strategies — especially when it came to using popular opinion to gain leverage.[1]

Picketers and Local 594 supporters, however, expressed frustration with how their story was portrayed and lamented that the company's message was helping to shape the dominant narrative about the lockout. On a number of occasions, local media headlines and stories falsely referred to the dispute as a "strike," for example.[2]

In looking at how the traditional newsmedia covered the lockout, there is an obvious need for independent journalism in developing a more comprehensive approach to the "labour beat." We wanted to track the decline over time of labour beat reporting in newsmedia in Canada, especially focusing on Saskatchewan. So, we studied coverage of the lockout across 435 articles at five major newsmedia outlets in Saskatchewan from a political and economic perspective. It became clear that both right- and left-wing sources have been establishing their labour-focused reporting by filling in the space vacated by the mainstream media.

We argue that traditional newsmedia has been so devastated by decades of newsroom cuts that it is now incapable of producing the kinds of reporting required for ordinary news consumers to understand the nuances of labour disputes and the issues that bring the respective parties to an impasse. In addition, we contend that newsmedia's commitment to "objective" journalism is flawed and easily manipulated by public relations campaigns advanced by employers with professional communication teams. The entrenchment of what Shane Gunster calls "extractive populism" in western Canada means that the media is heavily influenced by the interests of the oil and gas industry on matters of ecological justice and labour relations. With this in mind, we suggest that independent newsmedia and organized labour can play an important role in re-establishing labour beat reporting, without which economic shifts away from fossil fuels will lack a labour lens.

It is important to start by acknowledging our relationship to the lockout, newsmedia, and why we are well situated to comment at length on the subject. During the dispute, we both worked for *Rankandfile.ca*, an independent, not-for-profit labour research and news project founded in 2012. This is the kind of embedded journalism that labour activists and writers, such as Steve Early, have long advanced as a means of shedding light on the complex internal realities that define unions and union movements.[3] Co-founded by Doug Nesbitt and Andrew Stevens in 2011, *Rankandfile.ca* was inspired by *Labor Notes*, a labour publication established in 1979 to promote democratic union reform and workplace militancy in opposition to conservative "business unionism" in the United States.[4] Emily Leedham was, at the time of the lockout, hosting and producing the weekly program *Rank and File Radio — Prairies Edition* while also publishing investigative articles. Leedham now works at *PressProgress*, which is an independent investigative newsroom established in 2013 by the Broadbent Institute, a think tank founded by former New Democratic Party leader Ed Broadbent. Nesbitt continues to contribute to *Rankandfile.ca* as a Kingston-based labour activist and researcher.

We had followed labour relations at the Co-op Refinery Complex for several years and were anticipating a work stoppage prior to the breakdown of negotiations in 2019. Informed by various parties in Regina, we tracked the outcome of the 2016 round of bargaining between the CRC and Unifor Local 594, during which a "scab camp" on the refinery grounds was originally conceived. In December 2015, prior to the 2016 bargaining, *Rankandfile.ca* published a video presentation by Dr. Sean Tucker of the University of Regina discussing the explosions and fires that had plagued the refinery between 2011 and 2013. In 2019, Nesbitt and others, on behalf of Unifor Local 594, comprehensively reviewed the CRC and its parent company, Federated Co-operatives Limited (FCL) to better understand developments within the only co-operatively owned oil refinery in the world.[5] Their review suggested that FCL's departure from co-operative values was reflected in its vilification of Local 594 (and Co-op workers) during the 2016–2017 negotiations.[6]

When retail strikes broke out at Co-ops federated with FCL in 2018 in Moose Jaw and Saskatoon, *Rankandfile.ca* had led the related coverage. During the Saskatoon Co-op strike against the employer's two-tier contract proposal, Leedham's reporting exposed a *Saskatoon StarPhoenix* story, which profiled one of the replacement workers who crossed the picket line during the strike, for failing to report that the scab was the son of FCL board member Shannan Corey.[7] Meanwhile, Nesbitt was researching the history of Unifor Local 594 and oil worker unionism more generally leading up to the dispute.[8] When bargaining between the CRC and Local 594 reached an impasse and headed toward a lockout, the media team at *Rankandfile.ca* was ready to provide in-depth coverage and commentary resting upon a foundation of historical, political, and economic knowledge of the industry, union, and employer.

The traditional newsmedia, however, was largely incapable of arming readers with the broader knowledge necessary to understand the dispute as well as the issues that brought both parties to a standstill at the bargaining table. This was particularly true at the beginning of the lockout, when union and company press releases shaped the media's messaging about the conflict. For example, although the CRC's releases consistently referenced the coming "low-carbon economy," traditional media missed the opportunity to investigate the links between energy transition and the CRC's bargaining strategy. Despite being a two-person operation working out of Winnipeg, Manitoba, and Kingston, Ontario, *Rankandfile.ca* was able to cover the lockout. Despite its limited resources and no full-time staff, we believe *Rankandfile.ca* provided essential contextual and historical reporting that was absent in mainstream accounts of the lockout.[9] We argue that independent media should pursue dedicated labour coverage and that independent coverage such as ours could help unions understand the wider new media landscape and how to fight back against corporations with deep pockets, sophisticated public relations teams, and the capacity to take advantage of an often-hapless mainstream newsmedia. On that note, we begin the next section with an obituary for the labour beat reporter.

BEHIND THE DEATH OF THE LABOUR BEAT

The lockout exposed the absence of any dedicated labour reporters in Saskatchewan — or, for that matter, in the three-thousand-kilometre distance between Vancouver Island and Thunder Bay where CRC petroleum products are sold at Co-op and other service stations. As newsroom cuts accelerated throughout the 1990s, institutional memory was lost with the elimination of beat reporting, and not just in labour, but in coverage of city halls, health care, the courts, education, and rural and regional issues. At best, smaller papers, like Regina's *Leader-Post*, are left with a single columnist and newer journalists with little experience. This can result in surface commentary on a range of political issues, as well as a lack of deeper knowledge and expertise on many subjects. Young journalists who may be interested in labour reporting lack the time and resources to develop a specific knowledge base and skill set or to build relationships with workers, organizers, labour leaders, and experts. This reality deserves attention.

As late *New York Times* labour reporter William Serrin put it, the problems confronting labour journalism "go to the heart" of what is wrong with "all American journalism." Serrin described himself as "hopelessly overcommitted" as a labour reporter. "Other departments had far greater resources. The business section had forty or fifty reporters. Labor had me, plus a guy in Washington."[10] The lack of resources, disrespect for the beat, and neglect by management described by Serrin's experiences in the 1980s came to define journalism more widely.

In the early 1990s, Ontario alone had half a dozen labour reporters.[11] Today, only Canada's two largest-circulation English-language dailies have dedicated labour reporters. For nearly a decade, Sara Mojtehedzadeh at the *Toronto Star* has focused primarily on low-wage workplaces and employment standards in the Toronto region. In January 2022, Vanmala Subramaniam became the *Globe & Mail*'s "Future of Work" reporter in the Report on Business.

The labour beat in Canada became an early casualty of three decades of newsroom cuts and greater ownership involvement in editorial direction. This process started in earnest during the 1990s as a deep recession coincided with large investments in new high-quality colour printers. Saddled by debt and declining revenues, Southam and other large newspaper owners enacted cost-cutting measures, resulting in a frenzy of asset sales. According to veteran reporter John Miller, this crisis "drove many of them [newspaper owners] into the clutches of large corporate owners, who were beholden as they never were before to lenders and shareholders."[12]

The most significant of these large corporate owners was Conrad Black's international newspaper company, Hollinger.[13] By 1996, Hollinger had secured a controlling stake in the Southam newspaper chain and, by the end of the decade, came to own 61 of Canada's 101 daily newspapers and control more than 50 percent of Canada's daily newspaper circulation,[14] including the *Regina Leader-Post* and Saskatoon's *StarPhoenix*. Conrad Black's openly conservative and anti-union politics featured prominently in his disdain for journalists and his decimation of newsrooms. The imposition of concessions by Hollinger sparked significant labour disputes, such as the 1999–2000 *Calgary Herald* strike.[15] Between 1993 and 1999, more than 2,100 of 7,800 Southam newspaper staff were axed.[16] Media consolidation and concentration is nothing new. In the first half of the twentieth century, local newspaper monopolies in many major cities were created through the merger of competing outfits. Today's *Regina Leader-Post* was the outcome of two papers being merged in 1930. Two years earlier, Saskatoon's *Daily Star* and *Daily Phoenix* were combined to form today's *StarPhoenix*. For more than half a century, Regina and Saskatoon have been one-newspaper cities.

Conditions for investigative reporting worsened through the 1990s, as corporate interests like Conrad Black's Hollinger expanded their influence. Under Hollinger, newsrooms were cut, workloads increased, and specialized beats, notably labour, were scrapped. But the assault on journalism was not merely a product of Hollinger's corporate debts; it also had a political dimension. Black was an outspoken critic of professional journalists. He believed they were too powerful and abused the moniker of "freedom of the press." They were, in his words, "the rogue elephants of western society."[17] Black consciously followed the union-busting, cost-cutting path of Rupert Murdoch, whose breaking of the British printers' union in the mid-1980s ushered in a newsmedia revolution that was carried on by Black and his successors in Canada. "Once the unions were broken," writes veteran British investigative journalist Nick Davies, "the new corporate owners simply applied the logic of commerce — cut costs and increase revenues," resulting in a "chain reaction of internal changes which have had a devastating effect on truth-telling journalism."[18] The result has been the rise of "churnalism," according to Davies, caused by new corporate owners who have "cut editorial staffing while increasing editorial output; slashed the old supply lines which used to feed up raw information from the ground; and, with the advent of news websites, added the new imperative of speed."[19]

Under these conditions of reduced staff, fewer beats, more editorializing, and a general speed-up, journalists have less time to develop contacts and leads, and they have become more reliant on outside information, notably wire agencies and public relations. "In these circumstances, the news factory will produce an effective and reliable product for its readers and viewers and listeners only if those outside suppliers are delivering an effective and reliable account of the world."[20] Davies concludes with the essential question, "Are they?"

Unable to pay off the debt it inherited from the Southam chain, Black's newspaper, magazine, and internet empire faltered and was largely sold to Canwest Global in 2000 for $3.5 billion. Under the direction of Canwest's politically conservative CEO Izzy Asper, the editorial independence of local newspapers was further constrained and newsrooms suffered more rounds of cuts. Once more, the debt of the newspaper monopoly proved too large, and under bankruptcy protection in 2009, Canwest sold its newspapers and broadcasting assets to Postmedia for $1.1 billion.[21] Postmedia subsequently spun off its broadcasting arm to Shaw Communications (now Corus Entertainment) and consolidated and expanded its newspaper holdings by buying up Sun Media, the country's second-largest newspaper chain, in 2014. Since this expansion, Postmedia has largely contracted, closing down newspapers, merging ostensibly competing newsrooms in Edmonton and Ottawa, and conducting numerous rounds of layoffs.[22] Since at least the time of the Sun Media merger, Postmedia had been majority owned by American hedge fund GoldenTree Asset Management. In 2016, Chatham Asset Management, which specializes in ownership of newsmedia, bought GoldenTree's controlling stake and now reportedly commands two-thirds of Postmedia's shares.[23]

This extreme concentration of newspaper ownership has failed to reduce Postmedia's debt. One study reports that newspaper revenues in Canada between 2010 to 2020 have declined about 60 percent.[24] This parallels McChesney's findings from the United States, which suffered an unprecedented wave of newspaper closures and newsroom job losses during and immediately following the Great Recession of 2007–2009, and these have continued steadily since.[25] Long-time Canadian journalist Ian Gill reported in 2016 that upwards of ten thousand journalism jobs in Canada had disappeared "in less than a decade."[26] Canada's public broadcaster has not been immune to these changes, either. According to Gill, the CBC "has long been thought of as a safe harbour from the tendency of corporate media to bow to the biases of advertisers, and to locate only where news businesses can turn a profit. However, the publicly funded model is under severe stress as resources dwindle."[27] Despite the absence of private sector commercial pressures, CBC's independence was first subjected to cutbacks under Pierre Trudeau on the grounds that its news coverage was too favourable to separatism. According to veteran journalist Alain Saulnier, five decades of politically motivated cutbacks have transformed CBC's newsrooms and news gathering processes in ways similar to private sector newsrooms.[28]

As the traditional newsroom continues to be squeezed through corporate directives and loss of advertising revenue, low-cost online publishing platforms have given rise to a new generation of newsmedia outlets across the political spectrum. *Rankandfile.ca*, *PressProgress*, *Halifax Examiner*, *Canadaland*, *Rebel News*, *Post Millennial*, *The Narwhal*, *The Tyee*, *The Breach*, and many more have come to fill gaps left behind in the editorial shifts in major newsrooms, including the loss of particular beats such as labour. This experimentation has extended into newsprint, with the 2022 launch of *The Grind*, a Toronto-based bimonthly. Freelance journalists are also beginning to publish directly online using new paid subscription platforms such as Substack and Patreon. A growing number of unemployed and freelance reporters have also given birth to many new independent newsmedia outlets, but these outlets have yet to rival the otherwise reduced output of traditional newsmedia. These outlets played an important role during the Co-op Refinery lockout, but they did so alongside the independent news platforms documenting issues that were missed by the big corporate newsrooms and government-funded broadcasters. As we will detail here, it became clear that the traditional newsmedia covering the lockout was heavily influenced in the opening weeks of the dispute by the public relations strategy of CRC.

FCL'S MEDIA STRATEGY DURING THE 2019–2020 LOCKOUT

FCL clearly appealed to "extractive populism" — a popular belief perpetuated by industry and right-wing politicians that expansion of the oil and gas sector is needed for economic growth — in their media messaging during the lockout. The Saskatoon-based business framed their own workers as a threat to the industry, justifying multiple "defensive" measures to protect the refinery: flying scabs over the picket line, a restrictive picketing injunction, and later, direct intervention from police and anti-union protestors. Little attention was paid to FCL's interventions into other co-op disputes, like the ones that unfolded in Saskatoon and Moose Jaw in 2018, which resulted in unfair labour practice charges being levelled against the employer.[29]

Just days after the CRC lockout began, FCL began using what *Rankandfile.ca* has called the "union thug" narrative, whereby Unifor 594 workers and their picket line were cast as engaging in what the parent company claimed to be "inappropriate and dangerous behaviour."[30] FCL also invoked the concept of "western alienation" by arguing that Unifor's "Toronto-based leadership" did not hold "Western Canadian values" and were a "threat" to "Western Canadians' fuel supply." Combined with the "union thug" narrative, FCL sought to mobilize people against the union to "defend" the Co-op. Whether or not this line of messaging succeeded requires further investigation. *The Rebel*, a far-right media outlet friendly with the "United We Roll" convoy, set up the website UnionThugs.ca to host its coverage of Unifor's secondary picket lines in Alberta, where a "reporter" boasted about crossing the picket line.[31] Then, a United We Roll organizer expressed intent to dismantle secondary picket line fences while another member threatened to run over picketers in a public Facebook group hosted by UWR.[32]

Even after these threats went public, FCL CEO Scott Banda organized a press conference in Carseland, Alberta, at the same time United We Roll planned their protest. Banda acknowledged UWR at the event, hinting at that organization's alignment with FCL values and interests. Banda had successfully harnessed extractive populist energy by framing unionized oil workers as a threat to his western Canadian oil company — just like the carbon tax. As a *Regina Leader-Post* article on December 9, 2019, reads:

> But the refinery sees these actions as "Unifor's Toronto-based leadership" making it clear "that they do not share our respectful Western Canadian values, and it's time they took their business elsewhere.... We take our responsibility for the safety of our community and to Western Canadians' fuel supply seriously. Any threat to the well-being of our people, and to the operational integrity of the refinery, will not be tolerated," it [the CRC] stated.[33]

A MEDIA ANALYSIS OF THE LOCKOUT

To understand the mainstream media's coverage of the lockout, we analyzed published content from five major newsmedia outlets in Saskatchewan. This included online print articles from Global Regina, CTV Regina, and CBC Saskatchewan, and the two major daily newspapers in the province, the *Regina Leader-Post* and the *Saskatoon StarPhoenix*. Global, CTV, and CBC have distinct ownership, while the *Leader-Post* and *StarPhoenix* are both owned by PostMedia. Both of the latter routinely republish each other's articles.

We scrutinized reporting over a two-year period, from January 1, 2019, to December 31, 2020, to ensure pre- and post-lockout coverage. We focused on these five outlets because of their online access and because of the difficulties and resources required to analyze television and radio news. We searched for and selected any article mentioning "Co-operative Refinery Complex." In all, we examined 435 unique articles and categorized them according to 38 themes. The *Leader-Post* published 143 articles, CTV 38, CBC 74, and Global 73. The *StarPhoenix* published 107 articles, of which 94 were republished from the *Leader-Post*. The vast majority of the articles (404) were published during the lockout, from December 2019 through to the end of June 2020.

Several trends emerged from our analysis. First, the concept of "safety" emerged as a dominant theme in the dispute and was mentioned a total of 220 times in the 435 articles. Many of the safety concerns focused on interactions between locked-out workers and scabs in and around the refinery complex. Unifor members were framed as aggressors in 139 articles. We also learned from this analysis that the media's coverage was balanced in terms of who is quoted in articles. There is no evidence of Unifor or FCL/CRC being disproportionately excluded or included from coverage. Most of FCL/CRC's quotes come from CRC spokesperson Brad DeLorey (95), press statements, or unattributed statements (89). On the union side, former Unifor Local 594 president Kevin Bittman is quoted most (143), followed by senior Unifor National official Scott Doherty (110) and Unifor National president Jerry Dias (80).

Third, both sides of the dispute employed a disciplined media strategy. Unifor Local 594 messaging was streamed through the local executive and national leadership (with the exception of social media commentary), and as a result, "rank-and-file" 594 members only appear thirty-eight times throughout the study period. This union discipline is about the control of messaging and publicized information, not unlike restrictions that employers would place on managers and other out-of-scope workers. It also serves to protect union members from intimidation during the lockout and the potential for targeted retaliation afterwards.

FCL/CRC also employed a disciplined media strategy in terms of restricting corporate voices cited in the media to high-ranking executives. CRC executive Brad DeLorey is quoted ninety-five times and Gil Le Dressay, forty-four times. FCL CEO Scott Banda is referenced thirty-five times in the media, but only once before the January 20 arrests of Local 594 members on the picket line around the refinery complex.

These figures conform with the traditional principle of journalistic "objectivity" in which both sides of an issue are cited through official sources. However, this idea of "balanced" journalism failed to provide readers with insight into the dispute beyond official statements. As a result, media consumers were dependent on selected quotes and statements from the employer and union representatives to understand otherwise complex issues related to pension plans, the company's financial well-being, and the complex dynamics that define the collective bargaining process. In fact, this journalistic framework of "balance" was wielded by FCL/CRC to their advantage in the opening weeks of the lockout. As the dispute evolved, some in the mainstream newsmedia developed a more skeptical approach to coverage of FCL/CRC claims and conducted an independent review of facts about pensions and items on the bargaining table, but within certain limits.[34]

In seeking to understand the evolution of the mainstream media's coverage, we identified three distinct periods of reporting. The first period began with the lockout in early December 2019 and ended on January 20, 2020, with the arrests of fourteen Unifor members, including national president Jerry Dias, by the Regina Police Service (RPS). The events of January 20, 2020, catapulted the lockout into a national and international news story, which marked the second period of intensive coverage; that wanes in early March with the declaration of the COVID pandemic. A third period of sparse coverage continued through to mid-May, when coverage refocused on news of a bomb threat against picketers and a refinery oil spill into Regina's sewers.

PERIOD ONE: DECEMBER 2019 TO JANUARY 20, 2020

The first coverage period saw quickly escalating tensions in December of 2019 around allegations of intimidation, harassment, violence, and vandalism by Unifor picketers against CRC scabs, managers, and truckers. Much of the media coverage of these incidents assumed a connection with the lockout and inferred that picketing workers (or their allies) might be involved. None of these claims were substantiated in the courts, though, and the union repeatedly denied the allegations. Nevertheless, these incidents helped to build political momentum in support of the company's objective of securing an injunction against the pickets, as Chapters 1 and 4 of this collection demonstrate.

In the first few days of the lockout, an occupational health and safety consultant, Jared Savage, was hired by the CRC. Savage claimed he was harassed and assaulted by Unifor members when they grabbed from him a list with names and contact information of replacement workers. CTV Regina ran a story with the headline: "OHS contractor alleges harassment, assault, from Unifor 594 members." It quoted Savage as saying, "It's almost like he checked me into his shoulder, I smashed into the guy, we smashed heads and with an overhand strike...."[35] However, a video of the alleged incident later emerged showing no contact.[36] CTV and other media did not conduct a follow-up story on the incident.

Suggestions of criminal activity committed by picketers, such as the dropping of caltrops on roadways adjacent to the refinery, are raised in fifty-three of the ninety-three news articles spanning December 4, 2019, to January 21, 2020. None of the allegations made against the union were ever substantiated in our period of study — a fact that is never explicitly noted in any newsmedia reports we read. Nor did the media confirm that incidents of vandalism, for instance, had any reasonable connection to the lockout or CRC employees.

These and others claims, however spurious, were considered newsworthy and linked to the dispute. The vast majority of these published allegations came from CRC spokespeople and statements or from their allies in the trucking industry. In most cases, specific allegations feature in the headlines of the articles, as part of a common "clickbait" strategy used to solicit online readers.[37] However, this type of coverage was not limited to the first period. An example surfaces again in a February 5, 2020, article in the *Regina Leader-Post* that reported the paintballing of seven homes belonging to CRC managers. The story runs the claims made by CRC spokesperson Brad DeLorey that the homes were targeted, with no mention of who targeted them or if these statements were true. The article confirms a police investigation and states that the police believe the incidents are connected to the labour dispute. To date, no charges have been laid in connection with this incident. The two articles on the matter feature two photos of paintballed homes taken by a *Leader-Post* photographer. One article concludes with Unifor's Scott Doherty denying the allegations and making clear that the union "doesn't condone the acts."[38] There is no follow-up report or analysis of whether the acts resulted in charges being laid.

These incidents and others in the first phase of the dispute raise important questions about how reporters and news editors cover such allegations, especially given that initial claims from the CRC and Saskatchewan Trucking Association laid the foundation for Judge McMurtry's injunction limiting Unifor 594 picket activity.[39] The steady stream of allegations against the union and its membership without evidence ought to have strained the credulity of reporters, news editors, and any seasoned labour beat reporter. Manufacturing allegations to elicit police-enforced injunctions against picketers is a common-enough practice in labour disputes. Even the courts cast doubt on claims made by the employer about the actual hardship caused by the blockade of Gate 7. Such a discussion, however, was not broached by the media.

PERIOD TWO: JANUARY 21 TO MARCH 2020

After the arrest of fourteen Unifor picketers on January 20, 2020, media coverage shifted significantly as the dispute gained national attention. In response, and with a court injunction now on their side, CRC spokespeople and statements, as well as statements from trucking companies and their industry representatives, adopted a remarkably coherent message appealing to "law and order." Of the 168 articles published between January 22 and March 3, 2020, there are 82 mentions of such appeals to law and order, and 69 inferences of union harassment, intimidation, and violence. Fifty-four of the 168 articles in this period, almost one in three, contain both an appeal to law and order and inferences of union harassment, intimidation and violence. This was also the period of the dispute in which the RPS initiated intensive policing of picket line activity.

After these two distinct periods of news coverage, a couple of important developments surfaced: the COVID-19 pandemic was declared and the provincial government introduced special mediation to resolve the lockout, appointing Vince Ready and Amanda Rogers to spearhead the process. Allegations against Unifor members and appeals to law and order disappeared almost entirely from media coverage after the second week of February. It appeared that the FCL/CRC media strategy was thrown off by the premier's support for special mediation. Using the special provisions of the province's labour laws, specifically Section 6-35(1) of the *Saskatchewan Employment Act*, the CRC forced a so-called "final offer" vote on the union membership. It was rejected by 89 percent of voting members.[40] As with the December injunction, there was no in-depth reporting of this special one-sided provision for a forced vote or FCL/CRC's Energy Roadmap and its relationship to the lockout. Indeed, the absence of informed beat reporting within the ranks of mainstream media outlets extended to the topic of climate change and a "just transition" in the CRC case.

PERIOD THREE: MAY TO JUNE 2020

A third period of coverage began in mid-May of 2020 with the disclosure of a prior bomb threat against the union. The bomb threat letter, dated February 18, 2020, only came to light after Unifor released the findings from its own freedom of information (FOI) request submitted to the City of Regina and RPS.[41] The Regina Police Service, then-mayor Michael Fougere, and labour minister Don Morgan all received copies of the threat but chose not to reveal it to the union or to the public. Yet four of the seven May 19 headlines in our study contained the phrase "not credible" or "non-credible" when referencing police dismissal of the threat — similar caveats rarely if ever preceded claims levied against union members. The seven stories also made no mention of the fact that Minister Morgan received a copy of the bomb threat directed at the union. There is no follow-up reporting on the bomb threat, either.

The media similarly failed to draw any connection between the ongoing lockout and the sixty-thousand-litre hydrocarbon and water spill that damaged the city's wastewater treatment facility. Omission of critical information seems to have been a defining feature of media coverage as the lockout drew to a close.

GAPS IN MEDIA COVERAGE

In covering "both sides" of the dispute, nearly all mainstream media demonstrated a failure to pursue lines of inquiry that went beyond immediate events and the comments issued by official organizational representatives. Consistent with this approach, we found that during the lockout, only eight out of 435 articles made any mention of labour relations at the refinery prior to the lockout. This includes the 2016 round of bargaining in which the union took pension concessions, the 2013 explosion, and the 2011 explosion that injured fifty-two employees. Readers were in effect denied any historical context to the dispute. Nor did the media speak about the financial state of the company, which had benefited from a lack of pipeline capacity and the low price of western crude to achieve record profits.

There was also no mention in any of the articles of Local 594's long history dating back to 1942, before FCL was even formed and less than a decade after the Co-op Refinery came online.[42] However, Nesbitt and Stevens published a lengthy *Rankandfile.ca* article in the first weeks of the lockout entitled "Local 594 and the Lost History of Oil Worker Unionism," which traced the story of how Local 594 and Saskatchewan's trade unionists were the wellspring of oil worker unionism in Canada.

The fact that Unifor had to uncover the bomb threat through an FOI request further exposes a profound weakness in the mainstream media's efforts to investigate and understand a historic dispute that dominated Saskatchewan news for nearly three months. The apparent failure of the media to conduct their own FOI requests and pursue the bomb threat story and its cover-up is a damning indictment of Saskatchewan's news-media institutions. And this is not the only aspect of the lockout that received almost no mainstream coverage.

Two weeks before the bomb threat was made, Leedham broke the story on *Rankandfile.ca* of social media death threats by United We Roll/Yellow Vest activists against picketing workers. These stories, published February 4 and February 6, were not picked up by the mainstream media. Only the *Globe & Mail* ran a story referencing this connection on February 7, with no reference to *Rankandfile.ca* breaking the story. In the 435 articles we examined, there was only one reference to Banda's relationship with the Yellow Vests and UWR organizations who attended his speech at the Carseland Co-op fuel terminal on February 5, 2020. This reference was made in passing in *Leader-Post* columnist Murray Mandryk's February 8 column.[43] Local media did not report on this story despite their regular coverage of earlier UWR and Yellow Vest protests in the province and the well-established links between these movements and far-right activists.[44]

The mainstream media also seemingly failed to investigate the companies that had partnered with FCL/CRC to hire and transport scabs to the camp despite the hardship the lockout was causing local residents and their families. It was widely known among Unifor 594 members that multinational union-busting firm AFIMAC was central to the scab operation, which also involved 24/7 surveillance of the union picket lines.[45]

Unifor 594 took numerous complaints of harassment and intimidation by AFIMAC staff to the RPS, but this was never covered by the media. Only Regina's *Briarpatch Magazine*, an independent progressive publication in circulation since the 1970s, gave the matter any serious attention.[46] Other omissions appeared in our media scan, as well.

The scab camp, built on property owned by the City of Regina only weeks before the lockout, was subjected to no investigation by the mainstream media. It took an FOI by non-media sources to uncover this. And it was not until the COVID-19 pandemic erupted in March 2020 that Regina City Council and health and safety experts began pressuring the Saskatchewan Health Authority to investigate health protocols in the on-site replacement camp.[47] Even with late mainstream media coverage of the work camp, it was never mentioned during the entire lockout that CRC had secured approval to establish a similar camp in 2016. The absence of a meaningful historical overview of bargaining at one of Saskatchewan's most important workplaces offers a clear example of what happens when labour beat reporting is abandoned by the newsmedia. Journalists become dependent upon official spokespeople and local experts for a meaningful understanding of the relationship between these respective parties.

EXPERIMENTS IN LABOUR REPORTING: THE LEFT AND RIGHT CONVERGE IN REGINA

Independent media outlets on both the left and the right of the political spectrum advanced their own beat reporting projects to cover the lockout. By January of 2020, Leedham, representing *Rankandfile.ca*, started reporting from the picket lines in Regina. With limited resources, we filled the gaps in information left out by the mainstream media with extensive on-the-ground reporting and analysis. Where *Rankandfile.ca* is unique is in its coverage of not only labour struggles, but also inter-union politics, resulting in criticism from both employers and union officials.

Leedham's coverage of labour relations with FCL had started in 2018 with the Moose Jaw Co-op strike and the subsequent five-month Saskatoon Co-op strike through winter 2018–2019. Both strikes were waged by UFCW Local 1400 members.[48] Co-op sought to implement a two-tier wage system on its retail workers. This struggle sparked Saskatoon Co-op Members for Fairness, a movement of Co-op members (the consumers) who opposed the Co-op's treatment of workers and its move away from "co-operative values." The movement ended up packing a Saskatoon Co-op Annual General Meeting and electing two new board members. The refinery lockout was part of this broader historical context. Unearthing this history allowed us to stitch together a narrative that had otherwise been obscured by company messaging and the substantial gaps in traditional newsmedia coverage.

Rankandfile.ca's coverage also broke stories that highlighted a significant crack in the established narrative about the dispute — specifically the connection between an allegedly pro-worker truck convoy movement, United We Roll, and its threat to violently dismantle Unifor's secondary pickets in Carseland, Alberta.[49] Banda's convenient allegiance with this right-wing group is noteworthy, and it was a focus of *Rankandfile.ca*'s reporting. Conservative politicians like Premier Moe and then-leader of the Opposition, Andrew Scheer, provided tacit support for United We Roll and the Yellow Vests but said nothing to support the over seven hundred oil workers who walked picket lines throughout western Canada. The mainstream media paid little attention to what should have been a political controversy. However, new right-wing media outlets also had a voice in reporting the dispute.

Following the January 20 blockades and subsequent police crackdown, right-wing outlets such as *Rebel News*, *True North*, and *The Post Millennial* began to cover the lockout. These editorial "news" organizations promoted FCL's extractive populist "union thug" narrative. *The Rebel*'s coverage began on January 29 with a video by correspondent Keean Bexte, entitled "Keean crosses the Unifor picket line for Co-op gas in Alberta."[50] The next day, *The Rebel* published a video of United Conservative Party MLA Joseph Schow crossing what it called Unifor's "illegal" secondary picket, referring to Unifor members as "union thugs." Two videos published February 3 report on United We Roll's meetup in Carseland, one titled, "Keean Bexte: Unifor's refinery protest spills from Saskatchewan into Alberta" and the other "'We can't have unions holding everyone hostage': Unifor's Co-op fuel protest meets resistance."

Two of *True North*'s Unifor lockout stories vilified the union. On January 3, it published "Unifor accused of vandalism, spiking tires of Co-op refinery trucks" and followed this on February 8 with "Refinery manager's property vandalized as Unifor standoff continues." *The Post Millennial*, meanwhile, published "WATCH: Unifor boss Jerry Dias arrested" on January 20, "Unifor found guilty of contempt of court, fined

$100,000" on January 22 and "Homes of seven Regina Co-op Refinery managers vandalized" on February 5. Again, no evidence was used to support allegations inferring Local 594 members' involvement in these incidents.

What merits further research is the effect of this type of subversive, right-wing journalism on popular opinion about work and labour. It too emerges in the context of disenchantment with the corporate media, but with a decidedly different narrative. These sources would regain significance during the Freedom Convoy in 2022, when supporters of this anti-Trudeau and anti-vaccine mandate would demonstrate their distrust of journalists and the media at large, relying instead on live social media feeds and outlets like *The Rebel*. Whether or not they shifted public opinion about the Unifor Local 594 lockout is uncertain.

On June 12, 2020, *The Post Millennial* did, however, publish a surprising article, "RCMP officers 'add another level of fear' for workers in their six-month battle to protect their pensions and jobs," by Sam Helguero, who cast refinery workers in a sympathetic light and as victims of intimidation from FCL and AFIMAC. The subhead also drew attention to facts that had been largely neglected by the media: "Dead rabbits on their doorsteps. Spouses being stalked; their pictures taken in their yards and communities. Bomb threats that police kept secret. Now workers have been getting regular visits from the RCMP." The article explicitly challenges the union thug narrative with a quote:

> The RCMP answers appear to follow an old stereotype of 'union thugs,'" responded Ronni Nordal, a Regina-based labour lawyer. "Do the RCMP conduct a 'possible mischief investigation' every time a group of people gather for a common cause?"[51]

The article is the first news report of AFIMAC's role in the dispute despite AFIMAC's mention in Unifor press releases. An in-depth look at AFIMAC's role in the refinery lockout would not appear again until a *Briarpatch Magazine* feature by Mitchell Thompson, published May 3, 2021, entitled "The strike-breakers playbook." In the article, Local 594 president Kevin Bittman highlights AFIMAC's role in the lockout surveillance: "We told all our members on the line, 'Talk like you are being heard because they're listening to everything that's going on.'"[52]

THE AGE OF MISINFORMATION AND LESSONS LEARNED

When the so-called Freedom Convoy arrived in Ottawa on January 28, 2022, it was plain to see the many connections between the convoy organizers and the United We Roll activists who had threatened and confronted Local 594 picket lines two years earlier. This insight and analysis was published in *Jacobin* by Emily Leedham in her article "Canada's 'Freedom Convoy' is a Front for a Right-Wing, Anti-Worker Agenda."[53]

Mainstream newsmedia, however, failed to connect the Freedom Convoy and the anti-worker petro-populists. Instead, newsmedia outlets largely repeated the claims that this was a working-class uprising of truck drivers, while it was alternative grassroots media that reported on the links between the organizers and funders of the Freedom Convoy and the populist pro–oil and gas organizations.[54] The mainstream media, with virtually no institutional knowledge or understanding of labour issues, became unwitting participants (or worse) in ginning up the spectacle by focusing on sensational incidents like the waving of Nazi flags at a demonstration in Ottawa.[55]

The absence of a labour beat in Canada's mainstream media has allowed large employers, such as FCL and CRC, and allied right-wing political organizations to turn reality on its head in pursuit of a traditional corporate agenda of union busting and retaining power and prerogative over economic and political affairs. Similar shortfalls exist in the coverage of FCL's Energy Roadmap and the company's "greenwashing" initiatives. The dominant mode of news reporting, "objective" journalism, has proven incapable of addressing corporate and right-wing forces that have learned through years of experience to manipulate "objective" journalism to its advantage. It is also apparent that the editors and managers of mainstream newsmedia are incapable or unwilling to challenge or address this problem for structural reasons related to corporate ownership of media and a meek public broadcaster.

The danger posed to organized labour is the strength and breadth of the mainstream newsmedia to broadcast this propaganda and misinformation into the ranks of labour and sew or deepen divisions among union members and sympathizers. In an age of misinformation, re-establishing labour beats and developing new independent media institutions will be essential in combating this pervasive problem. A new labour journalism must also face the failure of "objective" journalism as it is practised in the mainstream newsmedia, along with inevitable accusations of being "biased" and peddling "misinformation." Now that Canada's political and media elites have become the arbiters of what constitutes misinformation and seek to throttle and censor social media like Facebook and Twitter, they will use these communication platforms as a cudgel against reporting and investigative journalism that challenges the corporate status quo. Creating space for critical discussion of the "just transition" in the heartland of Canada's oil and gas industry, and what this means for local communities and workers, requires similar attention. The 2019–2020 lockout of refinery workers in Regina is instructive for these reasons, especially when the influences of "extractive populism" and a right-wing, anti-labour narrative dominates the political horizons.

Endnotes

1. Arthur White-Crummey, "Unifor vs. Co-op: Who's Winning the Battle for Public Opinion?" *Regina Leader-Post*, January 17, 2020 <leaderpost.com/news/local-news/unifor-vs-co-op-whos-winning-the-battle-for-public-opinion>.
2. See, for example Stefanie Davis, "Co-op Refinery Workers Locked Out after Strike Begins," CTV News, December 5, 2019, <regina.ctvnews.ca/co-op-refinery-workers-locked-out-after-strike-begins-1.4717592>.
3. Steve Early, *The Civil Wars in US Labor: Birth of a New Workers' Movement or Death Throes of the Old?* (Chicago: Haymarket Books, 2011).
4. Labor Notes, "About," n.d., <labornotes.org/about>.
5. Andrew Stevens, Doug Nesbitt, and Varun Makkar, *The Union Effect: Unifor Local 594's Economic and Community Impact* (Regina: Centre for Management Development, 2019).
6. For a more comprehensive analysis of the corporatization of Saskatchewan's co-operative movement, see Sara Birrell, "What Happened to the Co-op?" *Sask Dispatch*, June 15, 2019, <saskdispatch.com/articles/view/what-happened-to-the-saskatoon-co-op>.
7. Emily Leedham, "The Scab, His Mom, and the Soul of the Co-op," *Rankandfile.ca*, September 2, 2019, <rankandfile.ca/the-scab-his-mom-and-the-soul-of-the-co-op/>.
8. Doug Nesbitt and Andrew Stevens, "Local 594 and the Lost History of Oil Worker Unionism," *Rankandfile.ca*, December 12, 2019, <rankandfile.ca/local-594-history/>.
9. Charles Smith and Andrew Stevens, "Opinion: The Importance of 'Beat' Reporting," *Saskatoon StarPhoenix*, February 12, 2020, <thestarphoenix.com/opinion/letters/opinion-the-importance-of-beat-reporting>.
10. William Serrin, "Labor and the Mainstream Press: The Vanishing Labor Beat," in *The New Labor Press: Journalism for a Changing Union Movement*, eds. Sam Pizzigati and Fred J. Solowey (Ithaca: Cornell University Press, 1992), 11.

11 Findings from Douglas Nesbitt, "Days of Action: Ontario's Extra-Parliamentary Opposition to the Common Sense Revolution, 1995–1998" (unpublished doctoral dissertation, Queen's University, 2018), <qspace.library.queensu.ca/bitstream/handle/1974/24271/Nesbitt_Douglas_J_201805_PhD.pdf>.
12 John Gordon Miller, *Yesterday's News: Why Canada's Daily Newspapers Are Failing Us* (Halifax: Fernwood, 1998), 13.
13 David Skinner and Mike Gasher, "So Much by So Few: Media Policy and Ownership in Canada," in *Converging Media, Diverging Politics: A Political Economy of the News Media in the United States and Canada*, eds. David Skinner, James R. Compton, and Michael Gasher (Lanham: Lexington Books, 2005), 52.
14 Robert McChesney, *Rich Media, Poor Democracy: Communication Politics in Dubious Times* (Urbana: University of Illinois Press, 1999), 89.
15 Alberta Advantage, "The 1999–2000 Herald Strike, 20 Years Later," January 12 2020, <albertaadvantagepod.com/2020/01/12/the-1999-2000-herald-strike-20-years-later>.
16 Brenda Dalgish, "Southam Opts for Layoffs to Relieve Squeeze," *Financial Post*, January 17, 1996.
17 Miller, *Yesterday's News*, 35.
18 Nick Davies, *Flat Earth News: An Award-winning Reporter Exposes Falsehood, Distortion and Propaganda in the Global Media* (London: Chatto & Windus, 2008), 62.
19 Davies, *Flat Earth News*, 73.
20 Davies, *Flat Earth News*, 73.
21 See Marc Edge, *Asper Nation: Canada's Most Dangerous Media Company* (Vancouver: New Star Books, 2007).
22 Deborah Richmond, "Contracts, Outcry Reduce Forced Layoffs at Some Postmedia Papers," CWA Canada, March 3, 2023, <cwacanada.ca/2023/03/03/contracts-outcry-reduce-forced-layoffs-at-some-postmedia-papers/>.
23 See Chapter 1 of Marc Edge, *The Postmedia Effect: How Vulture Capitalism is Wrecking Our News* (Vancouver: New Star Books, 2022).
24 Global Media and Internet Concentration Project, "Media and Internet Concentration in Canada, 1984–2020," 10th ed., <cmcrp.org/media-and-internet-concentration-in-canada-1984-2020>, viii.
25 Robert McChesney, *Digital Disconnect: How Capitalism Is Turning the Internet Against Democracy* (New York: New Press, 2014), 176–77.
26 Ian Gill, *No News Is Bad News: Canada's Media Collapse — And What Comes Next* (Vancouver: Greystone Books, 2016), 11–12.
27 Gill, *No News Is Bad News*, 62.
28 See Alain Saulnier, *Losing Our Voice: Radio-Canada Under Siege*, trans. Pauline Couture (Toronto: Dundurn, 2015); David Taras and Christopher Waddell, *The End of the CBC?* (Toronto: University of Toronto Press, 2020).
29 David Giles, "Saskatoon Co-op Files Unfair Labour Practice in Ongoing Strike," Global News, November 9, 2018, <globalnews.ca/news/4649220/saskatoon-co-op-unfair-labour-practice-strike-ufcw-craig-thebaud/>; *Saskatoon Co-operative Associated Limited v United Food and Commercial Workers, Local 1400*, LRB Files 199-19 & 208-19, September 30, 2020 <sasklabourrelationsboard.com/-/media/project/lrb/documents/publications-and-policies/decisions/recent-reasons/2020/19919--20819september-30-2020.pdf>.
30 Austin Davis, "Co-op Refinery Transporting Staff Via Helicopters after Alleged

'Dangerous' Acts by Union Members," *Regina Leader-Post*, December 9, 2019. https://leaderpost.com/news/local-news/co-op-refinery-transporting-staff-via-helicopters-after-alleged-dangerous-acts-by-striking-union-members; "union thug" was typically repeated on social media channels by what were likely troll accounts generated during the disputes. For example, see: "Locked-out @CoopRefinery workers know Western Canadian values better than some suit from Saskatoon. Watch as they take on @CoopFCL CEO Scott Banda in their own words," Twitter/X, @UniforTheUnion, February 6, 2020.

31 Tamara Khandaker, "Andrew Scheer Criticized for Support of United We Roll Convoy," *Vice.com*, February 19, 2019, <vice.com/en/article/a3bjb4/andrew-scheer-criticized-for-support-of-united-we-roll-convoy>.
32 Emily Leedham, "United We Rollback Pensions: Refinery Lockout Exposes Right-wing Hypocrisy," *Rankandfile.ca*, March 2, 2020, <rankandfile.ca/uwr-pensions/>.
33 Davis, "Co-op Refinery Transporting Staff."
34 When the lockout began in December 2019, the media cast this as a dispute about pensions, but little attention was given to the merits of the employer or union's claims. As the work stoppage dragged on, reporters with the *Leader-Post*, namely Alec Salloum and Arthur White Crummey, started to provide their own analysis of the specific issues on the table — as well as recognition that the CRC was experiencing record profits while also claiming financial hardship. Arthur White-Crummey, "Lockout Begins at Co-op Refinery as Workers Rally for Pensions," *Regina Leader-Post*, December 6, 2019, <leaderpost.com/news/local-news/lockout-begins-at-co-op-refinery-as-workers-rally-for-pensions>; Arthur White-Crummey, "Unifor vs. Co-op: What is the CRC Dispute Really About?" *Regina Leader-Post*, January 23, 2020, <leaderpost.com/news/local-news/unifor-vs-co-op-what-is-the-crc-dispute-really-about>.
35 Marc Smith, "OHS Contractor Alleges Harassment, Assault, from Unifor 594 Members," CTV News Regina, December 18, 2019, <regina.ctvnews.ca/ohs-contractor-alleges-harassment-assault-from-unifor-594-members-1.4735925?cache=yesclipId104062%3FcontactForm%3Dtrue>.
36 Larry Hubich, "Here's what really happened: youtu.be/K93FmXZNi38. Watch near the end of the clip where the guy in the green jacket reaches in from Savage's (in beige parka with black shoulder bag) left side and snatches papers. Virtually no contact," Twitter/X, @Lhubich, January 3, 2020.
37 Juliane A. Lischka and Marcel Garz, "Clickbait News and Algorithmic Curation: A Game Theory Framework of the Relation between Journalism, Users, and Platforms," *New Media & Society* 25, no. 8 (2021), <doi.org/10.1177/14614448211027174>.
38 Mark Melnychuk, "Homes of Refinery Managers Hit with Paintballs, Regina Police Investigating," February 5, 2020, <leaderpost.com/news/crime/homes-of-refinery-managers-hit-with-paintballs-regina-police-investigating>.
39 Andrew Stevens, "Regina Refinery Lockout is No 'Tea Party,'" *Rankandfile.ca*, December 30, 2019, <rankandfile.ca/regina-refinery-lockout-is-no-tea-party/>; *Consumer's Co-operative Refineries Limited and Unifor Canada Local 594, December 24, 2019*, accessed through *Rankandfile.ca*, <rankandfile.ca/wp-content/uploads/2019/12/Coop-594-injunction-QBG-3302-19.pdf>.
40 Unifor, "Unifor Unable to Accept the Co-op Refinery Final Offer," March 31, 2020, <unifor.org/news/all-news/unifor-unable-accept-co-op-refinery-final-offer>.

41 Allison Bamford, "February Bomb Threat against Unifor Local 594 Not Credible: Regina Police," *Global News*, May 19, 2020, <globalnews.ca/news/6961950/february-bomb-threat-unifor-local-594-regina/>.
42 Nesbitt and Stevens, "Local 594 and the Lost History."
43 Murray Mandryk, "Co-op lockout shrouded by far too much irrational nonsense," *Regina Leader-Post*, February 8, 2020.
44 Tamara Khandaker, "Andrew Scheer Criticized."
45 AFIMAC Global describes itself as provided services related to "[i]nternational security, crisis response, investigations, labor disputes and business continuity services for public and private sector organizations worldwide." The company's Labor Dispute and Business Continuity Services offer companies work stoppage planning advice, transportation services, and assist employers in "gathering evidence to obtain injunctions and temporary restraining orders." AFIMAC, "AFIMAC Global," n.d., <afimacglobal.com/>.
46 Mitchell Thompson, "The Strike-breakers' Playbook," *Briarpatch Magazine*, May 3, 2021, <briarpatchmagazine.com/articles/view/the-strike-breakers-playbook>.
47 Jennifer Ackerman, "Regina City Council to Ask SHA for Health Assessment of Refinery Work Camp," *Regina Leader-Post*, March 22, 2020, <leaderpost.com/news/local-news/regina-city-council-to-ask-sha-for-health-assessment-of-refinery-work-camp>.
48 Emily Leedham, "The Co-op strike: Big Solidarity in Little Martensville," *Rankandfile.ca*, November 25, 2018, <rankandfile.ca/the-co-op-strike/>.
49 Leedham, "United We Rollback Pensions."
50 Keean Bexte, "Keean Crosses the Unifor Picket Line for Co-op Gas in Alberta," *RebelNews.com*, January 29, 2020, <rebelnews.com/keean-crosses-the-unifor-picket-line-co-op-gas-station-alberta>.
51 Samuel Helguero, "RCMP Officers 'Add Another Level of Fear' for Workers in Their Six-month Battle to Protect Their Pensions and Jobs," June 12, 2020, <thepostmillennial.com/rcmp-officers-add-another-level-of-fear-for-workers-in-their-six-month-battle-to-protect-their-pensions-and-jobs>.
52 Thompson, "The Strike-breakers' Playbook."
53 Emily Leedham, "Canada's "Freedom Convoy" Is a Front for a Right-Wing, Anti-Worker Agenda," *Jacobin*, February 5, 2022, <jacobin.com/2022/02/canada-freedom-convoy-conservative-right-wing-anti-worker-anti-vaccine>.
54 Simon Enoch, "The Oil Industry's Frankenstein," *Briarpatch Magazine*, October 14, 2022, <briarpatchmagazine.com/articles/view/the-oil-industrys-frankenstein>.
55 Dylan Robertson, "Rejecting Unproven Claims Prevents 'Mob' Takeover of Convoy Inquiry: Murray Sinclair," *CTV News*, November 23, 2022, <ctvnews.ca/politics/rejecting-unproven-claims-prevents-mob-takeover-of-convoy-inquiry-murray-sinclair-1.6166254>.

8

TOWARDS A JUST TRANSITION FOR REFINERY WORKERS?
Taking Control of the Change

Emily Eaton

IN DECEMBER 2019, WHEN THE Co-op Refinery Complex locked out over seven hundred unionized employees, the world was already in the throes of a climate emergency. Saskatoon and Regina were, on September 27, 2019, sites of the Global Climate Strike movement by staging large rallies and "die-ins,'" Australia was on fire, India's wettest monsoon in twenty-five years killed 1,750 people, and the Bahamas were recovering from the devastation of Hurricane Dorian, the second strongest Atlantic hurricane on record. And as Unifor 594 members assembled their picket lines, world leaders were meeting in Madrid for COP25, the twenty-fifth meeting of the United Nations Framework Convention on Climate Change. While there is no arguing that the CRC lockout was an acrimonious labour dispute, it can also be understood as a window into the future of fossil fuel workers and the fossil fuel economy in an era of climate emergency.

Surprisingly, neither the media coverage of this historic lockout nor the union local itself engaged the connections between the climate emergency happening all around them and the union-busting attempts of the CRC — despite the CRC itself couching a significant portion of its communications about the lockout in the "transition to a low-carbon economy."[1] On November 16, 2019, as negotiations broke down but prior to the lockout, the CRC published an open letter in Regina's *Leader-Post* in which it directly tied its bargaining position of providing employees with "a choice to transition from the current Defined Benefit Pension Plan to a Defined Contribution Pension Plan" to changes that were required because of "a shift in our traditional fossil fuel market."[2] And since the deal that was finally reached in June of 2020, the CRC has continued to use the rhetoric of a low-carbon transition in their new announcements about layoffs. In October 2021, for example, the CRC communicated that it would be laying off fifty-four Local 594 workers over the next six months, stating, "the need for a workforce reduction is largely the result of operational efficiencies realized over the past number of years as the company prepares to transition to the low carbon economy."[3] It was also in October 2021 that FCL announced its plan to reduce greenhouse gas (GHG) emissions by 40 percent below 2015 levels by 2030 and achieve net zero by 2050.[4]

The coming energy transition, which is already being strategically planned by the CRC, offers the opportunity to make just transition central to union strategy, member mobilization, and communications with governments and the wider public. Leading up to and during the lockout, Local 594 was, understandably, employing all its resources and attention to deal with what members describe as a vindictive employer intent on forcing a punishing lockout or strike in an attempt to break the union. The presences and absences of energy transition, as a discourse, in this labour dispute are important in informing future struggles. Taking some lessons from the dynamics of the lockout, all workers in the fossil fuels sectors and beyond could be better positioned to fight for a coming energy transition that is just for workers and their communities.

Engagement with energy transition is now required for a wide range of organizations, from private businesses to public institutions, as they adapt to government targets and public pressure. The future of humans on this planet depends on whether the rapidly proliferating climate frameworks, plans, and actions of organizations actually achieve a transition from fossil fuels to a post-carbon economy that will reduce GHGs to near zero. Many organizations are using climate frameworks and aspirational plans that they have little intention of fulfilling to buy time, allowing them to stay in business by appearing to be consistent with a climate-safe future. In the fossil fuel sector there are at least two paths for engaging with energy transition. One could be led by fossil fuel corporations, where new technologies and processes (carbon capture, utilization, and storage [CCUS], biofuels, hydrogen, etc.) are used for the bosses' own ends — workforce reduction, efficiencies, reducing worker's benefits, and undermining unions. Such a transition will be chaotic and painful for workers and their communities. More importantly, it will not achieve the emissions reductions needed to avoid global warming. The second path is one that is led by workers themselves and involves significant government support and planning to wind down the fossil fuels sector, achieving the needed absolute emissions reductions in ways that are just and managed. By understanding that their interests are separate from those of their fossil fuel employers and the wider industry, refinery workers are more likely to win a just transition. This historic lockout may have inadvertently provided the necessary conditions for that work to begin.

THE NECESSITY OF ENERGY TRANSITION

The science on climate change has long been clear. In fact, fossil fuel companies such as Exxon commissioned some of the first science confirming global warming and then poured significant resources into denying these findings in the name of continuing profits. As reported by *Scientific American*[5] in 1977, eleven years before climate change become a public issue, Exxon's senior scientist warned management that there was significant scientific agreement that the release of CO_2 from burning fossil fuels was changing the climate. And one year later, this same scientist suggested average global temperatures would increase by two to three degrees Celsius if CO_2 levels doubled in the atmosphere. As documented by authors such as Naomi Oreskes, Erik Conway, and Geoffrey Supran, in the face of this knowledge, fossil fuel companies like Exxon and others engaged in concerted campaigns to deny the science and persuade the public and governments that fossil fuel production should go on unabated.[6]

Working against this organized and well-funded campaign of denial and influence, environmental movements and land defenders have long been pressing for drastic action to cut carbon emissions. But climate politics are entering a new phase. Today even mainstream organizations are readying themselves for the coming energy transition. Thanks to the Intergovernmental Panel on Climate Change's (IPCC) 2018 report on global warming of 1.5°C, there is international consensus that we must reach net-zero emissions by 2050.[7] And there is increasing recognition that rescuing a habitable planet requires more than fantastic accounting schemes to move emissions off government and corporate books through offsets and emissions trading; it necessitates stopping the production of the emissions in the first place. This was made abundantly clear when the International Energy Agency, the world's leading energy authority, released a ground-breaking report in June 2021 describing the remaining pathways to net zero emissions by 2050 as "narrow and extremely challenging" and premised on no new investments in fossil fuel infrastructure and phasing out three-quarters of current fossil fuel production and use by 2050.[8]

In fact, the necessity of phasing out fossil fuels is now recognized as essential to reaching net-zero emissions — after all, fossil fuels accounted for 86 percent of global greenhouse gas emissions in the last decade.[9] There is recognition among those studying emissions that it is more urgent to phase out fossil fuels that are combusted (in vehicles, planes, industry, and power plants for example) than the fossil fuels used as feedstock in plastics and petrochemicals. However, plastics and petrochemical products also need to be reduced in order to stay within 1.5°C of warming, and scientists and policy analysts are working on reducing fertilizer use in agriculture, phasing out single-use plastics and many other initiatives to reduce the use of non-combusted fossil fuels.

In 2021, the Conference of the Parties (COP) of the UN Framework Convention on Climate Change for the first time considered fossil fuels, rather than emissions, as a target for phase-out. Canada joined twenty countries and institutions in committing to end direct international public finance for "unabated" coal, oil, and gas by the end of 2022, meaning coal, oil, and gas that is combusted without measures like carbon capture to reduce GHG emissions. Before India's successful last-minute lobby to have the language changed to "phase-down," the final agreement of the COP called for phasing out coal. The 2021 COP also saw the launch of the Beyond Oil & Gas Alliance, "an international coalition of governments and stakeholders working together to facilitate the managed phase-out of oil and gas production" and comprised of eight national and subnational core members, including Costa Rica, Ireland, and Quebec.[10]

While Canada's Liberal government has been careful not to commit to phasing out oil and gas, they have announced a cap on oil and gas *emissions* from extraction and processing that will be lowered to net zero by 2050. With a focus on phasing out emissions rather than fossil fuels in Canada, oil and gas companies are rushing to introduce net-zero pledges. The Pathways Alliance was launched in 2021 as an initiative between Canada's six largest oil sands producers with the goal of reducing the sixty-eight megatons of CO_2 equivalent per year produced by its members in three phases to net zero by 2050. This would be accomplished primarily through (1) capturing the CO_2 emitted during extraction and processing and sequestering it underground in the Cold Lake storage hub, (2) carbon offsets, and (3) a substantial reliance on additional technologies that are not yet available.[11] It is unclear how much of the sequestered carbon will be used in enhanced oil recovery — a process where captured carbon is used to flood aging oilfields to stimulate new production of oil. The primary method of disposal and sequestration for captured carbon across North America is currently in enhanced oil recovery.

In short, governments and organizations of all kinds can no longer avoid engaging with energy transition. Yet exactly what energy transition requires is still an active site of contestation, with many organizations attempting to delay GHG reductions, deny that fossil fuels must be phased out, and greenwash their activities. As a major oil and gas producing country, Canada is attempting to hedge its bets and leave space and time for its oil and gas sector to show that it can produce fossil fuels with a net-zero carbon impact. Yet there are two potentially fatal flaws in Canada's approach. First, it is not at all clear that oil companies can deliver on these commitments. Their plans rely on as yet unavailable (direct air capture) and unproven (for example, in Saskatchewan, the carbon capture plant on Boundary Dam Three is capturing less than two-thirds of the carbon it promised) technologies, as well as carbon offsets, which are dubious schemes that allow companies to continue producing carbon pollution.[12] Second, since the emissions associated with the production of fossil fuels only account for 5 to 15 percent of the total emissions associated with the full life cycle of the products,[13] it is unlikely that Canada's oil and gas will continue to find markets as countries around the world intensify their efforts to reduce emissions to zero. Canada's hypothetical net-zero oil would still need to be consumed domestically or internationally in combustion engines or gas-fired power plants, both of which have no place in a zero-carbon future. In fact, new research is showing that more than 83 percent of Canada's fossil fuel reserves will need to be kept in the ground if we are to have a 50 percent chance of limiting global heating to 1.5°C.[14]

THE TRANSITION THEY WANT

One way or another, Canada is engaging in energy transition. Even private capital is signalling a switch to "green finance," with major financial institutions starting to report the emissions associated with the projects and companies they are financing.[15] But the nature of this transition is contested, and fossil fuel companies have already begun strategizing to win the "low-carbon" future that they want. Federated Co-operatives Limited (FCL), the parent company that owns Regina's CRC, is no exception. FCL has embarked on a program titled the "Co-op Energy Roadmap" with the goal of keeping its refinery in business until at least 2040 and building "a path to ensure $600m in annual revenue, which will allow [them] to provide $0.08/litre back to local Co-op owners."[16] Key to their goals, the roadmap suggests, will be responding to federal environmental regulations and reducing the company's carbon intensity and emissions.[17] To this end, in October 2021, the FCL announced that it would reduce its greenhouse gas emissions by 40 percent below 2015 levels by 2030 and achieve net zero by 2050. FCL's 2020 annual report estimated the emissions of the CRC and the Co-op Ethanol Complex at over 2.2 million tonnes in 2019.[18] Using the federal government's large emitter data, the *National Observer* places the CRC as the thirty-first biggest source of carbon pollution in the whole country.[19]

 The FCL's plans for a low-carbon economy mirror the broader oil industry's vision of energy transition. The Canadian Fuels Association (CFA) and Canadian Association of Petroleum Producers (CAPP), leading lobby groups, position their members as leaders in adopting technological solutions that will address climate change all the while growing their industry.[20] The CFA's "Driving to 2050" climate plan touts a commitment to emission reductions, capital investments, and jobs.[21] While sparse on details, the plans assume — indeed, insist — that there will be continued demand for fossil fuels well into the future regardless of the level of uptake in electric vehicles, redesigning of transportation systems, or building out of renewables. In making this claim, fossil capitalists, including the FCL, insist that renewable and zero-carbon technologies are not reliable, cost effective, or available in sufficient quantities to fuel a full transition. So, the industry reasons that fossil fuels will make up a significant part of the energy mix for decades to come. FCL is forecasting a strong market for diesel fuels to service farmers' and heavy industry's needs, and some reduced demand for gasoline, initially due to electric vehicle uptake (although the Energy Roadmap speculates that uptake of EVs in Saskatchewan might lag behind other jurisdictions because of long driving distances and lack of charging infrastructure) but mostly after 2035, when the announced federal ban on internal combustion engines is expected to come into force.

Given their plans to continue producing fossil fuels, FCL and the broader industry now focus on moving emissions off their corporate books through reducing the carbon intensity of fuel production and a range of schemes supported by federal and provincial regulations. CCUS and biodiesel are the two pillars of FCL's roadmap. It is only through CCUS that the company can make a claim to getting anywhere close to net zero. The company's announced plan involves sending captured carbon through a 120-kilometre pipeline to a Weyburn oil field, where it will be used to push oil, otherwise inaccessible, out of a depleted reservoir. Whitecap Resources, the Calgary-based oil company that operates the Weyburn unit, has agreed to accept the captured CO_2, and FCL claims it will eventually be sending the company 500,000 tonnes of CO_2 equivalent per year for enhanced oil recovery. In 2021, FCL estimated the cost of its carbon capture facility at $510 million, based on preliminary feasibility work.[22] At the time, former FCL president and CEO Scott Banda made clear that any final approval of carbon capture investment will only happen with the right market conditions and government support.[23] FCL is committing $50 million for constructing and operating two carbon capture facilities, one next to the CRC on its newly acquired ethanol complex, to be completed in 2024, and the other on the CRC, which is slated for commissioning in 2026.[24]

But CCUS is expensive and contingent on continued consumer demand for fuel well beyond 2030. To make FCL's planned strategy viable, the company must build costly new capture facilities. The company also requires significant infrastructure to transport the CO_2 about 120 kilometres southeast, to the Weyburn oil field. In other words, buy-in from governments is required. The Province of Saskatchewan has indicated it will invest in building a trunk line and CCUS hubs that FCL and other companies might use, and the federal government introduced a tax credit for investments in CCUS in 2022.²⁵ At issue is the federal government's prohibition on enhanced oil recovery in its CCUS tax credit — both the Saskatchewan government and opposition stand united in opposing the exclusion of enhanced oil recovery.²⁶ Then-minister of energy and natural resources Bronwen Eyre said Saskatchewan will "stand with the enhanced oil recovery aside [sic] of the carbon capture, utilization and storage narrative."²⁷ Saskatchewan has also announced that its royalty structure will keep enhanced oil recovery projects using captured CO_2 competitive relative to conventional extraction.²⁸ In sum, the CCUS strategy requires significant public subsidies and will produce additional oil and gas that would otherwise not be extracted.

In response to new clean fuel standards being developed by the federal government, which will require that the carbon intensity of liquid fuels be reduced over time by blending in biofuels, FCL is betting on biodiesel. In 2019, FCL acquired an ethanol plant, now named the Co-op Ethanol Complex (CEC). The company has negotiated the option to purchase 327 hectares of land from the City of Regina, where it plans to build a facility that would process canola for biodiesel in partnership with Saskatchewan-based agricultural company AGT Food and Ingredients.²⁹

Shifting to biofuel production is also costly and controversial. In addition to significant capital costs, the process is expensive. The CRC's internal preliminary estimates suggest that it may take three or four times as much hydrogen to hydro-treat canola to create the same molecule structure as traditional diesel.³⁰ FCL's plan hinges on government funding and it is noteworthy that the 2023 federal budget prioritizes examining "different support mechanisms that could support the [biofuels] sector in meeting the growing demand for low emissions fuels."³¹ The budget document also highlighted FCL's plan "to build the largest renewable diesel facility in Canada."³² However, it is unclear what the consequences are of increased demand for canola for agricultural land that is currently used for growing food. FCL and its partners have not disclosed what percentage of Saskatchewan's canola harvest will be needed as feedstock for the biodiesel upgrader or how much land may be shifted to grow more canola instead of other crops used for producing food and animal feed. There is also the question of the climate impact of fertilizer and others inputs used to grow canola for fuel production.

In addition to biodiesel and CCUS, FCL says it is exploring other methods to continue producing energy with fossil fuels, including producing more hydrogen. The CRC already produces some hydrogen from fossil fuels, which it uses internally as a fuel source, and according to the company, it is now also examining the possibility of building a new hydrogen plant that could produce "clean" fuel for sale.[33] However, putting carbon capture technology on its existing hydrogen plants — and adding a new plant — will be expensive, especially if it wants the high capture rate required to meet FCL's emissions reduction targets. FCL also plans to accrue carbon credits under federal regulations by buying offsets, paying into a clean technology fund, and building out its electric charging system across its retail gas bars. Finally, it is also worth noting that in 2021 FCL put up for sale, for the second time in five years, its crude oil production business, which produces three thousand barrels of oil per day across western Canada.[34] Selling its oil extraction business will help lower the emissions profile of FCL at the margin.

FCL is well aware that to stay in business until 2040 it will have to invest heavily in emissions reductions. It is using the significant costs associated with deep emissions reductions to justify cutting its total labour costs. This has become a central plank of its low-carbon strategy. And for this objective, Local 594 is seen as a significant barrier. The CRC's public communications have consistently framed layoffs, workforce reductions, and company cost cutting (for example, diminishing the CRC's contribution to the Local 594 pension plan) as the efficiencies required for the low-carbon economy. In addition to the examples above, CRC spokesperson Brad DeLorey said of the announced layoffs in 2021: "Obviously, our industry is changing. We are transitioning to a low carbon economy. We are investing a great amount of time and potential money into our energy roadmap, which will serve as the roadmap for our future in this ever changing industry."[35]

But well before the CRC had announced details on its plans to reduce its emissions, it had already begun cutting its labour costs. In fact, 594 members said they see breaking the union as the main goal of the company's labour relations leading up to and during the lockout.[36] No union means more management control over the CRC's workforce and much more "flexibility" in deploying workers during a time of significant changes in operations. It would almost certainly lead to downward pressures on wages and benefits and more differentiation in skill, compensation, and benefits within the workforce. Whether FCL is using the low-carbon transition opportunistically or not, it has repeatedly and clearly linked its labour relations strategies to energy transition and is mobilizing climate action to justify its agenda of reducing its workforce and labour costs. This is happening outside of collective bargaining, as there have been no discussions of transition at the bargaining table, or elsewhere, between management and union members. How should a union local representing fossil fuel workers respond to such tactics during a time of climate emergency?

OPPORTUNITIES FOR A JUST TRANSITION

Just as FCL and the broader fossil fuel industry are positioning themselves to address federal regulations that require reductions in carbon emissions, so too should fossil fuel workers. By not addressing the CRC's rhetoric of energy transition, the union local will concede an important arena of labour and political struggle. Doing so misses some strategic opportunities to communicate with the public, engage the government, and stand up for worker's interests in an economy that is already undergoing significant changes. Although Local 594 managed to minimize its concessions and return to work with the confidence of its members in 2020, the company has continued to mobilize the low-carbon future to plow ahead with layoffs and restructuring outside of collective bargaining. To date, neither Unifor National nor the refinery local has offered public comments about the company's Energy Roadmap or announcements on emissions reductions — despite a history of Local 594 charting an independent path for energy workers.[37] If union members are correct that the FCL is intent on busting the union, they need to develop a strategy to counter the FCL's planned "low-carbon" future and replace it with a transition that is just for workers and the environment.

FCL is currently fighting for an energy transition that paints the union and collective agreement as barriers to transition and that will give it new leeway to flexibilize its workforce. If it is successful in busting the union and/or removing positions from the union, the company will be able to hire more non-union employees, pay them at different rates, and reassign and redeploy workers with more ease, all while continuing to produce publicly subsidized fossil fuels into the indefinite future. FCL's vision of a low-carbon future is, thus, chaotic and painful for workers. It is a cover for throwing workers out of their jobs and making them work under increasingly precarious and dangerous conditions. For example, during the 2019–2020 negotiations, the CRC proposed eliminating the master operator position, the most senior position in the bargaining unit and one that Local 594 claims is crucial to the safe operation of the refinery. After the union and the arbitrator refused to accept the employer's attempt to eliminate the role and have comparable job duties covered by out-of-scope supervisors, the CRC withdrew the proposal. Yet since the conclusion of the negotiations, the CRC has nevertheless proceeded with layoffs and restructuring. According to workers, changes to the workforce complement required by a low-carbon transition ought to be negotiated with the union and applied to entry-level positions, yet FCL continues to pursue its transition outside of the collective bargaining process without support or even consultation with workers.

Energy transition is simply too powerful as a terrain and narrative for fossil fuel workers to concede to their bosses, as evidenced by comments issued by senior leaders at the CRC. Doug Mah, the refinery's director of the Energy Roadmap and business development, made clear in communication with us that "no in-scope workers were involved" in developing the company's low-carbon roadmap and suggested the union may see the refinery as a "slot machine making profits for the organization."[38] He speculated that new facilities, under different operating structures like joint ventures, could very well be non-union. Taken together, these moves — and the attacks on the union and its pension — represent an *unjust* transition, whereby greenwashing and attempts to break the collective power of labour are part of the rhetoric of the "net-zero" future. For these reasons is it imperative that unions like Local 594 become leaders in the just transition movement and help to mobilize the broad-based popular, political, and government support that will be needed to safeguard a bright future for their members and the planet, rather than corporations. Local 594 members are highly skilled — they include engineers, accountants, electricians, mechanics, machinists, pipefitters, welders, laboratory technicians — and many could feasibly find work in existing and new green industries. But to ensure a smooth transition to jobs of relatively equivalent benefits and compensation, they will need to advocate for their interests.

The Labour Movement Roots of Just Transition

Labour and environmental movements have had a fraught history in North America. Environmental non-government organizations (ENGOs) have often been rejected by people in rural resource peripheries (including unionized workers) when they have advocated for conservation of resources affecting the industries upon which these communities depend for jobs. For example, during the "war in the woods" in the 1990s in British Columbia, ENGOs and Indigenous Nations and organizations battled multinational forestry companies to preserve old growth forests from clear-cutting. In these protests, resulting in hundreds of arrests, forestry unions often sided with industry. In fact, their counterprotests in Clayquot Sound in 1993 were larger in size than those organized by the ENGOs, reflecting the local concerns about lost jobs.[39]

On the other hand, through their health and safety committees, workers in many toxic and dangerous industries have a long history of addressing the environmental effects of their industries as matters of workplace justice.[40] Environmental justice can overlap with struggles for workplace justice when polluting industries endanger not just the health of workers, but also the health of wider communities, with the most polluting industries often sited in Indigenous, Black, and otherwise racialized communities. In these cases, strong alliances between environmentalists and unions can emerge to counter industries that harm workers, community health, and the wider environment while advocating for workers to be transitioned to other jobs.

The concept of just transition originated in the labour movement, and energy workers have always been at the forefront of just transition campaigns. Advocates for just transition maintain that workers affected by environmental policies ought to be supported as they move into different jobs with unionized protections.[41] Tony Mazzocchi is credited with pioneering the concept, when, as the leader of the Oil, Chemical and Atomic Workers Union, he advocated for a "Superfund for workers" to provide support for workers affected by the environmental policies of the 1990s in the United States.[42] In Canada, large private sector unions, including the United Steelworkers, the Communications, Energy, and Paperworkers Union (CEP) and the Autoworkers developed early policy around climate change that focused on green job creation and actively sought to undermine the jobs-versus-environment frame.[43] In fact, the

CEP, which later joined the Autoworkers to form Unifor, was an early leader, with its 2002 Energy Policy and campaign to pressure Canada to ratify the Kyoto Accord and implement a just transition for Canadian energy workers.[44] The Canadian Labour Congress then followed suit and endorsed the CEP's calls.

At the national level, Unifor is now one of the unions that is doing the most to advance the just transition movement in Canada, at least in terms of policy positions and public discourse. In 2017, Unifor National released the *Unifor Energy Policy*, which supported carbon pricing and called for its revenues to be used to finance a just transition, including "labour market impact assessments, retraining, skills upgrading, income support, relocation assistance, pension bridging and employment insurance flexibility" for fossil fuel workers.[45] In 2019, Unifor held a national just transition conference in Saskatoon, with representatives from car manufacturing locals in Ontario, tar sands workers in Alberta, offshore oil workers in Newfoundland, forestry and heavy industry workers in Quebec, and refinery workers in Regina, among others. At this conference, which I attended, workers spoke of the need to work at the scale and speed of the climate crisis that confronts us and brainstormed ideas about how their union locals could advocate for their members and be leaders in transitioning their workplaces and broader communities. Discussion also pointed out the missed opportunity of the 2008–2009 financial collapse, when auto-manufacturing locals advocated for public ownership of the industry to manufacture electric vehicles and other "sustainable" goods. The conference, however, was not without a major tension, namely whether fossil fuel production needed to be phased out in Canada. As can be expected, some workers did not agree that the industry needed to be wound down; instead they advocated for finding efficiencies within their workplaces. Yet in April 2021, when Canada announced new emissions targets of 40 to 45 percent below 2005 levels by 2030, Unifor National joined Environmental Defence in calling for even more aggressive emissions reductions, provided that a just transition framework be put in place to help its twelve thousand members move out of the oil and gas sector.[46]

It is not just Unifor National that is calling on the federal government to introduce a robust just transition strategy. When the Canadian government announced, in 2016, the phase out of coal-fired electricity by 2030, it was calls from the Canadian Labour Congress that instigated

Canada's Task Force on Just Transition,[47] which toured coal communities and issued two reports in 2019. At the national policy level, United Steelworkers is still committed to climate action, and organizations like Blue Green Canada and the Green Economy Network are seeking to unite labour, environmental, and civil society organizations to put pressure on governments for a transition that is socially and economically just. The federal government responded to this pressure by announcing, in 2019, that it would bring forward Just Transition legislation and include action on Just Transition in the 2021 federal mandate letters.[48] However, the Act was delayed for further consultation and only introduced in June of 2023 as the more palatable Sustainable Jobs Act. It promises sustainable jobs action plans starting in 2025 and every five years thereafter.

Central to the calls for just transition coming from labour and its national coalitions is adherence to the International Labour Organization's "Guidelines for Just a Transition Towards Environmentally Sustainable Economies and Societies for All."[49] The guidelines emphasize the importance of tripartite social dialogues as a foundation for successful and equitable just transition. According to the ILO, these social dialogues, a form of ongoing and informed consultation and negotiation, should involve governments (including Indigenous governments), employers, and workers as well as other relevant civil society organizations. Together, the work done by national unions, including Unifor, national labour organizations and coalitions, and the ILO guidelines lays out a path for locals such as Unifor 594. However, as Local 594 members said, there is often a disconnect between the work being done at the national scale and the situation on the ground within energy workers' locals.

The Future of Local 594

Drawing on the support of Unifor National and other allies, Local 594 could use the CRC's "low-carbon" rhetoric to advance a vision of just transition — a low-carbon future led by fossil fuel workers themselves involving significant government support and planning. It is clear that broaching the question of the future of fossil fuels and the refinery with its workers does not make for easy work. One Local 594 member suggested that conversations need to start "on the shop floor" and another suggested that the local ought to start a committee on just transition to begin to explore the low-carbon future, the company's rhetoric, and how the union might intervene in wider conversations about transition.[50] It seems a union committee and shop floor conversations are the first step forward for locals like 594, but ultimately the union, governments, and the employer need to come to the table in a process of transparent social dialogue where they can have an equal voice in the future of their industry. Unfortunately, the VP of the CRC during the lockout is now responsible for leading FCL's Energy. This acts as a barrier to worker voices in transition processes.

As current and former refinery workers noted, they had not been engaged by management in the development of FCL's Energy Roadmap. According to 594 members, communication with members about the company's vision has been very scant, and although management signalled drastic changes to its operations in the Energy Roadmap, 594 members told us they believe energy transition is largely a pipe dream and that the refinery has a long life ahead of it supplying fossil fuels to western Canada. Through the establishment of a just transition committee within the local, members could educate themselves and their peers on the shop floor about the scale and timeline of the transformations coming. And they could agitate for the FCL to establish a formal process through which the union is informed and consulted about energy transition.

The ILO's Conventions (including the 1981 Convention on Occupational Health and Safety) codify the right of workers to know about their workplace operations, including any hazards and the measures the employer is taking to address them.[51] As Samantha Smith from the International Trade Union Confederation's Just Transition Centre makes clear, this principle of the right to know logically extends to the plans and pathways that industries and employers are taking for energy transition.[52] Importantly, a just transition committee could strategize about how to expose FCL's low-carbon transition communications as cover for workforce layoffs and pension concessions, and they could develop their own messaging about the obligations of the company to its workforce as it transitions. Unifor National is well equipped to play a supporting role for such a committee, sharing its research and expertise on just transition and advocating on the national stage for the interests of refinery workers in such a process. But building an environmental consciousness at the rank-and-file level will take strong leadership and meaningful engagement from locals and national unions if they wish to construct a formidable counterweight to the influence of industry and the dominant political narrative.

While exposing the CRC's rhetoric of energy transition as disingenuous, the local could strategically mobilize the "low-carbon future" discourse to its advantage in the lead-up to the next contract negotiations. With their current contract set to expire in 2026, the local has time to strategize about bargaining the types of protections and supports they will need from an employer that continues to foreground energy transition. By that point, energy transition and the climate crisis will be more central to public discourse, which might play in the union's favour. Members of Local 594 pointed out that their contract already contains provisions for severance, job protection, and layoffs, and it covers all work sites within the City of Regina limits by a Saskatchewan Labour Relations Board decision. But these provisions might be strengthened in new negotiations — an extended notice period for termination, increases in severance and retraining in portable skills on company time are all worth revisiting in contract negotiations — in an effort to secure a better future for members during what could rightly be described as a *just* transition. The union should also be thinking about how to ensure new assets and low-carbon infrastructure — like the biodiesel, hydrogen, and carbon capture plants — are covered by their bargaining unit and contract and that the bargaining unit is able to absorb and retrain existing members as operations shift. In other words, the union needs to bargain to retain, retrain, and redeploy workers across the FCL's energy sector. One member also suggested that the union would be wise to bargain a letter of understanding specifically related to energy transition, including a legacy fund to help with employee retraining and environmental cleanup as units are wound down over time.

Through a just transition committee, workers could also begin to strategize about how to assert their interests in the broader politics of energy transition. The City of Regina has begun implementing its 100 percent renewable civic strategy, and the refinery is one of the largest sources of emissions in the city. As a willing partner, Local 594 could engage city administration in holding the company to account for its promises to its workforce, to reducing emissions to zero, and to cleaning up its operations. In fact, the City of Regina needs rank-and-file employees to perform such a watchdog role because industry self-regulation has allowed ongoing environmental messes and serious occupational health and safety incidents.[53] The committee could form alliances with other labour unions and environmental groups working on issues of energy transition in Regina so that workers' interests achieve a prominent place in those conversations.

At the provincial level, workers could similarly insert themselves in the politics of energy transition. Demanding a tripartite social dialogue would be a strategic move for the union and could play well with the public — it seems commonsensical that energy workers should be included in their employer's and the government's plans for the future. The governing Saskatchewan Party loudly promotes its support for energy workers, mobilizing the welfare of energy workers to oppose federal policies such as carbon pricing and to attack the opposition NDP, as Premier Moe proclaimed in a letter to *Sask Today*.[54] There is a strategic opportunity for Local 594 members to draw attention to themselves as energy workers who have been abandoned by governments and employers in energy transition. Climate change policy is already a wedge issue in Saskatchewan, and Local 594 could exploit this wedge by pointing out that the CRC's low-carbon future is cover for throwing energy workers out of their jobs. Similarly, there is a strategic opportunity for the opposition NDP to champion the welfare of oil workers and press the government for social dialogues. It is, in fact, surprising that the opposition NDP showed up on the Local 594 picket lines but did not critically engage the employer's rhetoric around a low-carbon future. The NDP still has a tremendous opportunity to expose the company's plans to transition without consulting workers and to play up the government's abandonment of these energy workers.

In fact, the NDP could take a leadership role on the issue of employer-planned transitions by firmly siding with energy workers. They could point out that the provincial government is investing in carbon capture infrastructure and giving incentives for enhanced oil recovery, but they are not investing in the future of fossil fuel workers. This would be a change, of course, for the Saskatchewan NDP, which supported the industry when it was in power for decades in the province and has since actively supported the Sask Party's defence of the oil and gas industry against what they have painted as an overreaching federal government. For example, in 2022 the NDP stood united with the Sask Party against the federal government's exclusion of enhanced oil recovery in their CCUS tax credit. There is also an opportunity for Local 594 to push the provincial opposition on these issues, to both stand up for workers' rights and shame the government for its abandonment of energy workers. Alongside the NDP, workers could press for stronger labour rights (anti-scab legislation), bridges to retirement, employment insurance top-ups, education and retraining opportunities, community economic development and diversification, and more. Armed with the knowledge about the speed and scale of the coming transition, Local 594 could begin to advocate that governments invest in new supports through federal benefits such as employment insurance and in building out a new green economy with plenty of jobs and opportunities for the skilled trades. Advancing the vision of a worker-led low-carbon future is a strategic opportunity that should not be wasted.

As new federal climate change policy comes forward within the context of the Sustainable Jobs Act, union workers in Saskatchewan could band together to ensure that the low-carbon transition supports good, green, unionized jobs. Unions and trades have a lot at stake in this transition; it is in their interests to pressure governments to build out publicly owned green infrastructure that will support new unionized jobs and respect the integrity of the trades. There is concern, for example, that trades could become deregulated and split apart in many new green industries, creating a number of lower-paid, more precarious "technician" jobs that would displace, for example, the work of journeymen and skilled trades people. The strong advocacy and mobilization that is needed to protect good, public, unionized, and skilled jobs in the transition could be coordinated through organizations like the Saskatchewan Federation of Labour and Blue Green Canada, in an alliance between labour, environmental, and civil society organizations.

WORKERS LEADING TO NET ZERO

The world is in the throes of a climate crisis, and governments, private capital, and other interests are all vying to define and set the trajectory for energy transition. The federal government is bringing in net-zero climate policy that is forcing industries and consumers to respond. And at the municipal level, cities like Regina are putting in place plans to be net zero by 2050.[55] Crucially, these climate plans and policies leave a lot of the transition to market forces and they thus produce a lot of uncertainty for our collective future. The federal government, for example, has not announced a managed wind down of fossil fuels, despite the evidence that climate change cannot be arrested without phasing out fossil fuels from our economies. Instead, a cap on oil and gas emissions (the specifics of which have not yet been clarified) and the clean fuel standard will allow space for fossil fuel industries to put forward plans — based on far-off commitments using unproven technologies like carbon capture and biodiesel — to continue producing fossil fuels while zeroing out their emissions on paper. The fossil fuel industry's strategy to stay alive in Canada, and to keep exporting their products to the world, hinges on public subsidies and mechanisms within federal and provincial regulations that allow companies to move emissions off their books through credits, offsets, and carbon capture, while continuing to produce carbon pollution. This strategy puts workers in a tricky position.

Without a government-managed phase-out of fossil fuels, workers face a chaotic future based on individual companies' abilities to meet new regulations and propose paths to net zero. It is also an invitation to these energy companies to push the transition down the road to far-off targets achieved through unproven technologies and find ways of shaping policy to align with their short- and long-term interests. Clearly the interest of company owners is to continue producing fossil fuels while shifting the costs of transition onto workers and the public so that dividends can remain "sustainable." In their plans for a "low-carbon" future, companies like the CRC increasingly see unions and their members as hurdles to overcome. The need for large investments to keep fossil fuel production going and the uncertainties associated with new regulations and unproven technologies are increasingly being used to justify workforce reductions, decreased benefits, and layoffs.

Currently, workers in the fossil fuel sectors, especially those beginning or mid-career, are largely unprepared for the coming transition. Concerted campaigns, organized by fossil fuel industry associations like the Canadian Association of Petroleum Producer's "Canada's Energy Citizens," have successfully persuaded many fossil fuel workers to defend the interests of the fossil fuel industries. Many oil and gas workers have deeply held beliefs that economies cannot function without widespread use of fossil fuels and that attempts to transition to renewables are attacks launched by urban "liberal elites" against their ways of life. For example, workers in Saskatchewan's coal-producing communities will see their jobs phased out as part of the federal government's wind down of coal-fired electricity by 2030. The United Steelworkers have not been able to demand a satisfactory just transition program for their workers, so transition has thus far been abrupt and workers themselves have not received support from the federal monies set aside — in Saskatchewan the majority of the $20 million spent so far has gone to infrastructure projects rather than workers.[56] Engaging fossil fuel workers in contemplating energy transition is contentious work that must start within workers' organizations and ranks and ultimately involve social dialogues among governments, employers, workers, and communities.

While many fossil fuel workers in Canada understand their own interests as synonymous with the interests of their employers and the industry more widely, a visible rift in this marriage, at least at the CRC, has emerged. After the punishing lockout, Local 594 members see very clearly that their employer's interests are not their own: FCL wants to break the union, drive down wages and benefits, and reduce its workforce.

Key to its communications strategy around this is the low-carbon transition, and Local 594 is now well positioned to expose FCL's low-carbon rhetoric for what it is. Ultimately, if there is to be a just transition for workers in Saskatchewan and Canada, more workers will need to come to the same understanding as Local 594 members that their interests are different from those of their employers. In the coming energy transition, fossil fuel workers face a choice: they can be passive and reactive, accepting the industry's layoffs and decreased benefits while private companies abandon their communities. Or they can fight for a just transition alongside allies in other sectors and strategically engage with environmental movements. A just transition is one that would secure a climate-safe future while supporting workers and their communities in a managed wind down. To do this, workers will need to stand up to their employers strategically through their unions (though most fossil fuel workers in Saskatchewan are non-unionized), form coalitions with civil society and environmental organizations, and advocate for themselves with all levels of government. This work can't start soon enough.

Endnotes

1 The transition to a low-carbon economy featured prominently in Federated Co-operatives Limited's messaging in the lead-up to, and during, the lockout. See, for example, the next endnote; Federated Co-operatives Limited, "The CRC Disappointed Unifor 594 Membership Votes to Reject Best and Final Offer," April 29, 2020, <fcl.crs/news-reports/news/article/the-crc-disappointed-unifor-594-votes-to-reject-offer>; Federated Co-operatives Limited, "Questions on Offer to Refinery Employees," April 7, 2020, <fcl.crs/news-reports/news/article/questions-on-offer-to-refinery-employees>.
2 Scott D. Banda and Gilbert Le Dressay, "Open Letter: Preparing for the Future," *Regina Leader-Post*, November 18, 2019; also posted to FCL website: <fcl.crs/news-reports/news/article/open-letter-preparing-for-the-future>.
3 Alec Salloum, "Co-op Refinery Announces Layoff of 54 Unionized Employees," *Regina Leader-Post*, October 4, 2021, <leaderpost.com/news/local-news/co-op-refinery-announces-layoff-of-54-unionized-employees>.
4 Federated Co-Operatives Limited, "FCL Exploring Carbon Capture with Whitecap Resources to Help Meet New Emissions Targets," October 21, 2001, <fcl.crs/news-reports/news/article/fcl-exploring-carbon-capture-with-whitecap-to-meet-emissions>.
5 Shannon Hall, "Exxon Knew about Climate Change Almost 40 Years Agos," *Scientific American*, October 26, 2015, <scientificamerican.com/article/exxon-knew-about-climate-change-almost-40-years-ago/>.
6 Naomi Oreskes and Erik M. Conway, *Merchants of Doubt: How a Handful of Scientists Obscured the Truth on Issues from Tobacco Smoke to Global Warming* (New York: Bloomsbury, 2011). Geoffrey Supran and Naomi Oreskes, "Assessing ExxonMobil's Climate Change Communications (1977–2014)," *Environmental Research Letters* 12, no. 8 (2020). See also PBS *Frontline*, "The Power of Big Oil," 2022, <pbs.org/wgbh/frontline/documentary/the-power-of-big-oil/>.
7 Intergovernmental Panel on Climate Change, *Global Warming of 1.5oC*, 2018, <ipcc.ch/site/assets/uploads/sites/2/2019/06/SR15_Full_Report_Low_Res.pdf>.
8 International Energy Agency, *Net Zero By 2050: A Roadmap for the Global Energy Sector*, October 2021, <iea.blob.core.windows.net/assets/deebef5d-0c34-4539-9d0c-10b13d840027/NetZeroby2050-ARoadmapfortheGlobalEnergySector_CORR.pdf>, 3.
9 P.A. Arias, N. Bellouin, E. Coppola, et al., "Technical Summary," in *Climate Change 2021: The Physical Science Basis*, contribution of Working Group I to the Sixth Assessment Report of the Intergovernmental Panel on Climate Change, <ipcc.ch/report/ar6/wg1/chapter/technical-summary/>, 80.
10 Beyond Oil and Gas Alliance. "Redefining Climate Leadership," 2021, <beyondoilandgasalliance.org/#:~:text=REDEFINING%20CLIMATE%20LEADERSHIP&text=Raise%20the%20issue%20of%20fossil,of%20oil%20and%20gas%20production>.
11 No Author, "The Pathways Vision," *Oil Sands Pathways to Net Zero*, 2021, <pathwaysalliance.ca/net-zero-initiative/>.
12 Marc Lee, *Dangerous Distractions: Canada's Carbon Emissions and the Pathway to Net Zero* (Vancouver: Canadian Centre for Policy Alternatives, 2021), <policyalternatives.ca/sites/default/files/uploads/publications/BC%20Office/2021/06/CCPA%20report_Dangerous%20Distractions%20Net%20Zero.pdf>.

13 Amanda Luhavalja, "Equinor's Move to Halve Carbon Intensity, Scope 3 Emissions Both Praised, Panned," *S&P Global Market Intelligence*, 2020, <spglobal.com/marketintelligence/en/news-insights/latest-news-headlines/equinor-s-move-to-halve-carbon-intensity-scope-3-emissions-both-praised-panned-56984504>.
14 Dan Welby, James Price, Steve Pye, and Paul Ekins, "Unextractable Fossil Fuels in a 1.5 C World," *Nature* 597 (2020): 230–34, <doi.org/10.1038/s41586-021-03821-8>.
15 *The Energy Mix*, "'Financed Emissions' Take the Spotlight as Banks Slowly Begin Reporting Climate Risk," May 7, 2021, <theenergymix.com/2021/05/07/financed-emissions-take-the-spotlight-as-banks-slowly-begin-reporting-climate-risk/>.
16 Co-op Refinery Complex, "Co-op Energy Roadmap — FAQ," internal document, 2021, 4.
17 Co-op Refinery Complex, "Co-op Energy Roadmap."
18 Federated Co-operatives Limited, *Annual Report*, 2020, 42, <fcl.crs/news-reports/annual-report-2020>
19 John Woodside, "Canada's 100 Dirtiest Emitters," *National Observer*, October 21, 2021, <nationalobserver.com/2021/10/21/news/canadas-100-dirtiest-emitters>.
20 Canadian Fuels Association (CFA), "Environmental Commitment," 2023, <canadianfuels.ca/environmental-commitment/#overview; Canadian Association of Petroleum Producers (CAPP), "Industry's Climate Commitment," 2023, <capp.ca/explore/industrys-climate-commitment/>.
21 CFA, *Moving Forward Together: Update to CFA Driving to 2050 Vision*, 2022, <canadianfuels.ca/wp-content/uploads/2022/11/Moving-Forward-Together_2022-Update-to-CFA-Driving-to-2050-Vision.pdf>.
22 Reuters, "Canada's Federated Co-Operatives Plans C$510 Million Carbon Capture Facilities," October 21, 2021, <reuters.com/business/energy/canadas-federated-co-operatives-plans-c510-million-carbon-capture-facilities-2021-10-21/#:~:text=Canada's%20Federated%20Co%2Doperatives%20plans%20C%24510%20million%20carbon%20capture%20facilities,-Reuters&text=WINNIPEG%2C%20Manitoba%2C%20Oct%2021%20(,complex%20and%20refinery%20in%20Saskatchewan>.
23 In an interview with *Pipeline Online*, Banda is quoted: "Our final decision to move forward will be based on the project's economic competitiveness, which will require government support and approvals, as well as favorable market conditions"; see Brian Zinchuk, "Federated Co-Op Announces Carbon Capture MOU with Whitecap Resources for Refinery, Ethanol Plant," *Pipeline Online*, October 21, 2021, <pipelineonline.ca/federated-co-op-announced-carbon-capture-mou-with-whitecap-resources-for-refinery-ethanol-plant/#/?playlistId=0&videoId=0>.
24 William DeKay, "FCL Embraces Carbon Capture," *The Western Producer*, November 4, 2021, <producer.com/news/fcl-embraces-carbon-capture/>.
25 Government of Canada, "Budget 2022: Clean Air and Strong Economy," April 7, 2022, <budget.gc.ca/2022/report-rapport/chap3-en.html>.
26 Adam Hunter, "Sask. Government, Opposition Disappointed Enhanced Oil Recovery Excluded from Federal Tax Credit," CBC News, April 15, 2022, <cbc.ca/news/canada/saskatchewan/sask-enchanced-oil-emissions-1.6420272>.
27 Zinchuk, "Federated Co-Op Announces."
28 Government of Saskatchewan, "Government of Saskatchewan Announces Carbon Capture Utilization and Storage Priorities," September 7, 2021, <saskatchewan.ca/government/news-and-media/2021/september/07/saskatchewan-announces-carbon-capture-utilization-and-storage-priorities>.

29 Cole Davenport, "Co-op Refinery Strikes Land Deal with City of Regina for Renewable Diesel Project," CTV News, November 3, 2021, <regina.ctvnews.ca/co-op-refinery-strikes-land-deal-with-city-of-regina-for-renewable-diesel-project-1.5651313>.
30 These internal estimates are supported by Sergios Karatzos, James D. McMillan, and Jack N. Saddler, *Summary of the Report: The Potential and Challenges of Drop-in Biofuels*, International Energy Agency — Bioenergy, 2014, 3 <task39.sites.olt.ubc.ca/files/2014/01/Task-39-drop-in-biofuels-report-summary-FINAL-14-July-2014-ecopy.pdf>.
31 Government of Canada, "Budget 2023: A Made-In-Canada-Plan," <budget.canada.ca/2023/pdf/budget-2023-en.pdf?fbclid=IwAR3Qqvl_q-qttg3DywNC5rJVKsl9az-JnHVXHOYMmyjtEEDU8vexkoS3aq-Y>, 110.
32 Government of Canada, "Budget 2023," 110.
33 Doug Mah, September 22, 2021, personal communication.
34 Brian Zinchuk, "Federated Co-Op CEO Explains Rationale Behind Putting its Upstream Oil Producing Assets up for Sale," *Pipeline Online*, October 21, 2021, <pipelineonline.ca/federated-co-op-ceo-explains-rationale-behind-putting-its-upstream-oil-producing-assets-up-for-sale/#/?playlistId=0&videoId=0>.
35 Laura Sciarpelletti, "Co-Op Refinery Complex Begins Talks with Unifor 594 over Upcoming Layoffs," CBC News, May 28, 2021, <cbc.ca/news/canada/saskatchewan/co-op-refinery-begins-talks-with-unifor-594-over-upcoming-layoffs-1.6045130>.
36 See Chapter 2 for passages where workers express this.
37 Chapters 1 and 9 outline the independent path charted Local 594 energy workers.
38 Email correspondence with Dr. Emily Eaton.
39 Roger Hayter, "'The War in the Woods': Post-Fordist Restructuring, Globalization, and the Contested Remapping of British Columbia's Forest Economy," *Annals of the Association of American Geographers* 93, no. 3 (2003): 706–29.
40 Darryn Snell and Peter Fairbrother, "Unions as Environmental Actors," *Transfer: European Review of Labour and Research* 16, no. 3 (2010): 411–24.
41 Karen Cooling, Marc Lee, Shannon Daub, and Jessie Singer, *Just Transition: Creating a Green Social Contract for BC's Resource Workers*, January, 2015, Canadian Centre for Policy Alternatives, <policyalternatives.ca/sites/default/files/uploads/publications/BC%20Office/2015/01/ccpa-bc_JustTransition_web.pdf>
42 Béla Galgóczi, *Just Transition Towards Environmentally Sustainable Economies and Societies for All*, International Labour Organization, 2018, <ilo.org/wcmsp5/groups/public/---ed_dialogue/---actrav/documents/publication/wcms_647648.pdf>
43 James Patrick Nugent, "Changing the Climate: Ecoliberalism, Green New Dealism, and the Struggle Over Green Jobs in Canada," *Labor Studies Journal* 36, no. 1 (2011): 63.
44 Shannon J. Daub, "Negotiating Sustainability: Climate Change Framing in the Communications, Energy and Paperworkers Union," *Symbolic interaction* 33, no. 1 (2010): 115–40.
45 Unifor Research Department, *Unifor Energy Policy: A Progressive Vision for Canada's Energy Future*, 2017, 60, <unifor.org/sites/default/files/legacy/documents/document/energy_policy_2017_eng_final_web.pdf>.
46 Inayat Singh and Alice Hopton, "Union Representing Energy Workers Backs Stronger Emissions Cuts — As Long as There's a Transition Plan," CBC News, April 27, 2021, <cbc.ca/news/science/climate-targets-transition-oil-energy-1.6000224>.

47 Hadrian Mertins-Kirkwood and Clay Duncalfe, *Roadmap to a Canadian Just Transition Act: A Path to a Clean and Inclusive Economy*, Canadian Centre for Policy Alternatives, 2021, 22.
48 Vanessa Corkal and Estan Beedell, "Making Good Green Jobs the Law: How Canada Can Build on International Best Practice to Advance Just Transition for All," International Institute for Sustainable Development, 2022, <iisd.org/publications/green-jobs-advance-canada-just-transition>.
49 International Labour Organization, *Guidelines for a Just Transition towards Environmentally Sustainable Economies and Societies for All*, 2015, <ilo.org/wcmsp5/groups/public/@ed_emp/@emp_ent/documents/publication/wcms_432859.pdf>.
50 Chapter 2 provides more depth about what 594 workers see as the best ways to advance a just transition through their workplaces.
51 International Labour Organization, "C155 — Occupational Safety and Health Convention," 1981, <ilo.org/dyn/normlex/en/f?p=NORMLEXPUB:12100:0::NO::P12100_ILO_CODE:C155>.
52 Samantha Smith, "Implementing a Just Transition: Leading Global Practices for Just Transition," Parkland Institute, March 11, 2022, see 29:40–30:10, <youtube.com/watch?v=xQN7ZfoJJfw>.
53 See Chapters 5 and 6 for more on the environmental and occupational health and safety record of the refinery.
54 Scott Moe, "Premier Scott Moe Welcomes Anti-Carbon Tax Convoy to Regina," *Sask Today*, April 3, 2019, <sasktoday.ca/south/opinion/letter-premier-scott-moe-welcomes-anti-carbon-tax-convoy-to-regina-4131409>.
55 City of Regina and Sustainability Solutions Group, *Energy & Sustainability Framework: Energy & Emissions Reduction Action Plan*, City of Regina, January 2022, <regina.ca/export/sites/Regina.ca/about-regina/renewable-regina/.galleries/pdfs/Energy-Sustainability-Framework.pdf>.
56 Natasha Bulowski, "Canada Decides Where to Put Some of its Coal Phaseout Money," *National Observer*, January 18, 2022, <nationalobserver.com/2022/01/18/news/canada-decides-where-put-coal-phaseout-money>.

9

TRANSITION PATHWAYS
Workers Before Profits

Emily Eaton, Andrew Stevens, and Sean Tucker

> I think that you are going to see a lot of energy workers in Saskatchewan that, after they've lost their job, and then you go back and ask them about just transition and they're going to be like: "Ah I wish I paid more attention. So you need to be involved … 'cause if you don't go that extra step, you're just, you're politically dead in the water. (Unifor Local 594 worker)

ONE YEAR AFTER THE LOCKOUT at the Co-op Refinery Complex ended, Federated Co-operatives Limited announced that it was committed to "reducing greenhouse gas emissions by 40 percent below 2015 levels by 2030" and that it was "aspiring to achieve net-zero emissions by 2050."[1] To do this, the company developed what it calls an "Energy Roadmap."[2] Under this plan, the CRC and one other FCL facility would establish the "single largest anthropogenic carbon sequestration project in the world," capturing 500,000 tonnes of carbon dioxide annually. Another key part of the plan involves a joint venture (with FCL maintaining 51 percent control) to construct and operate a canola-crushing facility that "will supply approximately 50 percent of the feedstock required for a 15,000-barrel-per-day renewable diesel plant" at the refinery.[3] The estimated total cost of these and other transition projects is about $4 billion.[4] In one of FCL's media releases, Saskatchewan premier Scott Moe hailed the renewable diesel facility "a win for the economy, a win for workers, families and communities, and a win for the environment."[5]

But workers should be concerned about what the planned energy "transition" means for them and the communities in which they live. Locked-out energy workers represented by Unifor Local 594 experienced first-hand what happens when industry charts a transition pathway governed by profits over the interests of labour. What these workers experienced was not a win.

The architects of the refinery's Energy Roadmap speculated that new facilities, under different operating structures like joint ventures, could very well be non-union.[6] A transition towards the low-carbon economy, the company insisted in 2021, informed the decision to lay off fifty-four unionized workers in the interest of securing "operational efficiencies …."[7] Taken together, these moves, and the attacks on the union and its pension, represent an *unjust* transition, whereby attempts to break the collective power of labour are part of the rhetoric of the "net-zero" future.

Transition away from fossil fuels is inevitable. Whether this transition is fast enough or adequately reduces the production and use of fossil fuels to avert a climate catastrophe is another matter, but new regulations and changes in consumer demand are already taking shape. Electric vehicle sales are growing at a rapid pace in many countries, "green" hydrogen plans are unfolding in important economies like Germany,[8] the US Inflation Reduction Act has committed hundreds of billions of dollars to incentivize the transition,[9] and China's massive investments into sustainable technology overshadow American spending.[10] The deployment of alternatives to fossil fuels are accelerating rapidly around the world.[11] While these technologies have not yet displaced significant amounts of fossil fuel consumption and use, they are projected to start eating into the proportion of fossil energy used worldwide in the very near future.[12] Economies of the Global South are also wrestling with transition plans, despite lacking the wealth and technical capacity of advanced industrial countries.[13] In Canada, important questions related to how the transition will unfold for workers in the country's oil and gas sector are not unlike what has been experienced in other resource industries, like logging and fisheries. So far, the history of resource-based transitions in Canada has been deeply unjust, with the working class shouldering the burden of an industry's unravelling without interventions. A deviation from this track record requires labour to secure a seat at the table to ensure that a worker- and equity-focused lens is applied to current transition policy, so that Canada can do its share to avert a deepening climate emergency. In Saskatchewan and other fossil fuel-intensive regions, this requires challenging industry's hegemonic narrative — or what political economists have labelled the fossil fuel industry's "regime of obstruction."[14]

The 2019–2020 lockout at the CRC is an example of one pathway to transition: a financially well off company appropriates federal government climate policy to undermine their workers' union, repeatedly forces workers to accept layoffs and pension concessions, and bars workers any role in steering the company's transformation. For their part, governments in Saskatchewan and Alberta — Canada's two largest oil-producing provinces — employ the convenient trope of the oil and gas worker to defend the interests of the industry, casting fossil fuel corporations as job creators, even though they know such jobs will begin to disappear in the future. For these provincial governments and fossil fuel companies, environmentalists and the federal government are mobilized as scapegoats for job losses and economic fallout associated with transition policies.

The absence of meaningful coalitions connecting the interests of other workers, unions, environmental groups, and the community at large weakened the capacity of Local 594 to build real political power. This lesson needs to be heeded. Governments of Canada's "petro-provinces" offer little leadership in terms of either protecting the rights of workers or aggressively ramping up renewable energy projects, retraining, and labour market planning.[15] In this scenario, organized labour lacks the power and agency to independently develop and advocate for policies that support good jobs in the energy sector of tomorrow. *If* this becomes the dominant pathway to transition, oil and gas workers will be denied a voice in transition, exposed to abrupt changes dictated by their employers, and left to individually navigate the uncertainty of labour markets. We believe there are better, more just pathways to transition Canada's oil and gas workers.

Unions, to be sure, are right to be suspicious of how the transition will be managed. Citing an interview with former business manager of the BC Insulators Union, Lee Loftus, Seth Klein draws attention to the disconnect between established policy and the lived reality facing displaced workers.[16] "Transition in our Canadian environment has been an absolute failure," Loftus says. "You know, if you take a look at fisheries, you take a look at forestry, you take a look at shipbuilding, you take a look at asbestos. The list goes on."[17] But Loftus also recognizes the duplicity of the oil and gas sector and their appeal for support from workers for fossil fuel projects. Industry, he argues, is willing to go to a non-union contractor if labour organizations fall short of supporting employer interests. Not to mention that the oil and gas industry has been shedding thousands of workers since a price decline in 2014 prompted firms to pursue "efficiencies" through automation, attrition, and the adoption of new technologies.[18] Since 2012, employment in the sector has fallen by some thirty thousand jobs.[19]

What, then, are the characteristics of a just transition for Canada's oil and gas workers? We argue that an equity-focused transition includes improving basic standards of employment, like occupational safety, and the maintenance and expansion of existing entitlements like pension plans; using the labour and employment relations regime to advance "transition" language and to tackle precarious work; strengthening environmental regulations that benefit the community at large; and the prevalence of an objective, well-informed media landscape that can hold industry, governments, and labour to account.

A JUST TRANSITION

The idea of "just transition" was pioneered in the 1970s by the US trade union movement in response to environmental regulations that resulted in the closure of producers of certain toxic chemicals.[20] The idea was that workers in industries affected by environmental regulation should be supported to take up new lines of decent work. Within the labour movement, the term is now mostly used in relation to the changes in employment spurred by clean energy transition and the need to support fossil fuel and other impacted workers. "Just transition" is, however, as much about revitalizing a labour movement as it is about charting a path that addresses existential environmental challenges and delivers high-paying jobs to skilled oil and gas workers — it also requires attention to social inequalities and solidarity between unions, community members, and environmental actors. Labour is one part of the path forward.

In the United States, one of the world's largest per-capita emitters of CO_2, some states are beginning to advance their own "just transition" programs to buffer regions and workers from the pains of moving away from fossil fuels. For example, in Colorado, millions of dollars are being funnelled into a dedicated Office of Just Transition to finance a Coal Transition Worker assistance program to provide coal workers and their families with money to cover apprenticeship and retraining, childcare services, and housing assistance.[21] Recently, trillions of US federal dollars to support new infrastructure might serve the same objective as part of a historic executive order tackling climate change.[22]

Beyond the US, interest in just transition for fossil fuel workers is growing. In fact, it was part of a featured session at the 2022 COP27 meetings in Egypt.[23] Germany is advancing ambitious supports for coal-producing regions like the Ruhr Valley, where employment in the sector has been declining for decades.[24] The European Commission is even establishing a Just Transition Mechanism to address transition's socioeconomic impacts, although the process may have been hastened because of Putin's invasion of Ukraine and Europe's resolve to end energy imports from Russia.[25] Global union federations like IndustriALL have similarly been part of the coalition of labour organizations calling for more action to assist with the transition.[26] That means partnering with unions in wealthy economies and in the Global South that are invested in the oil and gas industry, like Norway's LO and Iraq's electricity sector labour organizations, to advance renewable energy production in these respective countries.[27] Their goal is to establish tripartite initiatives that bridge the efforts of governments and workers to finance a departure from fossil fuels. Part of this rests on International Labour Organization (ILO) Guidelines that shape decent work agendas, namely workers' rights, social dialogue, and social protection.[28]

Some suggest that Canada's climate agenda is now being outstripped by the US and European plans, just as billions of dollars continue to be pumped into supporting the Canadian fossil fuel industry.[29] Given that the industry has been "propped up by an elaborate system of subsidies, privileges, and favorable regulations," as legal scholar Ted Hamilton argues,[30] then it would only make sense that public money should be shifted to support the interventions needed to advance the "just transition" and that those companies currently experiencing booming profits should be forced to pay their fair share.[31] The oil and gas sector holds significant liability through its network of pipelines, wells, mines, upgraders, refineries, and other infrastructure; part of holding it accountable could involve a just transition program employing fossil fuel workers to clean up the industry's pollution.

With Ottawa's recent announcement and implementation of new clean air regulations that will affect the oil and gas industry, and the progress made on just transition in other countries, the time is ripe for Canadian unions to advance their members' interests in the energy transition. Historically, some unions and union federations have functioned as environmental actors, engaging with ecological concerns like climate change, clean water, better occupational health and safety, and air quality emissions standards. But, as Snell and Fairbrother suggest, organized labour must navigate the often-contradictory pressures of ensuring job creation and environmental responsibility to realize this potential.[32] The figure of the oil worker in western Canada, by comparison, is one that supposedly champions industry, not their own interests or the interests of workers in general.

JOBS FOR, NOT VERSUS, THE ENVIRONMENT

The prognosis for the Earth's climate and ecosystems is increasingly bleak. The completion of this book coincided with record global temperatures, record ocean temperatures, and record forest fire activity in Canada, with over 25 million acres burned as of late July 2023.[33] One headline read: "Summer 2023 is screaming climate change."[34] A 2021 report from the Intergovernmental Panel on Climate Change (IPCC) laid bare a grim reality: "unless there are immediate, rapid and large-scale reductions in greenhouse gas emissions, limiting warming to close to 1.5°C or even 2°C will be beyond reach."[35] Among the scenarios that could unfold is runaway climate change, whereby the average temperature on the planet rises by 4°C by 2100 (and continuously higher thereafter), with the highest increases (+9 to +11°C) experienced in the Artic regions.[36] All current IPCC scenarios paint a picture of increasing temperature, more frequent severe weather events, quicker melting of glaciers, rising and warming seas, widespread species extinction, and changes to the land (e.g., permafrost melt).[37] Research also shows a connection between increased CO_2 emissions and social inequality, which furthers the claim that fossil fuel dependence is in need of radical change.[38]

While the direct and indirect impacts of climate change on humanity, animals, and ecosystems are grave, world leaders meeting in November 2022 at the UN Framework Convention on Climate Change Conference (COP27) were unable to agree on concrete ways to address the issue.[39] Fossil fuel industry lobbyists attending the conference, including eight from Canada, claimed they have "green" solutions and cautioned politicians against radical policy changes that they said will lead to job losses.[40] For critical sociologists like William Carroll, this deepens the crisis. "As fossil capital and its allies redouble their obstructive endeavours," he writes, "prospects for a just transition seem grim, and resistance may face sharper repression."[41] This right-wing energy consensus furthers the gulf between environmental concerns and economic development.

Pitting jobs against the environment has been powerful and persistent in the recent history of Canada and elsewhere, often setting workers and the labour movement against environmentalists who, among other things, are trying to reverse the size of the fossil fuel industry in order to arrest climate change. The Government of Alberta under then-premier Jason Kenney tried to further this divide by commissioning the Public Inquiry into anti-Alberta Energy Campaigns (the Allen Report) — only to find that much of "the reduced investment [in Alberta's oil and gas industry] is therefore due to natural market forces," along with anti-tar sands activism.[42] This frame positions workers' interests as one and the same as industry's — to continue business as usual with large profits flowing to capital while nature absorbs the waste.

In response to the threat that burning fossil fuels poses to our collective future, capital is attempting to "green" itself. This is evidenced by FCL's recent proposals for large-scale carbon capture and biodiesel projects, which are contingent on federal government support.[43] Nicholas Graham argues this "greening" of carbon extraction is part of "carbon capital's accumulation strategy,"[44] in which the industry attempts to stave off political and economic threats by skilfully rebranding to delay action. Indeed, in 2021, FCL signalled its commitment to fossil fuels with the purchase of 171 Husky gas stations in western Canada for $264 million, the largest retail acquisition in its history.[45] Our view is that FCL's roadmap will have little meaningful impact on overall carbon emissions reductions in part because the promised and hugely expensive carbon capture plans may always only ever be on the horizon; if they ever do arrive, they will be used to extract more oil in southeast Saskatchewan. In November of 2023, the International Energy Agency warned that carbon capture utilization and storage technologies cannot be used to offset the projected demand for fossil fuels. According to the Agency, "If oil and natural gas consumption were to evolve as projected under today's policy settings, this would require an inconceivable 32 billion tonnes of carbon captured for utilisation or storage by 2050, including 23 billion tonnes via direct air capture to limit the temperature rise to 1.5°C. The necessary carbon capture technologies would require 26 000 terawatt hours of electricity generation to operate in 2050, which is more than global electricity demand in 2022."[46] The existential threat of global climate change means the business-as-usual scenario, dressed up with token "low-carbon" projects, is no longer tenable as we look ahead to 2030 and beyond.

Characteristics of a Just Transition for Oil and Gas Workers in Canada

What, then, does a just transition for workers at Regina's CRC and other fossil fuel workers look like? We propose the following characteristics:

- Revaluation of worker interests as independent from the interests of their employers
- Strong protection for collective bargaining rights
- Active bargaining of transition
- Increasing community unionism and strategic cooperation with environmental groups
- Alliance building
- Holding fossil fuel corporations accountable for their pollution by requiring them to pay remediation and related costs
- Increased state support for rapid expansion of renewable energy sources, job re-training, cleanup of contaminated sites, and other measures to the advance the interests of workers and vulnerable communities

Worker Interests

FCL has shown an ability to adapt to a changing regulatory environment at the expense of workers. It and other companies will continue to adjust their businesses to extract profits from the labour of those who do the work, while undermining workers' only source of independent power, their union. Most Unifor 594 workers now see that the refinery's primary concern is profitability and increased control over labour. As a retired process operator emphasized, "They really seemed to go out of their way to get you down. To break you. I think that was the idea — to break you." Labour's interests are forced to take a back seat as the industry crafts its own "low-carbon" sustainability plan. Meanwhile, the political right has successfully captured the social licence to speak on behalf of energy workers in favour of pipelines and in opposition to climate policies like the carbon tax, clean fuel standards, and other federal programs aimed at taking the climate emergency seriously. But there was a time when oil and gas unions charted a path independent from corporations. A socially just transition requires workers and organized labour to map out strategies that advance their own interests. History can teach us much here, as can Canada's labour relations framework. Local 594's historic parent union, OCAW (the Oil, Chemical and Atomic Workers International Union) and then ECWU (the Energy and Chemical Workers Union of Canada), had engaged with the future of oil and gas work while developing their National Energy Policy in the late 1970s. At the time, labour unrest was caused by efforts by the energy sector to undermine existing employment conditions. Perhaps it is time to return to a model of engagement that involves a mixture of collaboration, resistance, and, when required, militancy. In some cases that meant pushing the boundaries of legal norms and engaging in acts of civil disobedience.

Labour Laws and Benefits

Unions representing energy workers must have firm legal footing from which to assert demands for a just transition. Laws that enable the use of replacement workers, alongside court decisions curtailing picketing, render picket lines ineffective and diminish the bargaining power of workers. Stronger protections for collective bargaining will allow workers to dedicate more time and effort to negotiating transition. As we saw with the CRC lockout, workers cannot do this when they are fighting in court and at their labour relations board for the very existence of their union. The president of the Saskatchewan Federation of Labour, Lori Johb, reflected on this: "Nothing about the lockout at the refinery was fair and [it was] absolutely about union busting."[47] The CRC's safety record could also serve to spur labour to raise concerns about industry regulations and workplace safety — issues that are of concern for all workers (see Chapter 6). As relatively privileged workers, refinery labour should establish bonds of solidarity with unions and the rank-and-file down through the supply chain, so that pickets and boycotts might disrupt revenue generation at the top of the value ladder.

Bargaining Transition

With stronger protections for collective bargaining and a sharp sense of their interests, unionized oil and gas workers can turn attention to developing and asserting a vision for jobs of the future. To be clear, that vision is for oil and gas workers to determine themselves. At a local level, joint worker-management transition committees would give workers a voice into the transition process, as suggested in Chapter 8.

A "just transition" must consider the sustainability (and availability) of legacy entitlements, such as unfunded pension liabilities shouldered by major fossil fuel companies, as the industry shrinks. Outside of oil and gas extraction and refining, there is little reason to believe that "green" jobs, like EV production, are inherently just. Tesla's repeated violation of US labour rights, and the struggle by American unions to organize battery assembly workers, is a reminder that "green capitalism" is still capitalism.[48] Even visions for just transition promoted by coalitions of social justice organizations, like the Leap Manifesto, pay too little attention to the precarity and relative low pay of many of the green service-oriented jobs they celebrate.[49] A social dialogue model creates some possibilities for a tripartite transition, but worker power is a necessary element of ensuring that labour is a meaningful partner in this exchange.

These and other issues related to transition will become more prominent in 2026, when the current collective bargaining agreement between the CRC and Local 594 expires, and in the early 2030s when presumably bargaining will take place again. Reflecting on the historic lockout of 2020, one 594 member noted: "I would say we gained a lot of solidarity, I would say that it was the biggest teambuilding event Unifor 594 has ever participated in. We showed how strong we can be." Worker solidarity will be critical to amassing sufficient power to effectively bargain transition in the coming decade.

Community Unionism and Forging Strategic Ties with Environmental Groups

We believe that unions capable of advancing social or community union frames of action are more powerful and better situated to underwrite initiatives needed to address the justice-based elements of transition.[50] This is a fundamental characteristic of the "just transition" for labour. Unlikely allies of ecological justice, such as Unifor or OCAW, can join this struggle by finding ways of partnering with community-based environmental organizations to make a transition feasible for their members.[51] The same must be said of environmental groups that seek to transition our economy away from fossil fuels but otherwise marginalize the needs and interests of workers in the process. For Canadian legal scholar David Doorey, climate policy "will need to coordinate with labour policy moving forward, and this coordination can be strengthened with closer ties between environmental law and labour law communities."[52]

The absence of broad and strong community links and the onset of the COVID-19 pandemic weakened Local 594's position as the 2020 lockout dragged on. And as courts and other institutions sided with FCL, and media coverage failed to more deeply explore issues like workers' pension and the energy transition, public opinion shifted against the union. Stronger community ties increase strength and the possibility of solidarity. Richard Hyman, for example, suggests that unions could deploy social movement and radical unionism in mobilizing politically to advance working-class interests.[53]

Even if oil and gas workers reject the idea that their interests are one and the same with the fossil fuel corporations, it is still unclear how they might come to understand themselves as allied with environmental action — and, importantly, how environmentalists might become better allies. In his book *Climate Change as Class War*, Matthew Huber suggests that a focus on production can unite ecological and union movements into a mass popular movement. Environmentalists need to focus much more on the fact that a small class of capitalists produce the vast majority of emissions as they charge ahead with private profit.[54] That means curbing criticism of fossil fuel workers and the labour of carbon extraction, turning attention instead to the power centres (and power brokers) of this industry. It also means engaging with and advocating for supports for workers — acting as allies for a just transition. A working-class ecological politics to assert democratic control over life's necessities is needed — or as Huber puts it, a "proletarian ecology."

Ecological catastrophes associated with the extraction, processing, and transportation of fossil fuels, like the Lac-Megantic rail disaster or the CRC's decades-long contribution to water pollution and poor (local) emissions standards, can serve to ignite solidarity building between unions, workers, and community organizations.[55] All parties play a role here in pushing municipal and provincial governments into strengthening environmental standards in a regime where voluntary regulation is the norm for fossil fuel companies. In South Africa, labour federations like COSATU are successfully addressing the pollution caused by the country's coal industry while also confronting the reality that mining is a significant employer in a country beset by poverty and high unemployment.[56] The BlueGreen Alliance in the US and Canada similarly attempts to build bridges over the ideological rift between ecological justice and workers' rights.[57] We see potential long-term benefits for both oil and gas workers and environmental groups through exploring strategic cooperation. But civil society movements cannot be left to advance this transition alone. State intervention is required to provide the adequate regulatory structure and financial support for this massive societal and technological undertaking.

Making the Corporations Pay

A growing movement is trying to hold fossil fuel corporations accountable for their climate pollution and responsible for funding transitions to the low-carbon future. Richard Heede at the Climate Accountability Institute has found that just twenty fossil fuel companies (both state-owned companies such as Saudi Aramco and Gazprom and invest-or-owned firms like Chevron, Exxon, BP, and Shell) have contributed more than one-third of total global GHG emissions since 1965.[58] Modelled after successful litigation against tobacco companies, municipalities, states, classes of affected people (especially youth), and others are bringing lawsuits against fossil fuel corporations for continuing to produce products they knew were harmful to individual and collective health and indeed for covering up those harmful effects for decades. According to the *Guardian* there were over two thousand legal cases focused on the climate crisis in 2022, which is double the number of legal challenges in the year 2015.[59] Many of these cases are against the world's largest oil companies, but some of them also target state laws for failing to protect people and the environment. The long-standing "polluter pays" principle is at the heart of the growing consensus that fossil fuel companies should bear the burden and costs of repairing the damage their products have done and fund the transition off of fossil fuels.

In Canada, however, federal and provincial governments are still providing healthy subsidies to fossil fuel corporations through incentives and tax credits, including a new one, introduced in 2022, that specifically incentivizes investment in carbon capture.[60] Critics suggest there are large loopholes in the new federal plan to phase out "inefficient" fossil fuel subsidies — for example, the framework for evaluating subsidies allows incentives for "abated" production (production that includes CCUS) and projects that have a credible plan to achieve net-zero emissions by 2030.[61] Instead of subsidizing fossil fuel corporations, the federal and provincial governments could be taxing them more and investing this money into a variety of measures that will bolster a just transition, including supports for workers and others in fossil fuel–dependent communities. Blue Green Canada has also called for companies to directly support impacted workers and communities as part of their commitment to just transition.[62]

State Support for Transition

Throughout the 1980s and 1990s, US labour organizations formulated the concept of "just transition" to identify programs required to support workers who had been displaced as a consequence of environmental policies and the closure of offending industries. This meant advancing economic policy initiatives aimed at creating new well-paying jobs, reskilling, and establishing a floor of rights and income for affected workers.[63] There is now a broader conversation about the need for more robust social supports and industrial policy in order to transition to a more sustainable and clean economic system.

Unions from around the world are advocating for their interests in the energy transition. The ILO proposes tripartite social dialogues between governments, employers, and workers, and these are already happening, even in places with deep connections to fossil fuels. But in Canada, discussions about just transition are still in their infancy. Industry groups like Energy Safety Canada recognize that many of the skilled jobs in the fossil fuel industry are transferable to geothermal, hydrogen, and lithium development, along with the maintenance of solar, wind, and biofuel assets.[64] But since displaced workers over the age of fifty-five and long-tenure employees are less likely to secure new forms of employment, it means that meaningful public policies are required to mitigate the hardship of transition-induced job losses. Union movements have also been advocating that new jobs in renewable and green industries need to provide good wages and union representation.[65] Part of this involves safeguarding the integrity of existing trades so that they do not get split and deskilled in the process — swapping out journeymen electricians for lower-skilled solar panel installers, for example, can threaten workplace safety, union coverage, wages, and more.

It is noteworthy here that most of the work in the oil and gas industry, by number of jobs, is in the scientific and administrative fields, not in extraction or processing.[66] But these numbers provide little comfort to communities, families, and workers who are dispossessed of their livelihoods. Construction trades unions in California have recognized that wages in oil and gas are nearly double statewide private sector averages, which casts doubt over the income potential for these workers should they transition to other industries. The reality is much different in the rural communities where there are few alternatives. Even labour-friendly economists sometimes do not fully capture the human cost of industry redundancies with their analyses that displaced fossil fuel workers can simply be absorbed into the regional economy or other industries.[67]

Lori Johb notes that some discussions have taken place with the Government of Saskatchewan about transition but more are needed. She cautions that there is a lot at stake:

> Workers who are directly affected by the phase out of fossil fuels have not felt like they have been heard by governments at any level and are not taking their concerns seriously. It is about much more than losing their jobs/careers and livelihood. It is also about communities as a whole and about their future. These are well-paid, stable jobs and the loss of them will devastate communities.[68]

Johb also criticized the mixed messaging from government and companies about coal mines in Saskatchewan; in recent years, these were shuttered, but a number are now hiring new workers, and some coal mines in Alberta are reopening.[69] This, she said, "sends a very confusing message to the workers."

To date, Canada has had one major subnational experience with just transition policy. This involved workers affected by then-Alberta NDP premier Rachel Notley's decisions to phase out coal-fired electricity in the province, which involved negotiated supports like pension bridging, retraining and relocation allowances, enhancements to EI benefits, and grants for community economic development. Coal-fired electricity was also phased out in Ontario between 2014 and 2021, but there was no negotiated package of just transition supports for affected workers.

CANADA'S ENERGY TRANSITION (SLOWLY) TAKES SHAPE

Workers and unions in Germany, Spain, Australia, and other fossil fuel extractive countries have engaged in government-led processes of transition and won policies that mitigate the hardship of winding down coal extraction either as a response to corporate efficiencies and/or environmental objectives. In the 2020s, Canada is playing catch up.

The Canada Energy Regulator (CER) finally projected Canada's energy landscape under scenarios of net-zero emissions. In *Canada's Energy Future 2023*, the CER considered three scenarios: one in which all nations strive towards net zero emissions by 2050, one in which Canada gets to net zero in 2050 but the rest of the world decreases their emissions more slowly, and a third where Canada fails to achieve net-zero emissions, implementing no new climate policies beyond what is currently in place.[70] The CER found that in both net-zero scenarios there is a decline in oil and gas production in Canada by 2050. In the first scenario, where all countries mobilize toward net zero, Canadian oil and gas production declines most — 76 percent for oil production and 68 percent for gas production below 2022 levels. However, both net-zero scenarios show Canadian oil and gas production beginning to decline by 2030, meaning that policies that do not plan for a contraction of oil and gas production in Canada are betting against the future of the planet and the human and non-human creatures that inhabit it.

In 2019 the federal government promised a Just Transition Act but did not deliver the legislation until June 2023, shying away from the term "just transition" after it became politicized by conservative politicians, especially by Danielle Smith in Alberta.[71] However, Bill C-50, the Sustainable Jobs Act,[72] accomplishes very little in its present form, amounting mostly to a "plan to create a plan" in 2025 (after the next federal election) and every five years thereafter.[73] The government states that these action plans advance the legislation's three main goals: economic growth, the creation of sustainable jobs, and support for workers and communities.

In addition, the legislation created two new bodies. The sustainable jobs partnership council is a fifteen-member volunteer council, co-chaired by a trade union representative who will engage stakeholders and offer advice and recommendations to ministers in annual reports. The Sustainable Jobs Secretariat is charged with developing the action plans and coordinating legislation implementation across the government.[74] While there is mention of the importance of social dialogue in the work of the Sustainable Jobs Partnership Council, there is as yet no indication that these processes will in any way approach the kind of dialogues advocated by the ILO, where governments, workers and employers would sit down sector by sector and negotiate a transition.[75]

The federal government's 2023 budget provides further insights into the contours of Canada's energy transition plan for workers. While nowhere in the 270-page document is the term "just transition" used, the government has linked "clean energy" tax credits to labour requirements and signalled its support for biofuels and hydrogen under the slogan "Clean Fuels for a Clean Economy." The document highlighted FCL's proposed "renewable biodiesel" plant and noted:

> In the months ahead, the federal government will engage with the biofuels industry to explore opportunities to promote its growth in Canada. This will include an examination of different support mechanisms that could support the sector in meeting the growing demand for low emissions fuels.[76]

An announced $520 million tax credit for CCUS over five years will include a labour requirement as will a similar hydrogen tax credit. The requirement specifies that "businesses must pay a total compensation package that equates to the prevailing wage," where the prevailing wage is "based on union compensation, including benefits and pension contributions from the most recent, widely applicable multi-employer collective bargaining agreement, or corresponding project labour agreements, in the jurisdiction within which relevant labour is employed."[77] While CCUS and hydrogen are often deployed to delay phasing out fossil fuels, we see the tying of these tax credits to labour requirements as a positive step and anticipate biofuels tax credits will fit into this regime. More rigorous standards are needed, though, as none of FCL's anti-labour actions would disqualify it from receiving tens of millions of dollars in federal tax credits.

Appropriate just transition policy includes robust industrial planning with a large role for the federal government in steering industrial transition as well as social programs and safety nets that will support a wide variety of workers and people broadly affected by energy transition. The Regional Energy and Resource Tables, introduced in 2022, could play a pivotal role in establishing policies and supports relevant to local economies. Nine provinces and territories had joined the regional roundtables by mid-2023, with Saskatchewan, Alberta, Nunavut, and Quebec holding out on working with the federal government.[78] Pursuing a just transition will require a dramatic shift from the right-wing, anti-climate science that dominates the conversation about fossil fuels and energy in western Canada's oil-producing regions.

TOWARDS A NEW POLITICS OF TRANSITION IN WESTERN CANADA

Challenging right-wing hegemony and its grip on the fossil fuel narrative is a major task embedded within a just transition strategy. In western Canada, the very notion of energy transition, never mind a just transition, is contested by politicians, political parties, and powerful individuals that defend at all cost the fossil fuel economy. It primarily accounts for why there was no discussion of climate change and energy transition before, during, or after the 2019–2020 lockout.[79] The fossil fuel narrative persists years after the dispute: one of Saskatchewan's stated 2030 goals remains to "increase oil production by 25 per cent to 600,000 barrels per day" and adaptation is the province's de facto approach to climate change.[80] But the writing is on the wall and sooner or later Saskatchewan (and Alberta) will need to acknowledge the seriousness of climate change and take significant steps to cut their greenhouse gas emissions.

In both Saskatchewan and Alberta, centrist New Democratic Parties compete with the political right for legitimacy and support from the fossil fuel industry. They do so by paying lip-service to "net zero" and "sustainability" while seemingly disengaging from efforts to craft a "just transition" policy. This is done to secure public support for an industry that is cast as the life blood of the region.[81] As Nesbitt and Leedham (Chapter 7, this collection) demonstrate, Canada's under-resourced media landscape fails to adequately confront extractive populism, allowing employer narratives to define public understanding of a dispute and an industry. A counterhegemonic movement will need communicative prowess to generate alternative, more holistic accounts and narratives.

Public opinion, however, is remarkably split despite the narrative that the entire region must pay fealty to oil and gas. Polls in Alberta reveal that there is strong support for the province to achieve net-zero carbon emissions by 2050,[82] yet residents there also support legal challenges against President Joe Biden's decision to shut down the Keystone XL project.[83] Research in Saskatchewan yields a similar result. Residents are supportive of a transition to renewable energy and foresee a winding down of fossil fuels over the next half-century.[84] However, as Andrea Olive, Emily Eaton, and Randy Besco conclude in their report for the Canadian Centre for Policy Alternatives, "residents of oil producing communities frame their complaints within an overall acceptance and identification with the oil industry and its discourses on energy and climate change."[85] Lori Johb mirrored the position of many of the 594 members who were interviewed for this book: "I believe there will be a phase out," Johb remarked, "however, not enough has been done to find adequate and sufficient replacement to ensure there is an energy source that can replace fossil fuels."[86]

What is most problematic — and relevant — to the refinery lockout is that conservative tendencies have near absolute hegemony over the issue in western Canada — part of Gunster's extractive populism.[87] But oil labour is not inherently conservative, as our discussions with Local 594 members revealed and as other fossil fuel economies like Norway demonstrate. And there was a time when Saskatchewan's NDP aligned oil with public ownership under Premier Allan Blakeney and the formation of SaskOil in 1973.[88] There are alternatives, and workers and their unions have the capacity to construct political frameworks and talk about good jobs and environmentalism.[89] A genuine shift towards a "just transition" framework will take political mobilization within the ranks of energy unions and energy workers more broadly. Labour has a role to play in creating this alternative discourse through engagement and organizing.

The 2020s mark the beginning of a period of accelerating transition away from fossil fuels to non-greenhouse gas–emitting forms of energy. While the nature, scope, and speed of this change is yet unknown, we know that it is happening now and that it will, over time, have a significant impact on oil and gas workers, their families, and their communities. In this context, the 2019–2020 lockout at the CRC was a bellwether event. However, surprisingly absent from past and current accounts of the dispute is any discussion about the company's stated reason for the lockout: the need for transition. While the pathways to a just transition for fossil fuel workers in Canada are still somewhat unclear, awareness and mobilization among these workers is absolutely necessary to creating clarity and action.

Endnotes

1   FCL, "FCL Exploring Carbon Capture with Whitecap Resources to Help Meet New Emissions Targets," October 21, 2021, <fcl.crs/news-reports/news/article/fcl-exploring-carbon-capture-with-whitecap-to-meet-emissions>.
2   FCL, "Fuelling a Sustainable Future," 2023, <fuel.crs/commercial/detail/fuelling-a-sustainable-future>.
3   FCL, "FCL to Enter Joint Venture to Construct Integrated Agriculture Complex," January 17, 2022, <fcl.crs/news-reports/news/article/FCL-to-construct-Integrated-Agriculture-Complex>.
4   Brian Cross, "FCL Unveils 'Energy Roadmap,'" *Western Producer*, March 2, 2023, <producer.com/news/fcl-unveils-energy-road-map/>.
5   Cross, "FCL Unveils 'Energy Roadmap.'"
6   Email correspondence with Dr. Emily Eaton.
7   FCL, "The Co-op Refinery Complex to Proceed with Involuntary Separations," October 4, 2021, <fcl.crs/news-reports/news/article/The-Co-op-Refinery-Complex-to-Proceed-with-Involuntary-Separations>.
8   International Energy Agency, "Package for the Future: Hydrogen Strategy," May 25, 2023, <iea.org/policies/11561-package-for-the-future-hydrogen-strategy>.
9   Environmental Protection Agency, "Summary of Inflation Reduction Act Provisions Related to Renewable Energy," June 1, 2023, <epa.gov/green-power-markets/summary-inflation-reduction-act-provisions-related-renewable-energy>.
10 Sara Schonhardt, "China Invests $546 Billion in Clean Energy, Far Surpassing the US," *Scientific American*, January 30, 2023, <scientificamerican.com/article/china-invests-546-billion-in-clean-energy-far-surpassing-the-u-s/>.
11 International Energy Agency, "Global Government Spending on Clean Energy Transitions Rises to USD 1.2 Trillion since the Start of the Pandemic, Spurred by Energy Security Concerns," December 9, 2022, <iea.org/news/global-government-spending-on-clean-energy-transitions-rises-to-usd-1-2-trillion-since-the-start-of-the-pandemic-spurred-by-energy-security-concerns>.
12 Liam Denning, "Keeping the Lights On Is About to Get Less Deadly," Bloomberg, May 9, 2023, <bloomberg.com/opinion/articles/2023-05-09/keeping-lights-on-is-about-to-get-less-deadly-as-emissions-peak?leadSource=uverify%20wall>
13 Kim Harrisberg, "Can South Africa Become a Model for Developing Nations Ditching Coal?" *Global Citizen*, September 30, 2021, <globalcitizen.org/en/content/south-africa-coal-fossil-fuels-just-transition/>.
14 William Carroll, ed., *Regimes of Obstruction: How Corporate Power Blocks Energy Democracy* (Edmonton: Athabasca University Press, 2021).
15 Emma Graney, "Alberta to Pause New Solar and Wind Power Projects for Six Months amid Review of End-of-life Rules," *Globe and Mail*, August 3, 2023.

16 Seth Klein, *A Good War: Mobilizing Canada for the Climate Emergency* (Vancouver: ECW Press, 2020), 228.
17 Klein, *A Good War*, 228.
18 Lewis Lai, "Supporting Young Oil and Gas Workers in Alberta: Lessons from Just Transition" (unpublished master's thesis, Simon Fraser University, 2020).
19 Statistics Canada, "Job Displacement in the Oil and Gas Industry in Canada" (Ottawa: Statistics Canada, 2020). https://www150.statcan.gc.ca/n1/pub/11-627-m/11-627-m2020068-eng.htm
20 Peter Newell and Dustin Mulvaney, "The Political Economy of the 'Just Transition,'" *The Geographical Journal* 179, no. 2 (2013): 132–40.
21 Chase Woodruff, "As Coal Burning Goes Away in Colorado, Money for Coal Workers Goes Up," *Colorado Newsline,* April 30, 2022, <coloradonewsline.com/2022/04/30/just-transition-colorado-coal-workers-rural-communities-advanced/>; The White House, "Executive Order on Tackling the Climate Crisis at Home and Abroad" (Washington, DC: White House, 2021), <whitehouse.gov/briefing-room/presidential-actions/2021/01/27/executive-order-on-tackling-the-climate-crisis-at-home-and-abroad/>.
22 Ella Nilsen, "Joe Biden's $2 Trillion Infrastructure and Jobs Plan, Explained," *Vox,* March 31, 2021, <vox.com/2021/3/31/22357179/biden-two-trillion-infrastructure-jobs-plan-explained>.
23 *Roundtable on "Just Transition,"* November 7, 2022, <cop27.eg/assets/files/days/COP27%20JUST%20TRANSITION-DOC-01-EGY-10-22-EN.pdf>.
24 Lili Pike, "What Should Coal Communities Do When Power Plants Shut Down? Ask Germany," *Vox,* March 31, 2021, <vox.com/energy-and-environment/22349104/coal-climate-change-biden-infrastructure-plan-germany-just-transition>.
25 "The Just Transition Mechanism: Making Sure No One is Left Behind," European Commission, <ec.europa.eu/info/strategy/priorities-2019-2024/european-green-deal/finance-and-green-deal/just-transition-mechanism_en>; Reuters, "Germany Aims to Get 100% of Energy from Renewable Sources by 2035," February 28, 2022, <reuters.com/business/sustainable-business/germany-aims-get-100-energy-renewable-sources-by-2035-2022-02-28/>.
26 IndustriALL, "Unions Want Social Dialogue on the Just Transition for Workers," August 4, 2022, <industriall-union.org/unions-want-inclusive-social-dialogue-on-the-just-transition-for-workers-0>.
27 IndustriALL, "Unions want."
28 Samantha Smith, *Just Transition: A Report for the* OECD (Brussels: Just Transition Centre, 2017).
29 Dale Marshall, "It's Not About Canada. Biden is Getting Real About Fossil Fuels," *Policy Options,* February 26, 2021, <policyoptions.irpp.org/magazines/february-2021/its-not-about-canada-biden-is-getting-real-about-fossil-fuels/>.
30 Ted Hamilton, *Beyond Fossil Law: Climate, Courts and the Fight for a Sustainable Future* (New York: OR Books, 2022), 156.
31 Kyle Bakx, "Historic Profits in Oilpatch on Track to Continue as Global Oil Demand Set to Jump Yet Again," CBC News, February 16, 2023, <cbc.ca/news/canada/calgary/bakx-oil-profit-cashflow-climate-iea-1.6750496>.
32 Darryn Snell and Peter Fairbrother, "Unions as Environmental Actors," *Transfer* 16, no. 3 (2010): 411–24.

33 Matt McGrath, "Climate Change: World's Hottest Day Since Records Began," BBC News, July 4, 2023, <bbc.com/news/science-environment-66104822>; Helena Horton, "Ocean Surface Hits Highest Ever Recorded Temperature and Set to Rise Further," *Guardian*, August, 4, 2023, <theguardian.com/environment/2023/aug/04/oceans-hit-highest-ever-recorded-temperature>; Nadja Popovich, "How Canada's Record Wildfires Got So Bad, So Fast," *New York Times*, July 18, 2023.
34 Bob Weber, "'Something's Changed': Summer 2023 is Screaming Climate Change, Scientists Say," CBC News, August 5, 2023, <cbc.ca/news/canada/calgary/climate-change-something-changed-summer-2023-canada-1.6929271>.
35 Intergovernmental Panel on Climate Change, "Climate Change Widespread, Rapid, and Intensifying — IPCC," August 9, 2021, <ipcc.ch/2021/08/09/ar6-wg1-20210809-pr/>.
36 IPCC, "Climate Change Widespread"; M. Collins, R. Knutti, J. Arblaster, et al., "Long-term Climate Change: Projections, Commitments and Irreversibility," in *Climate Change 2013: The Physical Science Basis. Contribution of Working Group I to the Fifth Assessment Report of the Intergovernmental Panel on Climate Change*, 2013, <ipcc.ch/site/assets/uploads/2018/02/WG1AR5_Chapter12_FINAL.pdf>.
37 H.O. Pörtner, D.C. Roberts, E.S. Poloczanska, et al., "IPCC, 2022: Summary for Policymakers," in *Climate Change 2022: Impacts, Adaptation and Vulnerability. Contribution of Working Group II to the Sixth Assessment Report of the Intergovernmental Panel on Climate Change*, 2023, 3–33, <ipcc.ch/report/ar6/wg2/>.
38 L. Chancel and Thomas Piketty, *Carbon and Inequality: From Kyoto to Paris* (Paris: Paris School of Economics, 2015).
39 *Roundtable on "Just Transition,"* November 7, 2022.
40 Matt McGrath, "COP27: Sharp Rise in Fossil Fuel Industry Delegates at Climate Summit," BBC News, November 10, 2022, <bbc.com/news/science-environment-63571610>.
41 William K. Carroll, "Conclusion: Prospects for Energy Democracy in the Face of Passive Revolution," in *Regime of Obstruction: How Corporate Power Blocks Energy Democracy*, ed. William K. Carroll (Edmonton: AU Press, 2021), 487.
42 Government of Alberta, *Report of the Public Inquiry into Anti-Alberta Energy Campaigns* (Edmonton: Government of Alberta, 2021), 13.
43 FCL, "FCL Purchases True North's Assets," April 9, 2021, <fcl.crs/news-reports/news/article/fcl-purchases-true-norths-assets>.
44 Nicolas Graham, "Fossil Knowledge Networks: Science, Ecology, and the "Greening" of Carbon Extractive Development," *Studies in Political Economy* 101 (2020): 94.
45 FCL, "Co-op Investing in Western Canada with Retail Fuel Sites Acquisition," November 30, 2021, <fcl.crs/news-reports/news/article/co-op-investing-in-western-canada-with-retail-fuel-sites-acquisition>.
46 International Energy Agency, "The Oil and Gas Industry in Net Zero Transitions: Executive Summary," 2023, www.iea.org/reports/the-oil-and-gas-industry-in-net-zero-transitions/executive-summary.
47 Email correspondence with Sean Tucker, June 27, 2022.
48 Dan DiMaggio, "Battery Jobs Must Be Good-Paying Union Jobs, Says New UAW president," *Labor Notes*, May 18, 2023, <labornotes.org/2023/05/battery-jobs-must-be-good-paying-union-jobs-says-new-uaw-president>; Daniel Wiessner, "Tesla Broke US Labor Law By Silencing Workers, Official Rules," Reuters, April 26, 2023,

<reuters.com/business/autos-transportation/tesla-broke-us-labor-law-by-silencing-workers-official-rules-2023-04-26/>.
49 *Leap Manifesto: A Call for a Canada Based on Caring for Earth and One Another*, <leapmanifesto.org/en/the-leap-manifesto/>.
50 Geoff Evans and Liam Phelan, "Transition to a Post-Carbon Society: Linking Environmental Justice and Just Transition Discourses," *Energy Policy* 99 (2016): 329–39.
51 Jim Young, "Just Transition: A New Approach to Jobs vs. Environment," *Working USA* 2, no. 2 (1998): 42–48.
52 David J. Doorey, "Just Transitions Law: Putting Labour Law to Work on Climate Change," *Journal of Environmental Law and Practice* 30, no. 2 (2017): 201–39.
53 Richard Hyman, *Understanding European Trade Unionism: Between Market, Class and Society* (London: Sage, 2001).
54 Matthew Huber, *Climate Change as Class War: Building Socialism on a Warming Planet* (London: Verso Books. 2022).
55 Bruce Campbell, *The Lac-Megantic Rail Disaster: Public Betrayal, Justice Denied* (Toronto: James Lorimer Company Ltd., 2018).
56 Harrisberg, "Can South Africa Become a Model for Developing Nations Ditching Coal?"
57 BlueGreen Alliance, "About Us," <bluegreenalliance.org/>.
58 Matthew Taylor and Jonathan Watts, "Revealed: The 20 Firms Behind a Third of All Carbon Emissions," *Guardian*, October 9, 2019, <theguardian.com/environment/2019/oct/09/revealed-20-firms-third-carbon-emissions>.
59 Dharna Noor, "'Game Changing': Spate of US Lawsuits Calls Big Oil to Account for Climate Crisis," *Guardian* June 7, 2023, <theguardian.com/us-news/2023/jun/07/climate-crisis-big-oil-lawsuits-constitution>.
60 Government of Canada, "Additional Design Features of the Investment Tax Credit for Carbon Capture, Utilization and Storage: Recovery Mechanism, Climate Risk Disclosure, and Knowledge Sharing (Ottawa: Department of Finance, 2022), <canada.ca/en/department-finance/news/2022/08/additional-design-features-of-the-investment-tax-credit-for-carbon-capture-utilization-and-storage-recovery-mechanism-climate-risk-disclosure-and-k.html>.
61 Thomas Gunton, David Wheeler, Kyla Tienhaara, "Trudeau Government's Plan to End Fossil Fuel Subsidies Does Not Actually End a Single One," *Globe and Mail*, August 2, 2023, <theglobeandmail.com/business/commentary/article-trudeau-fossil-fuel-subsidies/?utm_medium=Referrer:+Social+Network+/+Media&utm_campaign=Shared+Web+Article+Links>.
62 J. Kirkpatrick, "Climate Plans Must Include Just Transition for Environment and Economy to Thrive," Blue Green Canada, February 24, 2016, <bluegreencanada.ca/press-release/climate-plans-must-include-just-transition-for-environment-and-economy-to-thrive/>.
63 David McKie, *Labour Market Outlook 2021 to 2023: Canada's Oil and Gas Industry* (PetroLMI, March 2021), <documentcloud.org/documents/20534517-labour-market-outlook-2021-to-2023-final#document/p4/a2025707>.
64 McKie, *Labour Market Outlook 2021 to 2023: Canada's Oil and Gas Industry*.
65 Canadian Labour Congress, "Canada's Unions: Canadian Sustainable Jobs Act an Unprecedented Opportunity for Collaboration," June 14, 2023, <canadianlabour.ca/canadas-unions-canadian-sustainable-jobs-act-an-unprecedented-opportunity-for-collaboration/>.

66 Statistics Canada, "Employment Characteristics for the Oil and Gas Sector," August 26, 2021, <www150.statcan.gc.ca/n1/pub/11-627-m/11-627-m2021063-eng.htm>.
67 Jim Stanford, *Employment Transitions and the Phase-out of Fossil Fuels* (Vancouver: Centre for Future Work, 2021).
68 Email correspondence with Sean Tucker, June 27, 2022.
69 Trina Moyles, "In Alberta's Rocky Mountains, an Australian-owned Coal Mine is Quietly Forging Ahead," *The Narwhal*, May 25, 2023, <thenarwhal.ca/grande-cache-coal-mine-alberta/>.
70 Canada Energy Regulator, *Canada's Energy Future 2023: Energy Supply and Demand Projections to 2050*, 2023, 13, <cer-rec.gc.ca/en/data-analysis/canada-energy-future/2023/canada-energy-futures-2023.pdf>.
71 Jason Markusoff, Danielle Smith, "'Just Transitions,' and What Lies Beyond Truth," CBC News, January 20, 2023, <cbc.ca/news/canada/calgary/smith-just-transition-jobs-claim-lies-beyond-truth-1.6720064>.
72 Bill C-50, An Act Respecting Accountability, Transparency and Engagement to Support The Creation of Sustainable Jobs for Workers and Economic Growth in a Net-Zero Economy, 1st sess., 44th Parliament, June 15, 2023, <parl.ca/DocumentViewer/en/44-1/bill/C-50/first-reading>.
73 Hadrian Mertins-Kirkwood, "Sustainable Jobs Act: Another Plan to Make a Plan," *The Monitor*, Canadian Centre for Policy Alternatives, June 22, 2023, <monitormag.ca/articles/sustainable-jobs-act-another-plan-to-make-a-plan/>.
74 Mertins-Kirkwood, "Sustainable Jobs Act."
75 ILO, *Guidelines for a Just Transition towards Environmentally Sustainable Economies and Societies for All*, 2015, <ilo.org/wcmsp5/groups/public/@ed_emp/@emp_ent/documents/publication/wcms_432859.pdf>.
76 Government of Canada, "Budget 2023: A Made-In-Canada-Plan," <budget.canada.ca/2023/pdf/budget-2023-en.pdf?fbclid=IwAR3Qqvl_q-qttg3DywNC5rJVKsl9az-JnHVXHOYMmyjtEEDU8vexkoS3aq-Y>, 89.
77 Government of Canada, "Budget 2023," 96.
78 Jeremy Simes, "Wilkinson Urges Collaboration after Saskatchewan Rejects Federal Energy Table," *Toronto Star*, June 8, 2023, <thestar.com/news/canada/2023/06/08/wilkinson-urges-collaboration-after-saskatchewan-rejects-federal-energy-table.html>.
79 Jeremy Simes, "Workers Demand Clarity as Sask. Weighs Future of Coal Power Stations," *Regina Leader-Post*, January 16, 2023, <leaderpost.com/news/saskatchewan/workers-demand-clarity-as-sask-weighs-future-of-coal-power-stations>.
80 Government of Saskatchewan, "30 Goals for 2030," 2020, <saskatchewan.ca/government/budget-planning-and-reporting/plan-for-growth/30-goals-for-2030>.
81 Emily Eaton and Simon Enoch, "Oil's Rural Reach: Social License in Saskatchewan's Oil-producing Communities," *Canadian Journal of Communication* 43 (2018): 53–74.
82 Pembina Institute, "Two Thirds of Albertans Support Reaching Net-Zero Emissions by 2050," January 15, 2021, <pembina.org/media-release/two-thirds-albertans-support-reaching-net-zero-emissions-2050>.
83 David Korzinski, "Pipe(line) dream? Albertans Want Ottawa to Keep Fighting for Keystone XL; But Most Canadians Say It's Time to 'Move On,'" Angus Reid Institute, January 26, 2021, <angusreid.org/keystone-biden-trudeau/>.
84 Andrea Olive, Emily Eaton, and Randy Besco, *Winds of Change*, April 2018,

Canadian Centre for Policy Alternatives, <policyalternatives.ca/sites/default/files/uploads/publications/Saskatchewan%20Office/2018/04/Winds%20of%20Change.pdf>.

85 Olive, Eaton, and Besco, *Winds of Change*, 7.

86 Email correspondence with Sean Tucker, June 27, 2022.

87 Shane Gunster, "Extractive Populism and the Future of Canada," *The Monitor*, Canadian Centre for Policy Alternatives, July 2, 2019, <policyalternatives.ca/publications/monitor/extractive-populism-and-future-canada>.

88 Emily Eaton and David Gray-Donald, "Could an Episode from Saskatchewan's Socialist Past Be the Answer to the Climate Crisis and Demands for Decolonization?" *Briarpatch Magazine*, April 2018, <briarpatchmagazine.com/articles/view/socializing-and-decolonizing-saskatchewans-oil>.

89 Andreas Ytterstad, Camilla Houeland, and David Jordhus-Lier, "Heroes of the Day after Tomorrow: 'The oil worker' in Norwegian Climate Coverage 2017–2021," *Journalism Practice* 16, no. 2–3 (2021): 1–17.

INDEX

Aamjiwnaang First Nation, 106
actuarial evaluations,
    employer claims, 31, 43nn23,26, 44n30
    shifts in practice, 26–7, 31, 43n29, 45n56
AFIMAC (private security force), 49, 156–9, 138n55, 164n45
AGT Foods, 108, 172
air pollution,
    CRC emissions, 89–91, 96, 102–5, 123
    monitoring of, 102, 106–8, 124, 194
    odours, 107–8
Alberta, 177, 202–3, 206
    oilsands production, support for, 103, 191
    secondary pickets in, 80, 150, 158
    separatism in, 13–14, 150, 195, 205
anti-unionism, 74, 149, 160–1, 182
    governments' and employers', 10, 52–3, 70, 204
    media, 50, 146
arbitration, 175
    Unifor request for binding, 15, 79–80
    see also mediation
asbestos exposure, 119–20, 192

Banda, Scott, 12, 151–2, 171
    on CRC culture, 62, 117–18, 121
    on pension concessions, 7, 54–5
    on police intervention, 77, 79
    right-wing alliances, 150, 156, 158
bargaining, *see* collective bargaining
benzene, 91, 104, 120
Bexte, Keean, 158
Beyond Oil & Gas Alliance, 168
biodiesel, 58, 108, 171–3, 180–3, 195, 204
biofuels, 167, 201
    FCL commitments to use, 3, 108, 171–3, 195, 204
Bittman, Kevin, 63, 74, 78, 81, 129, 151

bitumen exports, 5
Black, Conrad, 146–7
Blue Green Canada, 178, 182, 201
bomb threat, 13, 86n48, 131
    media coverage of, 152, 155–6, 159
boycotting, 9, 197
    Unifor calls for, 12, 34
Briarpatch Magazine, 157, 159

caltrops, alleged use of, 13, 129, 153
Canada Energy Regulator (CER) net-zero scenarios, 203
Canada Pension Plan (CPP) 24, 29
Canadian Association of Petroleum Producers (CAPP), 124
    lobbying and campaigning of, 6, 170, 183
Canadian Auto Workers, 28, 31, 176–7
Canadian Fuels Association, 109, 119, 170
Canadian Labour Congress, 13, 177–8
canola (for biodiesel), 108, 172, 189
capital, 92, 182
    assets, 53
    carbon, 5–6, 195
    green technology, 170–2, 195
    investment, 5, 170–1
    mobility, 25, 170–1
    state protection of, 16, 49, 52, 69–70
capitalism,
    CRC actions and, 70, 199
    green, 170–2, 198
    neoliberal, 24–5, 199
    preserving power dynamics of, 70, 81–2
carbon capture, utilization, and storage (CCUS), 58, 167–9, 172–3
    FCL commitments to use, 3, 195
    strategies for integrating, 180–3, 195–6, 200–1, 204
    Weyburn project, 110, 171

214   Unjust Transition

carbon dioxide, 192–4
    atmospheric concentration of, 3, 167
    CRC emissions of, 3, 55, 90, 104, 110
    sequestration, 169–74, 189
Carroll, William, 195
Carter, Angela, 3, 5
city council, Regina,
    CRC relations with, 14, 93–102, 121–3 131, 139n69
    oil and gas hegemony versus, 5–6, 108–10, 131–2
    planning, 93–4, 104–5, 123, 172, 180
    trucker anti-union appeals to, 12–13
    worker camp land leasing, 11, 52–3, 73, 127, 157
class,
    consciousness, 23, 47
    power, shifting, 27, 38–40
    reinforcing hierarchies of, 50, 69–70
    struggle, 70–1
    working, 40, 70–1, 160, 190, 199
Clean Air Act, 102–3
climate emergency, 205–6
    deepening, 1, 3, 165–8, 177, 182, 191–4
    fossil fuel industry responses to, 1–2, 23, 41, 170–4, 195–7
    just transition in, 184, 200
    lack of media attention, 155, 165–6
    policymaking and, 10, 55, 176–82, 193–4, 199, 203
    regulatory frameworks for, 109–10, 166–7, 190
coal production, 183, 200, 202–3
    commitments to transition from, 168, 177–8, 193
collective agreement, Local 594: 141n85
    co-operative principles, 6, 48, 62
    FCL narratives on, 174
    worker losses and restrictions in, 28, 35, 62, 65–6, 71
collective bargaining,
    agreement (CBA), *see* collective agreement, Local 594
    bad faith, 15, 47, 80–1, 134
    commencement of, 7, 30–1, 48
    concession, 24–5, 31–4, 41, 84n18
    CRC actions outside of, 174–5
    CRC first round (2016–2017), 31–3, 36, 122, 126, 131, 144
    CRC second round (2019), 34–7, 127–8, 166
    employer pressure during, 7, 10–12, 14–16, 28–31, 127
    groundwork for protracted dispute in, 10, 22–3, 31
    just transition, negotiating, 174–5, 180, 196–7, 204
    on master operator position, 47, 69, 122, 134, 175
    media coverage of, 50, 144–5, 152, 157
    national-pattern, 9–10
    on pensions, *see* pension plans
    right to, 49, 71, 196–7
    union strength during, 37–9, 42, 63, 68, 78–9, 196–200
Communications, Energy and Paperworkers (CEP) union, 9, 31, 176–7
community, local, 56, 198
    divisions, 1, 6, 13, 176, 191
    media coverage of, 142–3, 156, 161, 192
    refinery health impacts on, 90–6, 110, 123, 199–200
    safety risks to, 118, 121–6
concessions, pension,
    employer demands, 2, 8–11, 14–17, 37–8, 118
    employer justification of, 2, 7, 80, 174, 179, 191
    FCL bringing back withdrawn, 44n43, 79
    lockout due to, 22, 72–3, 80
    significant, 23, 31, 33–4, 146, 155
    union defeat in, 32–3, 69, 81, 84n18, 155
Conference of the Parties (COP), 165, 168, 193–4
Conservative Party of Canada,
    politicians, 53, 158
    support for oil and gas industry, 6, 102
conservativism, political,
    anti-unionism and, 28, 72, 81, 144, 146–8
    citizen, 24, 52
    government, 5, 72, 81, 158, 203
    narratives on fossil fuel workers, 6, 28, 52, 66

oil and gas industry and, 26–8, 206
right-wing movements and, 14
see also Saskatchewan Party
Consumers' Co-operative Refineries
  Limited (CCRL), 2, 43n26, 93,
  103–4, 129
constitutional rights, workers', 16, 68,
  70–1
  employers' rights versus, 72, 75–8,
    81–2, 84–5
  freedoms of expression and association, 68, 70–1, 76–7, 83, 86n48
contribution holidays, employer, 26, 30,
  37, 43nn23–4
Co-operative Commonwealth Federation
  (CCF), 5, 9, 24, 29, 94
co-operative principles,
  in collective agreement, 62
  FCL/CRC legacy, 2, 19n32, 29, 73, 93,
    144
  FCL transition away from, 2, 6–9, 23,
    48–9, 70, 125, 158
  workers' shattered faith in, 10, 16,
    62–4, 66, 81
co-operatives,
  CRC financial position among, 8, 23,
    73, 96
  workers' shattered faith in, 10, 16,
    62–4, 66, 81
Co-op Refinery Complex (CRC), 46
  bad-faith actions, 15, 47, 69, 76,
    80–1, 134
  bargaining with union, *see* collective
    bargaining
  deflection of scrutiny, 2, 16, 117–18,
    123–4, 165–6, 173
  energy roadmap, *see* Energy
    Roadmap, FCL
  expansion of, 88, 96, 103, 108
  financial success of, 7–8, 16, 31–3,
    41, 44n38, 73, 163n34
  government/judicial support for,
    52–4, 66, 69, 77, 82–3
  health and safety hazards from,
    10, 96, 100–1, 106–7, 117–21,
    127–34
  history as farmer-based co-operative, 2, 8, 29, 58, 62, 93, 144
  injunction, seeking of, *see* injunctions

lack of emissions reductions, 3–4,
  15–16, 56, 88–91, 97, 104
legal cases launched by, 14, 74–80,
  158–9
local dominance of, 5–6, 108, 117–18
lockout, *see* lockout, CRC
media support for, 16, 50–2, 145,
  151–2, 160
pension plan at, *see* pension plans
police support for, 49–50, 78
public relations strategy, 7, 13–16, 57,
  122–34, 149–57
scab camp, *see* scabs
Unifor blockades, 1, 11–14, 34, 68,
  130–1, 154, 158
unionization at, 8–9, 29
wastewater pollution, *see* wastewater
worker use of "low-carbon" rhetoric,
  178–84, 196
Corey, Shannan, 144
Court of Appeal cases, 69, 81–3
court cases, 199
  contempt of, 14, 77–9, 158–9
  CRC arguments in, 14, 36, 70, 76, 121,
    152
  see also injunction; Supreme Court of
    Canada rulings
Court of Queen's Bench cases, 69, 75–7,
  88, 126
COVID-19 pandemic, 128
  CRC dispute during, 14–15, 22, 37,
    142, 199
  impacts on workers, 14, 80, 157
  lower fuel demands amid, 79, 90
  media coverage during, 152, 154
crude oil, 19n43, 173
  CRC processing of, 7–8, 93, 95, 119, 156
  vanadium in, 99–100

Davies, Nick, 147
defined benefit (DB) pension plan, 49
  actuarial assessments of, *see* actuarial
    evaluations
  betrayal of promises on, 32–4
  cost factors of, 25–7
  CRC demand for concessions on,
    22–3, 34–41, 72–3
  employer undermining of, 28–32,
    42n11, 47, 80–1, 166

guaranteed benefits through, 25, 29–30, 36, 65, 73
importance of, 29–32, 40–1, 65
defined contribution (DC) pension plan, 36
growth of, 31–4, 42n11
risk transfer through, 25, 73
stipulation for new workers to accept, 7, 23, 27–8, 35, 166
DeLorey, Brad, 139n40, 151–3, 173
democracy, 19n32, 82, 199
lack of, 7, 76
union, 9, 76, 143–4
see also social democratic government
Dias, Jerry, 28, 79, 151–2
arrest of, 1, 13, 34, 68, 77, 142, 158
Doherty, Scott, 44n43, 68, 151, 153
Doorey, David, 199
Douglas, Tommy, 9, 29, 94

Early, Steve, 5, 46–7, 143
education, 145
transition job, 57–60, 179, 182
union campaign, 9, 39
see also retraining
electricity generation, 56, 193, 196
coal-fired, 177, 183, 202–3
electricians, 175, 202
electric vehicles, 173, 177
demand for, 4, 170–1, 190
emergency alert systems, 5, 128
concerns about, 105, 130
see also notifynow emergency alert system
emissions,
carbon, 4, 110, 167, 170
commitments to reduce, 3, 16, 107–10, 166–74, 189
CRC, 16, 95, 101–5, 166–73, 180, 195
fugitive, 90–1, 103, 107, 110
greenhouse gas, see greenhouse gas (GHG) emissions
monitoring of, 89, 92, 102–5, 109, 170
movement off corporate books, 168–9, 171–3, 183
net-zero, 3, 57, 109–10, 168–9, 201–3, 206
reductions of, 90, 100
standards, 8, 104–5, 194, 199
targets, 174, 177, 172–3, 177
trading, 168
see also notifynow emergency alert system
employers,
aggressiveness from, 23, 27–9, 34, 37, 68
arguments for pension "sustainability," 23, 31, 40–1, 73, 183, 198
defined benefit pension plans, see defined benefit (DB) pension plan
police support for, 1, 12–16, 49–50, 68–9, 77–83
role in energy transition, 57–8, 190–2
union inadequacy versus, 23, 33, 37–9, 69, 72, 79, 81
see also Co-op Refinery Complex (CRC); Federated Co-operatives Limited (FCL)
Enbridge, 89, 100
Energy and Chemical Workers Union (ECWU), 9–10, 197
energy policy,
national 8–10, 197
Unifor, 8, 176–7
Energy Roadmap, FCL, 155, 160, 170–5, 179, 189–90, 195
environmental impacts, industry, assessment of, 94–5, 104, 107, 123–6
lack of oversight of, 89, 103, 109, 131
remediation, 57, 98, 103, 196
environmental movements, 41, 66, 165–7, 175–6, 184, 199–200
Environmental Protection Act, 108–9
Environmental Protection Plans (EPPs), 103
environmental regulations,
FCL conduct versus, 8, 108–10, 122, 170–4, 196–7
federal, 3–4, 7–8, 90, 109–10, 170–2
industry responses to, 2–3, 7–8, 174, 183
just transition strengthening of, 190, 192, 194
weak, 89, 102–3, 108–10, 180, 200
explosions, 74, 96, 105–6, 117–19, 125–6
cause of, 121–2
media coverage of, 155
Exxon, 167, 200

Fantasia, Rick, 47
federal government, 191, 200–1
  environmental regulations, 3–4, 7–8, 90, 109–10, 170–2
  provincial government regulatory relations, 4–5, 58, 181–3
  role in energy transition, 58–60, 177–8, 181–3, 193–7, 203–5
Federated Co-operatives Limited (FCL),
  centralization of power, 7, 108, 173, 189
  collective bargaining involvement, 10–12, 29, 34–5, 149, 175
  façade of financial hardship, 6–8, 31–2, 40–1, 55–6
  health and safety concerns, 120–3, 125–8, 131, 134–5
  local dominance, 50, 52–4, 77
  media coverage of, 149–52, 155–60, 199
  pension demands, 23, 29–32, 36–9, 133–4
  profits and retained earnings, 2, 8, 33, 41, 44n38, 53
  public relations strategies, 6, 32, 117–18, 170, 185n1, 190, 204
  role in energy transition, 4, 57–8, 166, 170–1, 189–90, 195
  structure, 2, 7–8, 43n26, 62, 93
  transition from co-operative principles, 6–9, 48–9, 62–4, 70, 125, 144, 158
  Unifor versus, 12–14, 127–30, 149–52, 184
Federation of Labour, Saskatchewan, 13, 72, 182, 197
Feltham, Perry, 118–19
fires, refinery, 95, 101, 119
  CRC, 117, 121–2, 125–6, 137n39, 144
  safety measures for, 11, 96
fossil fuel industry, 48, 155
  climate change responses, 1, 3–4, 170–4, 190, 195
  government relations with, 3–6, 47, 83, 92, 181–2, 204–6
  health and safety risks in, 30–1, 95–7, 118–21
  media coverage of, 51–2, 123–30, 143–5, 160–1, 190–2, 205
  phasing out of, 3–6, 16–17, 47, 60, 168–9, 182–3, 201–6
  policymaking on, 9, 110, 176–8, 181–3, 191–6, 201–5
  pollution from, 89–90, 95–9, 107–9, 169, 176, 200
  role in energy transition, 57–8, 182–3, 194, 198
  self-regulation in, 89, 102–3, 107, 124, 130–1, 180–3
  union relations with, 9–10, 13, 176–80, 194–200
  wages in, 25, 38, 59, 80, 157, 184, 202–4
fossil fuel workers,
  concessions by, *see* concessions, pension
  government relations with, 3–6, 52–4, 58–60, 177–83, 193–7, 203–5
  health and safety issues, 74, 92, 96, 101, 110, 117–26, 132–5
  interests versus industries', 47–9, 57–8, 132–3, 166–7, 180–4
  intergenerational solidarity, 23, 27, 37–8
  labour organizing, 8–9, 50–1, 64–6, 71, 143, 206
  media coverage of, 50–2, 144–5, 149–56, 159–61
  negotiating a just transition, 41–2, 54–62, 167, 175–80, 190–201
  pensions for, *see* pension plans
  replacement, *see* scabs
  rights and freedoms, restricted, 12, 49, 68–70, 72–83
  shattered faith in co-operatives, 10, 16, 62–4, 66, 81, 125
  transition facing, 2, 66, 135, 161, 174–5, 201–2
  violence against, *see* violence
Freedom Convoy, 159–60
Fudge, Judy, 70–1

General Motors (GM), 24, 28, 43n14
Gormley, John, 44n37, 50–1
greenhouse gas (GHG) emissions, 194
  CRC/FCL levels of, 110, 166, 170, 189
  fossil fuel industry regulation, 3–4, 55, 168–9, 200, 205

transition planning to reduce, 3, 34, 166, 170, 189, 205–6
see also net-zero emissions
greenwashing, 169
    by CRC, 2–3, 40–1, 160, 175
Gunster, Shane, 143, 206

harassment, picket-line, 74, 129, 152–4, 157
health care, public, 39–40
helicopters, use of, 11, 22, 64, 73–4, 129, 133, 149
Heppner, Nancy, 105
Hollinger (newspaper company), 146–7
Huard, Vic, 32, 44n37, 73, 121, 123, 127
Huber, Matthew, 199
Husky gas station acquisition, 7, 195
hydrogen production, 58, 167, 172–3, 180, 190, 201, 204
hydrogen sulfide (H$_2$S), 90, 120
    CRC exceedances of, 95, 104, 107, 123
    reporting emissions of, 96, 101, 105

industrial pluralism, 49, 71
Information and Privacy Commissioner, Saskatchewan, 69, 92, 126
injunctions,
    arrests for violating, 13, 34, 68, 78
    balance of convenience test, 76
    court documents from, 11–12, 74–5
    issuing of, 11, 22, 75, 129
    limiting workers' rights and freedoms, 12, 68, 72, 77–9, 149
    media coverage of, 34, 154–5
    rulings on, 72, 75–7, 81–3, 129
injuries, worker,
    hospitalizations, 119, 122
    lack of public information on, 120, 126, 136nn4,14, 138n39
    in plant explosions, 74, 105, 119, 121, 155
    preventing, 118, 121–2, 126
Intergovernmental Panel on Climate Change (IPCC) report, 168, 194
International Energy Agency, 4, 168, 195
International Labour Organization (ILO), 178, 193, 201, 204
intimidation, 151
    picket-line, 50, 76, 129, 152–4, 157–9

Johb, Lori, 197, 202, 206
Josephson, Dan, 32, 127

Keene, Timothy J., 77, 88
Kelly, Jason, 38
Kenney, Jason, 13, 195
Kraemer, Nathan, 37

labour journalism beat,
    absence of, 50–2, 143–9
    attentive reporting on, 98, 118, 143, 152, 160–1
    industry restrictions on, 46–7, 88, 125–6
    right-wing versus, 159–60
    see also media coverage
labour movement, 83n1
    just transition and, 176, 192, 195
    pension struggle lessons, 23–4, 28, 37, 40
labour organizations, 192
    calling for just transition, 178, 193, 201
law, the
    class struggle alteration of, 71
    just transition and, 178, 203–4
    preserving capitalist power imbalances, 54, 69–71, 78–9, 82–3
layoffs, 148
    bargaining discussions of, 62, 64, 180
    health and safety risks from, 110, 134
    low-carbon transition narrative for, 166, 173–5, 179, 183–4
    post-dispute, 80–1, 110, 166, 173–5, 191
Le Dressay, Gil, 11, 130–3, 151
Leedham, Emily, 144, 156–7, 160
Leo, Geoff, 126
Liberal Party of Canada, 56, 169
lockout, CRC, 106, 165
    amid COVID-19 pandemic, 14, 22, 154, 199
    employer preparations for, 8, 11, 30–1, 48, 53, 68, 131
    FCL messaging during, 7–8, 11–13, 74, 118, 149–50, 185n1
    gains and losses from, 23, 40, 64–6, 81, 197–8

health and safety during, 122–3,
    126–35
implications for transition, 15–17,
    110, 165–7, 205–7
lead up to, 30–3, 41, 55, 157–8
length of, 1–2, 22
media coverage of, 16, 34, 142–5,
    149, 151–60
mediation during, *see* mediation
as political-economic awakening,
    37–8, 46–7, 63–4, 81, 173, 184
state/judicial coercion in, 68–72,
    76–9, 83, 199
low-carbon transition, 12, 14
    company greenwashing in, 2–3,
        40–1, 160, 175
    employer/industry role in, 57–8,
        182–3, 194, 198
    employer justification of concessions,
        2, 7–11, 34, 80, 174, 179, 191
    government role in, 58–60, 177–8,
        181–3, 193–7, 203–5
    industry delaying action amid, 2–4,
        15–17, 169, 178, 195, 204
    pay and benefits in, 25, 38, 57–9, 80,
        157, 184, 202–4
    technology for, 3, 54–5, 108–10,
        167–73, 183, 195–6
    union role in, 9–10, 13, 60–2,
        173–80, 192–200
    unjust, 16–17, 41–2, 190–1
    workers' preparation for, 41–2,
        54–62, 167, 174–80, 190–201

Major Hazards Risk Assessment (MHRA),
    88, 105–6, 126
management, CRC/FCL,
    amid bargaining, 29, 33, 198
    on health and safety issues, 120–8,
        132, 135
    labour relations, 7–8, 10, 52, 62, 77,
        81, 179
    lack of accountability, 101–2, 110,
        167
    amid lockout, 22, 74, 127–8, 132–3,
        151–3, 158
    narratives of, 41, 55, 96, 142
    pensions for, 30, 43
master operator (MO) position, 175

bad faith bargaining over, 14–15,
    80–1, 134
elimination of, 10, 47–8, 69, 122
mayors, Regina, 94, 105
receipt of bomb threat against union,
    131, 155
trucker anti-union appeals to, 12–13
McMurtry, Janet, 75, 129, 154
media coverage,
    analysis of, 144, 150–7
    concentration of ownership, 146–8,
        160–1
    failure of investigative, 50, 145,
        153–6, 199
    flawed "objective" journalism, 143,
        152, 160–1, 192, 205
    of health and safety issues, 96, 99,
        106, 123–6, 132
    independent, 143–5, 149, 156–60
    industry influence over, 16, 50–2,
        126–7, 143–5, 149–54
    lack of analysis in, 2, 50–2, 154,
        157–60, 165
    of lockout, 13–15, 22, 128–30, 142–3,
        152–3
    misrepresentation of union in, 51–2,
        62–3, 69, 130, 143
    right-wing, 28, 143, 149–50, 157–9
    of Unifor arrests, 1, 152
    see also labour journalism beat; social
        media
mediation,
    appointment of representatives, 14,
        35, 69, 79, 154
    failure of, 11, 22, 127
    union acceptance of recommend-
        ations, 15, 35
    see also Ready, Vince; Rogers, Amanda
mesothelioma, 119–20
militancy, worker, 10–12, 15, 29, 77, 144,
    197
Ministry of Environment, 123, 130
    documentation from, 92
    industry self-reporting to, 89, 96, 104
    studies on pollution, 105–7
Ministry of Labour Relations and
    Workplace Safety (LRWS), 130–1
Moe, Scott,
    opposition to oil and gas regulation, 4

220 Unjust Transition

support for CRC, 52–3
Morgan, Don, 14–15, 35, 54, 79, 130, 155
municipal government, Regina, 14
  neighbourhood expansion, 92–4, 105–6, 123–4, 131, 137n29
  net-zero plans, 110, 180, 182
  permit for scab camp housing, 11, 32, 52–3, 73, 131, 157
  refinery expansion and pollution, 92–104, 131–3, 155, 172
  relationship with CRC, 5–6, 12, 49, 88–92, 110

National Pollutant Release Inventory (NPRI) data, 90, 92, 107
neoliberalism, 24–5, 40, 72–3, 103
Nesbitt, Doug, 143–4, 156
net-zero emissions,
  government commitments to, 3, 110, 168–70, 182, 203–6
  oil and gas operating plans for, 2–3, 110, 169–71, 183, 203
  questioning FCL commitment to, 57, 110, 170–1, 189–90
  refinery concession demands and, 16, 175, 183, 190
  scenarios of, 203
  vehicle sales, 4
New Democratic Party (NDP), 54, 144, 181–2, 202, 205–6
news media, *see* media coverage
Nordal, Ronni, 80, 159
Norway, 6, 193, 206
notifynow emergency alert system, 107, 124

Oil, Chemical, and Atomic Workers International Union (OCAW), 9, 176, 197–9
oil and gas production,
  branding of Canadian, 5
  carbon sequestration and, 169–74, 189
  continuation of, 56, 103–4, 169–71, 174, 205
  CRC, 90–1, 94, 103–4, 171–3, 183
  demand declining for, 2–4, 7, 14, 55–7, 79, 135, 170–2
  drilling, 93, 95

global commodity prices, 5, 156
  increasing Saskatchewan's, 4, 96–7, 103–4, 205
  planning for transition from, 117, 167, 177, 190, 200–3
  pollution from, 90, 100, 103–4, 133, 169, 173
  questioning hegemony of, 5–6, 41, 47, 191, 205–6
  replacement with biofuels, 108, 172–3
  Saskatchewan championing of, 5, 94, 205
  subsidization of, 174, 193, 201
  winding down of, 4, 16, 57, 167–8, 182–4, 203, 206
Oil Workers' industrial Union (OWIU), 9

Palmer, Bryan, 69
Pasqua First Nation, 98, 132
Pasqua Lake, 92, 97
pension plans,
  bargaining over, 24–5, 28–37, 48, 60–2, 73, 166
  cost factors, 25–7, 29–30
  cost sharing of, 23, 31, 34–6
  CRC provision of, 22–3, 27–30, 36–40
  defined benefit, *see* defined benefit (DB) pension plan
  defined contribution, *see* defined contribution (DC) pension plan
  employer concession demands, 2, 8–11, 14–17, 37–8, 118
  financialization, 25–6
  indexation of, 30, 34–6, 45n46, 65
  maintenance of, 1, 35, 41, 118
  notable negotiations of, 27–9, 48
  two-tier, 10–11, 27–34, 37–9, 65, 73, 144, 157
  universal, 24, 40–1
petro-populism, 3, 5, 8, 160
picket lines, 48, 81, 165
  alleged threats of violence on, 50, 74–7, 128–33, 152–60
  altercations on, 68, 138n55, 150, 155, 160
  arrests for, 1, 13–14, 34, 68, 77–8, 142, 158

attempts to weaken, 68–70, 75–9, 129, 152–3, 197
bomb threat for, 13, 86n48, 131, 152, 155–6, 159
criminalization of, 12–14, 66, 78, 133, 153
crossing, 68, 74, 133–4, 144, 150, 158
delays from, 11–12, 74–8, 82
drivers' exemption on, 12, 72–8, 81–3
employer request to ban, 74–5, 84n23
extended periods of, 22, 27, 37, 50
injunction to restrict, 11–12, 22, 34, 68, 72, 77–9, 149–54
media coverage of, 143–44, 149–54, 156–60
police presence, 13–14, 49–50, 154
scab workers and, *see* scabs
secondary, 80, 150, 158
solidarity on, 15, 32–4, 71, 181
trucker appeals to dismantle, 12–13, 68, 129
Unifor national support for, 1, 34, 68, 77–8, 130, 142, 158
workers' right to participate in, 12, 16, 68, 71–2, 82–3
pipelines, 171, 183
alleged pressure on crude supply, 7–8, 156
nearby, 89, 100
populism and, 5, 197
police, *see* Regina Police Service (RPS)
populism,
extractive, 143, 149–50, 158, 161, 205–6
petro-, 3, 5, 8, 160
Postmedia, 148, 150
Post Millennial, 149, 158–9
private welfare state, 24–5
provincial government, Saskatchewan, 80, 154
30 Goals for 2030 growth plan, 4, 205
anti-union stance of, 7, 53, 62–3, 72
championing oil and gas production, 3, 5, 16, 47, 66, 183, 191
federal government regulatory conflict, 4–5, 171–2, 199–200, 205
lax regulatory capacity, 102–3, 107–10, 123, 130, 171
municipal council versus, 5–6, 53

refinery requests to, 12–13
role in energy transition, 58–60, 171–2, 181
stance during dispute, 16, 65–6, 79, 82–3
subsidizing fossil fuels, 174, 193, 201
support for CRC, 8, 89, 93–5, 102, 126, 171
Unifor versus, 13, 35, 53, 79–81
public relations,
FCL strategy, 7, 128–9,
media coverage and 143, 145–7, 149
safety as, 118, 122–6

Rankandfile.ca reporting, 143–5, 149, 156–8
RCMP, 86n48, 131, 159
Ready, Vince, 14, 35, 40n44, 79, 154
Rebel News/The Rebel, 149–50, 158–9
Regina, 88
city planning, 93–4, 104–5, 123, 172, 180
CRC relations with, 14, 93–102, 121–3 131, 139n69
Manifesto, 24, 40
neighbourhood safety, 92–4, 105–6, 123–4, 131, 137n29
net-zero plans, 110, 180, 182
as refinery town, 5, 46–7
worker camp land leasing, 11, 52–3, 73, 127, 157
see also city council, Regina; municipal government, Regina
Regina Leader-Post, 95
consolidated ownership, 145–7, 150
refinery coverage, 150–3, 156, 163n34, 166
Regina Police Service (RPS),
arrests for, 1, 13–14, 34, 68, 77–8, 142, 158
blockade presence, 13–14, 34, 49–50, 77–80
bomb threat, 13, 86n48, 131, 152, 155–6, 159
initial hands-off approach, 13, 49, 77
intimidation by, 49–50, 149, 152, 158
justification of actions, 77–82, 153–4
support for CRC, 12, 16, 49, 66–9, 77, 130

Unifor 594 confrontations with, 1, 14, 49–50, 77–8
Reimer, Neil, 9
remediation, 4, 98, 180
   employer accountability, 56–7, 196
   self-policing for, 103, 109
retirement, 46, 135, 182
   DB versus DC pensions and, 23–30, 33, 73, 118
   employer plan costs, 25–6, 29, 35, 73
   health benefits, 39
   as individual responsibility, 24, 28–9, 73
   lack of funds for, 59
   universal pensions and, 39–40, 42
retraining, 177, 180
   transition need for worker, 57–8, 60, 182, 191–3, 202
rights,
   asserting workers', 181–2, 191–3
   Charter, 71, 77–9, 81–2
   collective bargaining, 196
   constitutional rights, workers', 16, 68, 70–2
   employers' versus workers', 12, 72, 74–8, 84–5, 198
   just transition and, 66, 198, 200–1
   labour, 5, 16, 32, 46
right wing,
   far, 14, 150, 156
   fossil fuel industry and, 149, 195, 205
   media, 28, 50, 150, 158–9
   movements, 158, 160–1
   political parties, 52, 149, 158
   see also Freedom Convoy; United We Roll; Yellow Vests
risk pooling, 38–40
Rogers, Amanda, 14, 35, 40n44, 79, 154
Rosenfeld, Herman, 29
RWDSU v. Pepsi 2001: 71, 75–6, 84n23

safety,
   CRC risks to community, 90–6, 105–6, 110, 118, 121–6, 199–200
   FCL management on, 120–8, 132, 135
   amid lockout, 122–3, 126–35
   master operator (MO) position and, 10, 47–8, 69, 122, 175
   media coverage of issues on, 96, 99, 106, 123–6, 132
   as public relations, 118, 122–6
   workers' concerns for, 74, 92, 96, 101, 110, 117–26, 132–5
Sarnia, Ontario, 106–7
Saskatchewan,
   anti-union sentiments in, 14, 61, 156
   increasing oil and gas production, 4, 96–7, 103–4, 205
   as petro-province, 3, 5, 94, 191, 205–6
   political economy of, 3–6, 69, 89, 101, 191
   see also provincial government, Saskatchewan
Saskatchewan Federation of Labour v. Saskatchewan 2015: 71–2
Saskatchewan Labour Relations Board, 84n23, 122, 180, 197
   decision against CRC, 15, 47, 69, 80–1, 134
Saskatchewan Party,
   anti-labour stance, 52–4, 72
   fossil fuel industry support, 102, 181
Saskatoon Co-op, 144, 157–8
scabs,
   camp for, 11, 22, 48, 52, 123, 131–4, 156–7
   COVID-19 health concerns for, 14, 139n69, 157
   legislation on, 53, 82, 84n23, 182, 197
   preparations for, 11, 32–4, 52, 73–4, 144
   profiling of, 138n54, 144, 153
   tension between workers and, 127, 129, 133, 151–2
   transportation across picket lines, 11, 22, 74, 77, 149, 156
   as underqualified, 127–8
   use of labour, 27, 68–72, 83n1
   weakening of picket line, 68–70, 75–9, 129, 152–3, 197
   see also helicopters, use of
Scheer, Andrew, 53, 158
Serrin, William, 146
sewage system, municipal,
   agreements on refinery waste in, 95
   CRC pollution of, 14, 96–101, 105, 132–3, 152

extension to refinery, 94
  lagoons, 96, 98, 105
  see also wastewater
social democratic government, 6, 9, 29;
  see also Co-operative Commonwealth Federation (CCF)
socialist left, 24, 39
  governments, 5, 9
  see also Co-operative Commonwealth Federation (CCF)
social licence, industry, 3, 110, 124, 197
social media use, 120, 132, 150–1, 159, 161
  anti-union, 14, 156
  CRC, 128
solar power, 9, 56, 100, 201–2
solidarity,
  as co-operative value, 19n32
  expressions of, 1, 15, 34, 47, 71–2
  extending, 40–1, 65, 192, 197–9
  undermining, 13, 37–9, 73, 83n1
Southam newspaper chain, 146–7
spills, refinery, 90, 95, 132–3
  lack of industry reporting, 96, 98, 102–3, 107, 124, 137n18
  media coverage, 152, 155
StarPhoenix (Saskatoon),
  consolidated ownership, 146–7, 150
  refinery coverage, 144, 151
state, the,
  coercive force of, 69–72
  debates about role of, 16, 24
  employer support by, 47–9, 52–3, 68–9
Stevens, Andrew, 46, 131, 143, 156
strikes, 74, 146
  constitutional right for, 16, 49, 68–71, 82
  employer preparation for, 11, 34, 68, 127
  major industrial union, 9, 27–9
  media coverage of, 143–4, 157, 159
  purpose of, 72
  undermining of, 39–40, 69–72, 166
  voting for, 32, 34, 38, 76, 127
Supreme Court of Canada rulings, 72
  workers' constitutional rights, 16, 68, 71, 75
Sustainable Jobs Act, 178, 182, 203–4

taxation, 9
  business-friendly, 5, 103
  carbon, 7, 56, 58, 150, 197
  credits, 172, 181, 200, 204
  exemption from, 93–4
  property, 6, 25
Technical Safety Authority of Saskatchewan (TSASK), 122, 130
Tesla, 55, 198
transition, low-carbon, *see* low-carbon transition
trucking companies, anti-union appeals, 12–13, 51, 74, 153–4
trucks,
  alleged vandalism of, 129, 152–3, 158–9
  convoys of, 158, 160
  delay due to picketing, 11, 75, 129
  needless dispatching of, 11–12
  worker tension with, 68, 129, 152
Tucker, Eric, 70–1
Tucker, Sean, 144
two-tier pension plans, 10–11, 65, 73, 144
  union lessons on, 23, 27–34, 37–9, 157

Unifor,
  CRC messaging about, 7
  Energy Policy, 177
  Local 594, *see* Unifor 594
  media coverage of, 151–2, 154
  national executive decision making, 12, 60
  role in just transition, 174, 177–9
  undermined solidarity actions, 70–1, 78–9, 81, 130
  see also Dias, Jerry
Unifor 594,
  attempts to break power of, 2, 47–9, 68, 81
  blockades, 1, 11–14, 34, 68, 130–1, 154, 158
  court case against, 14, 74–80, 158–9
  defeat of, 14–15, 23, 32–3, 37–8, 69, 81, 84n18, 155
  ensuring survival of, 1, 37–8, 41–2, 58–60, 175–84, 197–203
  history and organizing of, 8–9, 12–14, 127–30, 149–52, 184

unions,
  class-wide perspective, need for, 23–4, 40, 191–4
  energy sector, 3, 6, 9–10, 17, 176–7, 206
  lack of solidarity, 13, 191–2
  in low-carbon transition, 2–3, 16–17, 41–2, 58–60, 175–84, 197–203
  media coverage of, 143, 145, 158
  two-tier pension bargaining, *see* two-tier pension plans
  undermining, 37, 66, 147, 167
  worker consciousness of, 9, 38, 65
  worker right to, 8–9, 24, 29, 71
"union thug" narrative, 149–50, 158–9, 162n30
United Auto Workers (UAW), 24
United Nations Framework Convention on Climate Change, 165, 168, 194
United States, 4, 136n4, 176, 198
  business unionism in, 143–4
  low-carbon transition mobilizing in, 190, 192–3, 200–1
  newspaper closures in, 148
  pension plans in, 24–5, 28, 30
United Steelworkers (USW), 24, 118, 176–8, 183
  Local 6500, 27, 37, 39
United We Roll, 14, 150, 156–8, 160

Vale-Inco, 27, 37, 39
vanadium, 99–100
violence,
  alleged threats of picket-line, 11, 78, 76, 129, 152–4, 158
  police presence for, 49, 138n55
  scab use and, 74, 76
volatile organic compounds (VOCs), 91, 108–9

Wascana Creek, 14, 92, 97–8, 132
wastewater,
  CRC system to clean, 97–9, 101
  EPCOR treatment plant, 97–100, 132
  lack of public notice on contamination, 98, 132–3
  pollution, 89, 94, 96–100, 155
  sewage lagoons, 96, 98, 105
Watch, Daryl, 117, 120, 134

water,
  clean, 52, 94, 194
  drinking, 92–3, 96
  refinery use of, 94, 97–100, 108, 199
  treatment, 59, 94, 97–8, 155
  waste–, *see* wastewater
  see also Wascana Creek
Water Security Agency, Saskatchewan, 98–9
western Canada,
  as "carbon capital," 5–6
  fossil fuel narrative in, 5–6, 194, 205
  petro-populism in, 3, 194, 206
  separatism in, 13, 149–50
Whitecap Resources (Weyburn, Saskatchewan, project), 110, 171
Whittingham, James, 89, 100–1
wind power, 9, 56, 100, 201–2
workers, *see* fossil fuel workers

Yellow Vests, 156, 158